Liberalism
in
Australia

Liberalism in Australia

Ian Cook

OXFORD
UNIVERSITY PRESS

For Beryl Joyce Cook

OXFORD
UNIVERSITY PRESS

253 Normanby Road, South Melbourne, Victoria, Australia 3205
Oxford University Press is a department of the University of Oxford.
It furthers the University's objective of excellence in research, scholarship,
and education by publishing worldwide in

Oxford   New York

Athens Auckland Bangkok Bogotá Buenos Aires Calcutta
Cape Town Chennai Dar es Salaam Delhi Florence Hong Kong Istanbul
Karachi Kuala Lumpur Madrid Melbourne Mexico City Mumbai Nairobi
Paris Port Moresby São Paulo Singapore Taipei Tokyo Toronto Warsaw

with associated companies in Berlin Ibadan

OXFORD is a registered trade mark of Oxford University Press
in the UK and certain other countries

National Library of Australia
Cataloguing-in-Publication data:

Cook, Ian, 1960– .
   Liberalism in Australia

   Includes index.
   ISBN 019 553 702 5

   1. Liberalism—Australia.
   I. Title

320.510994

Edited by Venetia Somerset
Text design by Peter Shaw
Cover design by Stephen Horsley
Typeset by Desktop Concepts Pty Ltd, Melbourne
Printed in China through the Bookmaker Pty Ltd, Australia

CONTENTS

ACKNOWLEDGMENTS

First I would like to acknowledge the support, assistance, patience, and tolerance of Jill Lane of Oxford University Press. My association with her has been one of the true pleasures that came to me via this project. I am also deeply indebted to Venetia Somerset, whose thoughtful editorial comments and careful touches have made this a much better book than it would otherwise have been. I would like to thank Rodney Smith for his assistance in developing and completing this project, and for his friendship. I must also acknowledge the support and encouragement provided by my colleagues in the Department of Politics and International Studies at Murdoch University. In particular, I would like to thank Professor Hugh Collins for his encouragement of my work. I also acknowledge the support provided to me through a Murdoch University Special Research Grant. I acknowledge and value the research assistance provided for this project by Megan Edwards, Yvonne Haigh, Richard Barlow, Sarah Barns, Tauel Harper, and Jeremy Chenoweth. I am also indebted for the support given my work on Australian liberalism given by Geoff Stokes and the rest of the Australian Political Thought Research Group. The following institutions kindly agreed to give permission to reproduce material and I gratefully acknowledge their cooperation: HarperCollins Publishers, for extracts from *72 Essays: A Selection*, by Walter Murdoch, 1947, and from *The Forgotten People*, by Robert Menzies, 1943 (both published by Angus & Robertson, Sydney); Cambridge University Press for extracts from *Return of Scarcity*, by H. C. Coombs, 1990, Cambridge University Press, Cambridge; extracts from John Hewson's speeches reported in Parliamentary Debates, House or Representatives, Commonwealth Government Printer, Canberra, Commonwealth Copyright reproduced with permission. Finally I would like to thank my partner Sally Kirk, and children Jack and Nicholas, who tolerated my absences in the final stages of preparing this book.

INTRODUCTION

Liberal political theory came to Australia as an integral part of the colonisation process. It was adopted, developed, and applied in a variety of ways that reflected both the received political philosophy and the conditions under which it was interpreted and used in the development of political institutions and practices. Liberalism was not received as a completed or static political philosophy, however, and is continually interpreted and reinterpreted by successive generations of liberals. Like all political philosophies, liberalism provides general principles that require interpretation and application at specific moments. While it remains consistent with respect to those general principles, interpretations and applications can produce distinct versions of liberal political theory. To deal with liberalism in Australia, then, is to deal with a specific set of interpretations of certain general principles.

This book comprises ten largely separate studies of individual thinkers. While some relationships between the various thinkers' works are noted in the conclusions to each chapter and in the conclusion to the book, the studies are largely separate. No overview of a single doctrine articulated by a set of thinkers is attempted. Instead the book provides an indication of how a number of significant public actors in Australia have articulated versions of liberal political thought.

Some readers may detect a bias in the list of liberals included in this book in favour of Victorians. I was not conscious of this bias and, never having lived for any length of time in Victoria, can find no explanation for a predisposition in favour of Victorians. Yet the predominance of Victorians is an interesting phenomenon. It may be the result of the presence of more avenues for publishing work in Victoria, or it may result from a more intellectual culture in Melbourne than is to be found elsewhere in Australia. I have no evidence to support either claim.

I tend to the view that the form of liberalism that has dominated Australian politics has been that which was articulated and practised in Victoria (at least until the 1980s). That it often functions under the name of Deakinite liberalism is one indicator of its form, content, and derivation. This form of liberalism seems to be in decline in Australia and in the process of being replaced by that commonly called economic rationalism. But this is in its early stages. This process of transformation might be seen as a shift from a Victorian liberalism to one that finds its more natural home in New South Wales. This is another story and not one that I wanted to discuss in this book.

Organisation of the book

Chapter 1 deals with the question of what it is to be an Australian liberal, and thereby the meaning of the words 'Australia' and 'liberal'. A preliminary consideration of the denotation and connotations of these two words provides the basis for a discussion of the themes around which this book is organised.

The studies of the ten liberals in Chapters 2–11 have not been arranged chronologically but are organised around three issues or themes that are typical of liberal political theory. If I discuss thinkers in terms of their views on one particular issue or theme this is not meant to imply that their works could not have been dealt with in terms of another of the issues used to organise the chapters. It is meant to imply, however, that these works contain views that illustrate both the issue under consideration and a response to that issue that reflects the application of premises typical of liberal political thought.

The first group of studies presented in this book deal with character (in the sense of a person's qualities, especially good ones; see p. 21) and citizenship. These are closely related concerns that are central to liberal political thought. Since liberals seek to promote the expression of individuality, a person's character, and its improvement, is always an important issue in their thinking. An interest in the opportunities for participation reflects a liberal's concern with creating opportunities to express individuality in social and political situations. Citizenship is important to liberals both in terms of the expression of individuality and in response to the rise of democratic theories and institutions. As citizens in a country that adopted democratic institutions and broadened suffrage early, many liberals in Australia have tried to ensure that voters received a training that provided for effective and thoughtful political participation in society—in good citizenship.

The second set of studies is arranged under the rubric 'social stratification'. Social stratification refers to the existence in a society of systemically produced inequality. This, in turn, refers to inequality that does not relate to natural differences between people but arises from the advantages that members of certain groups have because of their social position or the resources at their disposal. Liberals are committed to the view that individuals ought to be treated equally, particularly in having the opportunity to pursue interests in economic, political, and many other pursuits. Liberals accept the existence of inequality but reject inequality that results from unequally distributed resources because it means that members of certain social groups are systematically privileged over and successful in competition against others. Liberals believe in equality of opportunity, though not in equality of outcome.

The final group of studies are presented under the heading 'Economics: governments and markets'. Economic issues have always been important in liberal political thought, reflecting both the general importance of economics for politics and the centrality of the satisfaction of material needs to a liberal's understanding of human nature. The basic questions that face liberals are how far markets, particularly in labour, goods, and services, ought to be left free to operate according to their own logic, and how far and in what ways governments should override market forces in pursuit of larger social goals.

Each of these parts deals with enduring issues that liberals face in every context in which they find themselves. They are essential, or perennial, issues in liberal political theory. To this extent, the analyses provided here constitute traditional studies of political theory. That is, they deal with issues that are understood to face liberal political thinkers no matter who or where they are. They function to unite liberals across time and culture, and the answers provided for these questions have significance beyond the particular time and place within which they were developed. (This is why I am giving no account of the European or British philosophical matrix from which this liberal thinking arose.)

I do not mean to suggest that these issues are always prominent when it comes to electoral politics in Australia or any other country. Indeed, contemporary political debate in Australia is dominated by economic issues. Far less attention seems to be paid in mainstream Australian politics to issues that concern either character and citizenship or social stratification. This is not to say that these issues have lost any actual relevance or cannot return to centre stage; that they are perennial issues means that they may lose their currency in day-to-day political discourse, but not their essential significance. Perhaps it is simply that economic rationalism has for the time being overtaken everything else in public discourse.

Part III, then, deals with what has become a dominant issue in late twentieth-century debates in Australian politics. Certainly liberals in schools, universities, and other 'training' institutions maintain concerns with character, participation, and citizenship and, in many cases, with issues of inequality. Australian politics, however, at least in the 1980s and 1990s, seems to have marginalised both of these issues.

To begin with Charles Henry Pearson, who was deeply committed to the relationship between politics and good character, and to finish with John Hewson, a former professor of economics, one-time leader of the Liberal Party of Australia and champion of free-market theory, is not accidental. Eight thinkers appear between Pearson and Hewson. Explanations of their significance and the general themes emerging in each of the parts will be left to the introduction to those parts. The book is organised thematically rather than chronologically to bring out the great importance of these three themes.

Despite this thematic emphasis, however, the book remains deliberately a series of studies of the works of ten separate individuals. These studies were intended to make available accounts of a set of thinkers who, in my view, have articulated, and influenced the articulation of, liberalism in Australia. The research notes at the end of the book were included to assist students with their research.

Some final observations

The main problems I encountered in writing this book stemmed from my training as a political theorist. Most political theorists in anglophone universities (i.e. universities where instruction is in English) are trained through reading and interpreting a canon, or set of 'great' works, of political theory. The courses I taught began with classical political theorists such as Plato and Aristotle, continued through medieval political theorists, including Augustine and Aquinas, and finished with modern political theorists like Machiavelli, Hobbes, Locke, Mill, and Marx. Courses in political theory sometimes include women and may even extend to postmodern theorists.

The point of all this, in the context of this book, is that no Australians appeared among the great thinkers included in the political theory courses I undertook. Thinkers from England, Scotland, Germany, Italy, Russia, and France regularly appeared and still appear, and those from the United States of America were and are sometimes included. Australians never appear. One conclusion that could be drawn from this is that Australians have not produced any 'great works' of political theory. Another is that there is little value in political theorists examining the ideas about politics produced by Australians, and certainly little value in studying these works in the way in which the 'great works' are studied

The second implication is the more important and seems a function of two related factors. The first is that those who teach political theory were trained in a political theory that contained no Australians. The second is that that those who might read Australians as political thinkers have only a limited sense of where they might look for Australian political thinkers. If, like me, they have little training in the techniques historians use for 'recovering' texts, then finding works written by Australians that might qualify for a book like this presents a real challenge. It certainly was for me and for my research assistants. I was not sure where to look and could not provide much advice to those who looked for me. We found people who I thought merited attention, definitely not the only people who might have been chosen, and possibly not always the 'best' people who might be chosen. An important factor in the selection process was whether the thinker had published material in sufficient quantity to provide the basis for this study. A secondary consideration was the general availability of their works. Nevertheless, a choice was made.

ON BEING AN
AUSTRALIAN LIBERAL

Given that this book is a set of studies of ten thinkers chosen as expressing particular aspects or forms of liberalism in Australia, it seemed necessary to spend a little time discussing the meaning of these two words, 'liberalism' and 'Australia'. To enquire into the nature of liberal political thought is to provide a framework within which the subsequent discussion of liberal thinkers might be understood. The variety in forms and manifestations of liberalism here and elsewhere precludes a simple and incontestable claim as to essential elements of liberalism. Certainly individuals are central to liberal political theory, but different liberals may have very different views on how individuals emerge and what it takes to be an individual. Reflecting on the nature of liberal political thought does allow for some suggestions about certain factors that unite liberals and the liberals studied here.

A discussion of the word 'Australia' may seem less obviously relevant. Australia can be treated as simply referring to a particular geographical phenomenon (and, for the purposes of selecting the thinkers studied here, I have tended to look to thinkers who wrote in Australia but who may not have been Australian-born). These apparently simple geographical notions require careful scrutiny, however. 'Australia' does not simply refer to a place. It also refers to something imported as part of a process of colonisation and to the colonised space itself. This is worth consideration, not simply because of the issues of identity raised for non-Aboriginal 'Australians', who find themselves in a place into which their forebears were introduced and with which they have had to come to terms (not always easily).

Non-Aboriginal Australians seem to have found it difficult to negotiate their identity as they do not 'belong' in some original sense and yet have little else through which to identify themselves. This difficulty in negotiating their identity is reflected in the fact of Australia's being in an Asian region, yet not seeming to belong fully to that region. As an Australian, I found it hard to avoid considering issues involved in the meaning of this term when it came to working on this book. The simplest problem was whether to include thinkers who had not been born in Australia (to which the answer was 'yes'). The deeper problem reflected the fact that 'liberalism' was part of the process of colonisation and that its articulation in Australia represents both a reflection of the derivative nature of non-Aboriginal Australian society and the specificity of that society.

The liberalism articulated in Australia is neither unrecognisable in relation to that articulated in other countries nor identical to it. It represents a particular form of this Western political philosophy, theory, or ideology. It is a form of liberalism that emerged in a particular colonised place among a colonising people and reflects this place and these people. To understand liberalism in Australia is not, however, a mechanical exercise in which we observe the chanting of a received doctrine, or passages from a received text, by people who recite the appropriate phrases under the particular conditions in which they find themselves. I have chosen to understand liberalism as a living and developing philosophy, as a way of understanding oneself and others that cannot simply be understood in terms of some simple form of derivation, but must be seen as part of individual liberals' attempts to come to terms with themselves.

The title of this chapter refers to the fact that the book deals with ten human beings for whom liberal political ideas represent important ways of understanding themselves and those around them. Creating and negotiating meaning and purpose within a community deeply influenced by liberal political theory often means relying on and reinterpreting core liberal notions and tenets.

Another reason for the particular approach taken in this chapter is that I wanted to express a commitment to the notion that political theories or philosophies are central to living and being. They are alive and functioning in all people. They condition how we see others and ourselves. They are central to any visions we may have of the future and of human possibility more generally. They motivate us to undertake many of our actions and are central to our explanations of success and failure in our enterprises. One chapter does not provide the opportunity for a full elaboration of these points in the context of liberalism in Australia, but, I hope, some sense of the living nature of liberal political philosophy will emerge.

The first section of this chapter is a discussion of the meaning of the word 'Australian'. The second deals with what being a liberal might mean. The third is an attempt to bring the preceding discussions together. At this stage, readers ought to be warned that little is offered by way of a resolution of the issues raised, in part because those things that make someone an Australian and a liberal are not easy to define and seem to change over time, in part because the discussions in this chapter were designed to serve as a preliminary to the following chapters, to introduce issues that deserved consideration.

On Being Australian

Writing about liberalism in Australia and about a set of Australian individuals immediately raises the issue of what made a person, in this case a liberal, an Australian. The question of what makes a 'liberal' is a familiar one, though not always an easy one to answer. The question of what made and makes an 'Australian' is less familiar—even for those like myself who have no other word for themselves—and much more difficult to answer. A variety of ways exist for addressing the question of what makes an Australian. I have chosen two ways of looking at the question. One is in terms of 'Australian' as referring to something that was or is being introduced or imported. In this sense, 'Australian' derives from some other category such as 'Briton', 'European', or 'Anglo-Celtic'. Another way of understanding the term 'Australian' is in terms of situation, geography, or place. This second sense makes meaningful phrases such as 'Aboriginal Australian' or 'Australian flora and fauna'. Obviously, the imported and the situational are deeply intertwined. Nevertheless, each offers a distinctive perspective for examining the question of the meaning of 'Australian'.

Derivation: 'Australian' as Import

'Australia' has always been characterised by derivation. 'Australia' was a conscious and deliberate construction created by people who were not native to the region. Whatever else was here before white settlement, it was not 'Australia'. That word was part of the process of colonisation. Colonisation by human beings is a multi-layered process. At one level it is genetic (colonisation might be understood as a virus-like infestation of a host body by a foreign genetic code). Genetic colonisation is the introduction of genetic codes where they were not present before. Human colonisation is also the introduction, or importation, of various cultural artefacts and practices. Genetic and cultural colonisation in Australia has been a continuing and changing process. One change has been a shift in the sources of importation. Another is that where once colonisation was externally controlled, Australian governments have now taken greater control over the importation of particular genetic and cultural forms.

Genetic colonisation

It may well be crude to understand colonisation as a process of genetic invasion; it is certainly an odd way of looking at early colonisation in Australia. The first exports to Australia could not be thought of as possessing desirable genetic codes. Perhaps it may be just as appropriate to understand colonisation in Australia as the expunging of undesirable elements of the British gene pool. In this case, colonisation is less like genetic transplantation and more like genetic disposal. The myth of a people leaving a society to seek new grounds to flourish free of the constraints of that society and who, ultimately, proved superior to the people from which it sprang has not been readily available in Australia (as it was, for example, in the United States of America).

But colonists may not have taken very long before they began to understand themselves in the more familiar understanding of certain forms of colonisation in which something of value is transplanted to a place where nothing else is growing (*terra nullius*). The 'White Australia' policy was a fairly self-conscious and explicit attempt to protect a particular genetic inheritance from being diluted by other genetic lines. Changes to the story of Australian colonisation may also have occurred when it became clearer that Aboriginal Australians had to be included in stories of colonisation. In this case, an understanding of colonisation as bringing the light of civilisation to 'underdeveloped' or 'primitive' people developed in some circles.

Cultural colonisation

Cultural colonisation is about the sort of people who colonise, not through their genetic characteristics but through the cultural products they possess and have brought with them. These cultural products belong to fields such as the natural and social sciences, religion, and education. The products that have been part of the formation of an 'Australian' culture include languages, ideas, questions, and texts.

One of the most important forms of cultural colonisation is the introduction of a new language. Introducing a new language, to which the word 'Australia' itself belonged, was part of the process of colonisation. Languages are not simply means of reporting about the world and its possibilities but also contain ways of looking at the world. Embedded in a language are particular ideas and questions that can be brought to mind and discussed through that language. These ideas lend themselves to the posing of particular questions.

Liberalism itself was one of the imports that have gone to shape Australian intellectual life. For many writers, such as Tim Rowse (1978), the Australian intellectual form is distinctly liberal and expresses its source in a particular set of ideas, questions, and texts that were introduced as part of the colonisation process. The introduction of liberal political ideas may be understood as part of the cultural colonisation process that occurred alongside genetic colonisation. Both of these may be understood to reflect the fact that 'Australia' refers to a derived genetic, social, and cultural form.

Situation: 'Australian' as People in Place

Derivation is not the only way to approach 'Australianness'. Rather than concentrate on the things that were brought to Australia, attention may usefully be directed to the community that grew from those imports.[1] In this case, attention shifts from those who created and operated the colonisation process to the people transplanted and their attempts to sustain life in their new environment. Obviously Australia was an import before it was a community. But once that import came to take hold in the region into which these people were exported, it took on a momentum or shape of its own. 'Australianness', in this case, derives from the specific character of the natural and social environment to which further imports were brought.

That the Australian community was geographically separated from other communities meant that it had to develop particular ways of organising itself so that things that had to be done could be done. People had to know how they stood in relation to each other. They had to know what they could expect of others and what others expected of them. This reflected the relationships that existed in the colonising society, but the colony had to do much for itself. The roles of 'prisoner', 'guard', 'priest', and 'administrator' pre-existed the colonisation of Australia. These roles provide only a general guide to behaviour, however, and the Australian community required guides to behaviour that were specific to the local situation. 'Prisoners', for example, are only sometimes responsible for the creation of social infrastructure as they were in Australia. Those responsible for the prisoners, or convicts, also had to develop their own guides to practice.

When colonists arrived who belonged to none of the groups that had already established themselves, they had to change to become members of the community. In a sense, the new arrivals might be said to have to become 'Australian' in order to become part of the community they found at their destination. This process of adjustment was required because no matter how hard they might have tried—and they seemed at times to have tried very hard—the colonists could not reproduce the culture from which they had come, and colonists who followed them had to adjust to a new society.

The colonists' inability to recreate their home culture and society was partly a product of their new physical environment. The style of architecture, for example, that was most conducive to human habitation in Australia was unlike that of most of the countries from which the colonists came. While they struggled to reproduce an architecture with which they were familiar, this architecture had to be modified. Similarly, the agricultural techniques effective in the Australian environment were different from those that were effective in 'home' countries.

Hartz's fragment thesis

The community that developed in Australia could not mirror the community that the first colonists had left. Even had the physical environment been no different, the problem of reproducing a community in another place, without transporting that community in total, was insurmountable. Certainly the community to be found in Australia did not contain even an accurate sample of British society, and therefore it could not reproduce that community. Indeed the transplanted community can hardly be said to have resembled the source community.

Louis Hartz (1964) has argued that colonised countries contained 'fragments' of their source society, which were separated at a particular moment in time and bear the imprint of that moment of separation. The derived society was isolated from many of the stimuli that produced changes in the source society and was dominated by the culture and ideology carried by the fragment at the moment of separation. Consequently the fragment tended to reflect a particular set of cultural conditions, including ideological conditions that changed slowly, if they changed at all. Hartz argued that there 'is a problem of traditionalism and change common' to the countries settled in the period in which Australia was settled. The cause of this problem he attributed to 'the fact that all of them are fragments of the larger whole of Europe struck off in the course of the revolution which brought the West into the modern world. For when a part of a European nation is detached from the whole of it, and hurled outward onto new soil, it loses the stimulus toward change that the whole provides' (Hartz 1964: 3).

Beyond Hartz

While Hartz may have been correct in his analysis, those who use the word 'Australian' to describe themselves have experienced cultural shifts that have rendered them less confident in their idea of what makes someone an 'Australian'. Australian society has undergone significant and long-term changes, especially over the last twenty years, which make difficult any attempt to use the word in a book such as this. A decline in the predominance of British culture, for example, has been matched with a significant increase in the impact of American culture.

This is a reflection of the increasing internationalisation of culture. It also reflects the fact that the sources of derivation have changed. The nature of the local environment has also changed (both because of these shifts in sources of derivation and because of the effects that colonists and their offspring have had on the environment in Australia). This process will become more rapid with further developments in information technology. Another factor that makes more difficult the definition of 'Australian' is more recent moves to recognise and accommodate Aboriginal Australian peoples and cultures. Finally, immigration by Asians and moves to engage more fully with the local region have also made less stable some of the earlier bulwarks of 'Australianness'.

In summary, then, 'Australianness' refers to a particular heritage, which can be understood to reflect a genetic and a cultural lineage. But a focus on derivation, in which Australia is understood in terms of the imports that were brought to it, may under-emphasise the distinctive character of both the circumstances into which these imports were brought and the community that had to develop for colonisation to be successful. From this perspective, 'Australian' refers more to the environment and community located in Australia, which acted as filters for all subsequent importation.

On Being Liberal

If ideologies, political theories, or political philosophies—and liberalism is all of these—are carried by people, then a question arises as to what liberals are like. These characteristics will be discussed in terms of the public/private distinction.[2] All that this means is that liberals hold particular personal or private views and philosophies that they may or may not actively pursue. If they keep these ideas to themselves, their liberalism is private. If they seek to express and implement these views, their liberalism becomes public.

'Liberal' as private philosophy (as a way of thinking)

To be a liberal is to have a certain sort of attitude to oneself, to others, to society, and to the 'world'. It is at this point that philosophy meets life. We can deny that we have a philosophy and that we live our lives according to fundamental principles. But we are probably fooling ourselves. At a minimum, we are likely to be living by principles of which we are unaware. Sometimes it is difficult for us to see ourselves as liberals, in the same way that it is hard to see ourselves as we are seen by others. Sometimes it is difficult to see others as liberals because they adopt more or less the same attitudes that we do—that is to say, it may be difficult to see another as adopting a liberal way of being when this is our own way of being.

Liberalism manifests itself as a way of thinking in a variety of ways. It is reflected in the way that a person looks at the world. It is reflected in the sorts of things that a person knows and the ways in which that person pursues further knowledge. It may also be reflected in the way people conduct themselves. This is not exactly the same thing as the things that they do and refers more to the motivations that move them to act and the demeanour they adopt when acting.

Individuals

Liberals look at the world in particular ways. Individuals are central to their world. Individuals stand out, such that societies are understood in terms of individuals. Societies are the result of individuals and exist for individuals. Nevertheless, liberals do not see individuals in exactly the same way. All tend to see them as self-centred; only some see them as selfish; others simply see them as beginning from a centre in the self but not having to endlessly promote that self over others.

Reason

All liberals understand people to be reasonable or capable of being reasonable. They divide, though, over the question of whether that reason will always be employed selfishly. Reason is a capacity to identify goals and to conceive of means to achieve those goals. It is an ability to order information and experiences to make sense of the world. It includes a capacity to predict future events based on inferences from current conditions and experience. Most liberals do not believe that all individuals have fully developed their reasoning abilities. Sometimes this reflects a lack of formal education. Sometimes it is due to a lack of opportunity for individuals to use and develop their reason.

Individuality and reason

For a liberal, life is a process in which individuals attempt to understand and realise their potential. Individuals are responsible for their own life and the directions that it takes. They are members of society and not, as a socialist might think, products of their society. People can choose and they can use reason to help them determine their choices. To conduct oneself properly is to take responsibility for one's self-development, or actualisation, and to use reason in choosing one's life path.

Freedom and rights

Two of the most important ways in which liberals attempt to have individuality respected and protected is through appeals to individual freedom and individual rights. Freedom is necessary if individuals are able to use reason to pursue their goals and to realise their potential. Only if they are left to choose and act for themselves, liberals believe, can they become truly individual. Rights are required in order to protect individuals from interference in their lives: from other individuals, who are pursuing their own interests and who may want to treat them in ways they do not want; and from governments, which may seek to treat them in undesirable ways.

'Liberal' as public philosophy (as way of acting)

Their views mean that liberals are often attracted to public positions as vehicles through which they can articulate or implement their private philosophies. Liberals may be or seek to become part of formal politics (such as politician or bureaucrat). They may be active in groups whose members seek to influence political decisions (sometimes referred to as pressure groups). They may also engage in less direct forms of political influence as commentators on or interpreters of politics. In this case they may be part of broader intellectual communities that have political effects.

Formal politics

Liberals can be found in the Liberal Party of Australia. This is not an automatic association, however, as the Liberal Party has become a party that expresses the interests of urban Australians who do not support the Australian Labor Party (ALP). The Liberal Party, like all 'catch-all' parties, encompasses people with a variety of ideological commitments. Indeed, other major and minor parties, including the ALP, may adopt positions attractive to liberals. Thus liberals may be found in almost all Australian political parties.

Liberals are also attracted to the Australian Public Service, for the Public Service can be seen as an institution through which liberals can put their philosophy into practice. Of course, the Public Service may simply be a place in which liberals have found work. To hold too strongly to this latter view would be to maintain that Australian habit of denying that people pursue careers in the Public Service because they are committed to public service.

Liberals may also find themselves attracted to the legal system and, in particular, the judicial system. The judicial system in Australia may be understood to be founded on liberal principles and to be a means for pursuing liberal principles. Decisions handed down in Australian courts, especially the High Court of Australia, reflect attempts by judges to defend or pursue certain social and political principles.

Informal politics

Liberal principles also lead people to engage in less formal political activities. Liberals join groups that are only occasionally active in promoting certain political principles, or that exist for a particular period and develop in order to influence the formal political processes. Pressure groups often form for particular purposes and cease to function when that purpose has been achieved.

Myriad groups form to exert pressure on the formal political process. Worker and employer groups are two of the most familiar to Australians. Primary and secondary producer groups are also active. Aboriginal Australians also mobilise to exert direct pressure on the political process. Pressure also comes from environmental movements, peace movements, and movements for equal treatment of individuals of different sexes, sexualities, races, and ethnicities. In a number of cases the principles of liberalism match the principles that unify these groups fairly closely. In such instances liberals will be highly motivated to pursue alternative forms of political participation.

Networks of intellectuals

Formal and informal political organisations are not the only places in which liberals figure in Australian politics. They have also been significant in shaping what might be called the Australian political culture. Their influence may be understood in terms of their membership of three types of community that have been important in shaping this culture: intellectual communities, business communities, and media communities. Universities have been important points in the networks of intellectuals, but intellectual networks are not limited to them. Various artistic and creative organisations and communities also help shape Australian political culture.

The business community contributes quite directly to shaping Australian political culture, in a variety of ways. It exerts influence, for example, by funding research organisations, while the fact that business leaders are often taken to be community leaders means that their views are often prominent in political debates in Australia.

The significance of the media for Australian political culture is unquestionable. Those who work in the media may be understood to constitute a somewhat coherent community, which has a culture shaped by its members. This community then has an important role in shaping Australian political culture more generally.

The thinkers dealt with in this book

The thinkers whose works are studied in this book have been active in a variety of formal, informal, and extra-political organisations and groups. Their principles predisposed them to public action and developed, possibly changed substantially, as a result of public action. Liberalism may be understood as a living political philosophy because it provides the motivation and agenda for public action. Each of the thinkers engaged in a variety of public actions. Indeed it was because of their public actions that they figure in this book.

Charles Pearson was a member of the Legislative Assembly in Victoria, taught at the University of Melbourne, was headmaster at the Presbyterian Ladies' College, and wrote a report for the Victorian government that examined the possibility of creating a system of free education in that colony.

Vida Goldstein was a leading figure in the women's suffrage movement in Victoria and formed the Women's Political Association (she was also well known in women's suffrage movements in the UK and the USA). She also edited the journal *Woman's Sphere* and twice ran, unsuccessfully, for the Senate.

Walter Murdoch taught at and was Chancellor of the University of Western Australia. He is best known for his newspaper columns and radio broadcasts. He was also president of a local, West Australian chapter of the League of Nations Union and fought strongly against Menzies' attempt to ban the Communist Party of Australia.

William Charles Wentworth was a leading figure in the Australian Patriotic Association, was a member of the Legislative Council of the colony of New South Wales, and edited the *Australian* newspaper.

Henry Bournes Higgins was a member of the Legislative Assembly in Victoria and the federal House of Representatives. He was a delegate to the Constitutional Conventions in which the Australian Constitution was devised. He was appointed to the High Court of Australia and was the first president of the Commonwealth Court of Conciliation and Arbitration.

Robert Menzies was a member of the Victorian parliament and Deputy Premier. Later he was elected to the federal parliament and became Prime Minister as leader of the United Australia Party. When that party collapsed he took part in the re-formation of the Liberal Party of Australia and became its leader and, in this position, Prime Minister.

Sara Dowse was press secretary for the Federal Minister for Labour. Later she was head of the Office of Women's Affairs (which became the Women's Affairs Office and then the Commonwealth Office of the Status of Women). She contributed columns to various newspapers and magazines and has written six novels.

Alfred Deakin was a member of the Legislative Assembly in Victoria and became Minister for Public Works and Minister for Water Supply. He joined federal parliament, was Attorney-General, and then became Prime Minister of Australia.

Herbert Cole Coombs was an adviser to a series of prime ministers, both Labor and Liberal. During the Second World War he was director of rationing and after the war became director-general of the Office of Post-War Reconstruction. He was Governor of the Reserve Bank of

Australia, Chancellor of the Australian National University, and headed the Royal Commission into Australian Government Administration.

John Hewson was an adviser on economic issues to two federal treasurers. He was a professor of economics at the University of New South Wales. He was elected to federal parliament and became leader of the federal parliamentary Liberal Party and Leader of the federal Opposition.

Liberalism in Australia

Australian liberals stand at something of a crossroad in which locality as derivation and situation meet as private philosophy and public action. They are bearers, creators, and adapters of a political philosophy that is both general, in being a form of liberalism, and particular, in being a form of liberalism articulated within and for a particular community. In some instances the thinkers studied in this book have applied liberal principles self-consciously to the Australian situation. In other cases they have developed personal philosophies and practices that reflect liberal principles but have not been self-consciously generated as 'liberalism'.[3]

As has been discussed, core principles of liberal political thought include a concern with promoting and facilitating the expression of individuality, a belief in reason, and the defence of freedom and human rights. While these principles are not always directly articulated, they condition the way liberals deal with political issues of a less fundamental nature. The studies presented in this book reflect this tendency for liberal principles to be expressed in terms of more immediate issues. Character and citizenship, social stratification, and economics (governments and markets) have been chosen as focal points for the expression and application of liberal principles.

Character and citizenship

Issues concerning character and citizenship are important for liberals in Australia for two reasons. First, they relate to the general problem of maximising each person's capacity to self-actualise within the Australian community. At another level, they relate to the interaction between liberal and democratic theory that arose in the very early stages of the development of the Australian colonies, in which liberals in Australia had to engage with democratic principles. Dealing with the challenge of optimising political participation within a society strongly influenced by liberal principles has created a number of problems for liberals in Australia.

As has already been discussed, liberals place great emphasis on individual self-actualisation. Their concern with character is in part a reflection of this desire to promote self-actualisation, and increasing powers of reason is seen as important to it. Most liberals, however, do not accept that all people have achieved a degree of rationality that allows them to properly perceive and adequately further their interests. Some seek to facilitate the achievement of good character as this reflects their desire to promote an individual's achievement of a fully rational state. Self-actualisation is not simply a function of improvement in reasoning power, however. It is also a reflection of active engagement in public discourse. People also require the ability to engage in effective public action. To do so they must acquire abilities associated with citizenship.

For a liberal, citizenship primarily involves a capacity for effective engagement in those public forums through which an individual's interests are articulated and defended. To some extent, this simply amounts to understanding the political system and the moments at which individuals can have their views recorded or otherwise registered. It also means the capacity, on the part of individuals, to express their opinions clearly and as fully as possible in public forums. This in turn requires the ability to communicate and persuade others of the validity of their views and interests. A final, though less obvious, ingredient of citizenship is a sense of political efficacy. For people to have a sense of this means they believe that what they think matters and can influence public discussions and policies.

The encounter between liberalism and democracy, in general and in Australia, provides another way to understand the significance of character and citizenship for liberals. Many liberals, especially in the nineteenth and early twentieth centuries, feared democracy and political participation from the masses. Their fears grew as voting rights were extended to the point where full adult suffrage became the norm rather than the exception. Improving people's character, then, may be understood as a way of ensuring that mass participation in politics was not as dangerous as it first appeared. Citizenship was important in ensuring that public participation in Australia was regulated by certain standards for 'proper' participation in politics.

Character and citizenship cover a variety of problems and practices for Australian liberals. The most obvious practice is an active participation in public education. Pearson, Goldstein, and Murdoch, the three liberals whose works are dealt with in Part I, were all active in providing and promoting education. Goldstein was co-founder of a school for girls in St Kilda. Her decision to close the school simply represented a move to raising women's consciousness more generally. She ran newspapers, organised women's forums, and ran for federal parliament in order to educate women. Pearson was also active in providing and promoting education for women, and he sought to create a comprehensive system of education in Victoria. Murdoch wrote guides to Australian politics and citizenship for use in Australian schools.

Liberals may also seek to facilitate participation in society and politics by those to whom it is not yet available: first, because this participation is taken to be educational for individuals themselves as well as for those who come to hear their voice; second, because a lack of opportunities for individuals to participate in society and politics would preclude the full expression of their individuality. Pearson and Goldstein sought to encourage and create opportunities for women to engage in various forms of social and political participation that were at that time denied to them.

Social stratification

While liberals may believe that people have equal rights, they do not assume that they possess equal abilities. Indeed, they believe the opposite. Part of the reason that liberals argue that individuals need freedom and opportunities for self-expression is so that they can express their fundamental differences. That individuals are different means that only some of them will have the skills and attitudes conducive to success in economic or material pursuits; some will attain more wealth than others. This does not present a problem until inequality becomes entrenched in society and results in members of particular groups being unable to pursue their interests effectively. At this point, social inequality ceases to reflect natural differences and begins to reflect artificial differences, or differences that are produced by society. Liberals are wary of, if not hostile to, these artificial differences as they mean that equality of opportunity is not available to all individuals.

Liberals expect that some people will be more successful in society than others. This may be taken for a good thing if it rewards each individual's abilities and efforts and encourages individual initiative. Under these conditions, social inequality is in everyone's interest.

But when inequality becomes entrenched, or systemic, it reflects membership of an advantaged or disadvantaged group and not individual ability or potential.

In this case, social strata can be said to have developed. Social strata represent forms of inequality that do not reflect ability but opportunity. Members of some groups in society possess greater economic and political resources than do those who belong to other groups. Greater economic resources can be used to give children opportunities to develop their abilities which are not available to children in other groups. These resources simply allow some people to create a far richer environment for themselves and their children. Richer environments are more conducive to individual development than impoverished ones. Greater political resources give certain groups more influence over public policy than others have, and this influence is often used to further the interests of members of that group. Neither of these advantages produces a society in which equality of opportunity exists for all people.

William Charles Wentworth, Henry Bournes Higgins, Robert Menzies, and Sara Dowse all argued that Australian society had become stratified. They believed, consequently, that equality of opportunity did not exist. In their view, certain groups whose privileged position allowed them greater opportunities for participation and reward than were available to members of other groups dominated Australian society. Wentworth believed that emancipated convicts and their offspring were denied opportunities to achieve wealth and influence because of the domination of a group that consisted of colonial administrators, former administrators, and wealthy free settlers who received their favour. Higgins thought that working men were denied opportunities to live full and healthy lives because of the economic power of employers. Menzies argued that an industrious and self-reliant middle class was being marginalised and discriminated against because of the domination of organised labour on the one hand and 'the rich' on the other. Dowse believed that women were being denied opportunities, rights, and the resources to which they were entitled because of male domination of politics and society.

Economics: governments and markets

Economics is central to any theory of social organisation. This may not be an essential connection in all forms of political theory, but in liberal political theory the nexus is direct. Part of the intellectual heritage of liberal political theory lies in classical economics, but the connection in liberal thought is more direct because the classical economists were very influential in early liberal political theory. Questions of the relationship between governments and markets are recurrent throughout the history of liberal political thought. While all liberals support some use of markets to optimise the production and distribution of goods and services within a community, they often disagree about the proper relationship between governments and markets. Liberal principles have been used to justify everything from a near complete separation of governments and markets to very significant government regulation of the market (in short, liberalism includes everything from *laissez-faire* policies to those that result in the creation of a welfare state).

In the end, the basic question for liberals with respect to government and economy is the degree of government regulation of, intervention into and other forms of involvement in markets. All liberals accept that markets could allow opportunities for individual initiative, but not all would consider those opportunities more desirable than other possibilities that might be created through government intervention. Some liberals favour minimal government involvement in markets; others believe that some resources should be extracted from markets and some involvement from government is required for a sound and healthy society; others again hold that market forces are necessary but often divisive and must be ameliorated, if not counteracted, through community-building forces generated by governments.

Alfred Deakin believed that the relatively undeveloped state of the Australian economy and society required extensive government intervention to promote and protect local markets and the people who depended on them. Herbert Cole Coombs argued that markets were sometimes inefficient and often unstable. They were certainly, in his view, unreliable mechanisms for producing a sound economy and society. To achieve these ends necessitated government control over, and interventions to alter, the operation of market forces. John Hewson, on the other hand, adopted a *laissez-faire* position. He argued that most, if not all, forms of government intervention into markets were economically and socially disastrous and believed that governments ought to facilitate market forces and not interfere with markets.

The three themes or issues around which this book has been organised are not unique to liberalism in Australia. They represent themes or issues that arise as a result of the basic principles of liberal thought and may arise at any time in any place. The specific form in which the ten liberal thinkers take them up, however, often reflects particular factors present in the Australian context. In this way, the derived forms of liberal political thought meet the specificities of the Australian situation and from this emerges liberalism in Australia.

---

1   Sadly, non-Aboriginal culture has been unable to absorb many elements, apart from words, from Aboriginal culture, and assimilation remains the dominant approach to Aboriginal culture and people.

2   This is not intended to indicate that public/private is somehow natural or that it is without problems, but that the distinction can be useful for certain purposes. For discussions of the public/private distinction, see Landes (1998).

3   Hartz has provided an explanation for this unconscious liberalism: 'the very triumph of the European ideology in the fragment traditions makes it unrecognisable in the old sense. We know the European ideology, indeed we name it, in terms of its enemies, in terms of the whole of the classical European social struggle. When fragmentation detaches it from this context, and makes it master of a whole region, all sorts of magic inevitably take place. First of all it becomes a universal, sinking beneath the surface of thought to the level of an assumption' (1964: 5).

Part 1

CHARACTER AND CITIZENSHIP

That liberals share a concern with promoting individual development and expression goes a long way to explaining their interest in character and citizenship. If individuals are to live the best and most fulfilling lives of which they are capable, they require, at least, the skills to achieve this. Most liberals, and almost all Australian liberals, believe that individuals are not born fully equipped for leading the most fulfilling life possible, and argue that they require assistance in order to attain the requisite abilities. A commitment to ensuring that all people have access to and undergo at least some degree of formal education is the most obvious manifestation of this aspect of liberal thinking. Those who lack formal education, from this perspective, are significantly less likely to be able to identify and effectively pursue their interests.

Rationality

Their belief in the potential for increased rationality at an individual and social level is also a motive for liberals to concern themselves with character and citizenship. Increased rationality may well be understood as being at the heart of improved character. But attention must be paid here to the fact that rationality may well have different forms and that only some liberals will see it in terms of identifying and satisfying material interests. Some liberals reject this instrumental rationality as the only form of rationality and understand improvement in character as increased awareness of and commitment to non-material interests. Having a good character, in this case, means something other than being able to satisfy material interests. It means being more thoughtful, being better able to appreciate cultural and artistic pursuits, and it may even include becoming more moral beings.

An important point to note in this context is that liberals understand individual development to provide the basis for, if not to represent, social improvement. Increased instrumental rationality can be related directly to increased productivity. People who are more rational are more efficient and effective economic actors and are essential to well-functioning markets. An ability to appreciate 'higher' cultural and intellectual pursuits, on the other hand, makes for a richer and more refined society. Greater morality in individuals produces greater social cohesion and a generally more humane society.

Voting

Of course the need for liberals to respond to greater political participation may also explain their interest in improving character. If more people were to be given the vote, society would suffer if they did not use this vote well. Liberals tend to assume that individuals who are more rational are more likely to use their vote well and to make decisions that are not a result of some unthinking whim or connivance on the part of clever manipulators of popular emotion. Rational individuals, from this perspective, are more thoughtful and reliable voters. If there was to be a democracy, many liberals argued, then the people had to be equipped to act wisely.

Citizenship may also be understood to constitute an aspect of good character. Expressing individuality and self-actualisation often requires public action. Developing oneself as a human being may also require public action. A significant increase in self-confidence may accrue to individuals who know that they can participate effectively in public forums and have their voice heard, if not heeded. Individuals can suffer if they know what they want or know what is right but cannot express this publicly when the need arises.

Pearson, Goldstein, and Murdoch

The liberals whose works are examined in Part I all sought to promote good character and citizenship. All engaged, at some stage of their career, in providing formal education. They also promoted good character and citizenship in less formal ways. Charles Pearson and Vida Goldstein were both responsible for overseeing schools—indeed both were involved in schools for women. Walter Murdoch taught at two Australian universities. Pearson and Goldstein were active in informal educational activities, whereas Murdoch tended to promote good character and citizenship through his books and newspaper columns.

Vida Goldstein's project was the most daunting of the three. Women faced a series of very real obstacles to their acquisition of good character and citizenship. Their socialisation was not conducive to public action. The range of interests that were constructed as legitimate for women was heavily circumscribed. They did not have as ready access to formal education as men. They were denied the vote for much of Goldstein's life and were otherwise precluded from full participation in the public sphere. Even when their life situations provided them with greater moral sensibility and higher powers of identification with others, they were prevented from expressing this. Goldstein's project was to create conditions under which women could fully develop their characters and to change political institutions so that women could act more effectively in the public sphere. She always understood her role as being both educational and political (though she may well have denied the validity of this distinction).

Pearson was interested in increasing the life possibilities and political participation of women and was also concerned with broader educational issues and policies and the general refinement of Australian society. He looked to general social improvement and directed his energies accordingly. Improving women's opportunities to achieve and express themselves was an important part of this process, but the objectives were broader and the obstacles less debilitating for his project than they were for Goldstein's.

Murdoch's objectives were probably more nebulous than Goldstein's, in that problems women faced in developing and expressing their individuality were immediate and obvious. Gaining the vote was a tangible and important aspect of Goldstein's project. Making education accessible to women and opening career paths to them, which meant that they could aspire to and actually attain careers of their choice, was also a tangible project. Murdoch's goal of raising the standard of private and public life in Australia was no less important, but was less tangible. His central objective was to make Australians into a more thoughtful people who were capable of appreciating a variety of dimensions of life. This does not allow for ready translation into specific policy objectives, but Murdoch's character was such that he would have resisted any calls for the introduction of specific policies designed to promote good character and citizenship. He thought that people had to be encouraged to think for themselves and could not be prescribed for by those who knew better. His approach had to be less direct, though his goals were just as important.

However their projects are understood, Pearson, Goldstein, and Murdoch all sought to improve the character of and capacity for effective citizenship on the part of all Australians. They all saw this as giving individuals the ability to recognise and further their true interests and otherwise enrich their lives. They also saw it as a means of creating a better Australian society. In this society, increasingly rational individuals could cooperatively and collectively pursue the creation of a way of life that was conducive to the well-being of all.

2

CHARLES PEARSON
(1830–1894)

I think the first lessons in history ought to concern themselves with what is exalted or tragical, adventurous or picturesque in human or national character, and to deal with the acts and words of men and women rather than with the growth of institutions or the rush and turmoil of revolutions. Is not national character, after all, the most real, and abiding of our possessions? (Pearson 1896: 213)

Charles Henry Pearson was born in England in 1830. He first visited Australia in 1864 and stayed between 1872 and 1888. He was an Oxford graduate and fellow of Oriel College. He held various lecture-ships in England before coming to Australia. In 1873 he held a lecture-ship in history at the University of Melbourne where he founded the Debating Society (which attracted a number of students who became future leaders in Australian politics, including Deakin and Higgins). In 1874 he took up the headmastership of the Presbyterian Ladies College in Melbourne, but was forced to resign after expressing views that were perceived as too radical by the governing body of the college. In 1877 he was commissioned to write a report on the best and most economi-cal way to establish a system of free education in Victoria. In 1878 he was elected to the Victorian parliament (where one of his contributions was to introduce a bill to admit women students to university). In 1878 he was appointed Commissioner to England. Between 1880 and 1881 he was a cabinet minister (without a portfolio).

Pearson saw Australia as a place for the application of the ideas he had been exposed to in English intellectual life. 'Although he had been prepared or forced to make compromises, Pearson still represented …

a Liberal tradition concerned with long-term objective as distinct from the immediate grasping of power—a kind of embodied Liberal conscience' (Tregenza 1968: 230). For Pearson, Australia was an open land in which the absence of the restrictions and other corrupting elements of British culture had produced a form of government and individual character that gave individuals opportunities and capacities for development not available in Britain, for instance secular instruction in state schools (see Tregenza 1968: 227–8). Thus while major progressive or liberal writers of the time 'are perhaps not as well known or judiciously estimated in Victoria as in England … they exercise incomparably more influence, because, when an idea, right or wrong, has filtered into the public mind through the press, it is much easier to apply it in a new country than in an old, in a country where the retarding forces are small, than in one where they are all powerful' (Pearson 1879: 690).[1]

Pearson's concern with character reflects an important disposition on the part of many English and Australian liberals of his time. In order to achieve social cohesion, progression, and sound democratic process it was vital that individuals were able to make the best use of their freedom, that they were fitted for this freedom, and that they manifested a capacity for personal development. All depended on their developing and improving their characters. The conditions under which individuals formed their characters were a crucial determinant of both their capacity to improve and that of society to progress. For Pearson and other liberals of this time, the 'case that good government was consistent with a larger electorate rested heavily on a vision of educational enlightenment in which intellectuals such as themselves were to play a central role in upholding morality and imbuing a self-governing people with responsibility and purpose' (Macintyre 1991: 143).

This chapter is divided into three sections. In the first, Pearson's ideas on the elements of good character are discussed. The second is an examination of his views on the sources of character. His views on the relationships between politics and character are dealt with in the final part. The first section is intended to provide a basic outline of the form of character Pearson considered desirable. In the second, practices and institutions are suggested that conduce to the acquisition of good character.[2] The final section is an examination of the political dimensions of character. This is dealt with in two ways: in terms of the role that political institutions play in character formation, and in terms of the opportunities that these institutions provide for the expression of good character.

The Elements of Good Character

Pearson's conception of the highest form of human character privileges a number of fundamental attributes. Those examined in this section are individuality, a capacity to learn from those who have attained higher characters, discipline, and patriotism. Individuality provides the essential ingredients of personal difference and the motivation to express and promote that difference. The ability to attune to higher minds allows individuals to develop and increase their appreciation of the higher aspects of life. Discipline fits individuals with both the capacity to live in a society and the wherewithal to achieve their goals. Patriotism evinces a capacity on the part of individuals for exertion to further a collective interest. Pearson provided something of an overview of his ideas on these subjects in the following quotation: 'First and last, we have to fall back on ourselves, and to ask whether the springs of will are stronger than they were, the purpose of life nobler, the mental vision keener, and if the habit of unselfish action has become more and more a part of our moral being' (Pearson 1896: 100).

Individuality

The first attribute of good character, in Pearson's view, was the ability to think and act for oneself. This did not necessitate selfishness, as the preceding quotation might suggest, but it did require an ability and desire to express individuality. Pearson 'could never look with any satisfaction on extensions of state authority which reduced the chances of individuals thinking and acting for themselves' (Tregenza 1968: 125). He sided with those who believed 'that the man[3] who cries to the State to help him, when he ought to help himself, will gradually suffer paralysis of strength and will' (Pearson 1893: 26).

Above all, individuals required freedom. They required protection from interference with their fundamental rights. For the right 'to think mistakenly, to speak foolishly, and to live within limits riotously … [is] also the right to believe on conviction, to denounce error fearlessly, and to lead sweet and wholesome lives' (Pearson 1893: 199). People could not be coerced or otherwise have their freedom of action limited. They had to be left to their own devices, even if this meant that they made mistakes.

People may seek protection from their own inadequacies. To provide such protection, however, would weaken them as individuals and make society as a whole worse off. Achieving individuality, especially the refined version Pearson promoted, was an onerous responsibility. It was particularly difficult to attain in a society that promoted facile amusements: 'What is a society that has no purpose beyond supplying the day's needs, and amusing the day's vacuity to do with the terrible burden of personality?' (Pearson 1893: 337). Pearson foresaw a situation in which modern societies offered increasing levels of protection and provision for their people. These societies may have been comfortable and affluent but they were 'deficient in the spiritual reserve which an older and more imperfect society possessed in the initiative and resource of its members' (1893: 262).

Interaction with other (higher) minds

Individuality, in Pearson's view, could not be developed fully in isolation. Good character required contact with others and particularly with more highly developed others. For Pearson, 'the contact of mind with mind is perhaps the main factor in intellectual development'. Thus 'the minds of the highest order are very sensible to the need of human intercourse, and are apt to feel their own want of criticism and sympathy to an extent that is sometimes incompatible with self-reliance' (1893: 148, 149).

The most important effects of contact with those of higher or more refined sensibilities were a result of the contagious nature of these sensibilities. Pearson believed that religion had been an important source in producing individual character. He lamented the decline among social elites of religiosity and of a concern for intellectual stimulation, both of which resulted in a decline in individuality in modern societies. 'The influence of deep religious feeling and the influence of exalted intellectual energy have been of such incomparable importance in moulding individual character hitherto, that if we assume them to be powerfully reduced it is difficult to see what can take their place' (1893: 320). A lack of opportunities for individuals to explore higher modes of being left society as a whole worse off. Pearson argued that 'there is positive sin facing us … in the absolute deadness of all society to the claims of a higher life' (quoted in Tregenza 1968: 180).

Pearson was horrified by the substitution in higher social circles of petty amusements and clever conversational gambits for greatness of mind and spirit. He believed that instead of pursuing activities that stimulated intellectual and moral development ,'the world of society prefers the small change of available and ephemeral talent to the wealth of great thoughts'. He longed for a cultural elite 'which shall not allow itself to be absorbed in the riot and the ennui of fashionable gatherings, which shall find better use for its thought than to tone it down into [the] commonplace, and nobler use for its style than affectation of epigrammatic smartness' (1893: 157, 158).

Discipline and self-discipline

Among the attributes of good character, self-discipline was the one that Pearson valued most highly. He believed it was a declining feature of society throughout the world, not just in Australia. A significant decrease in the extent to which people were capable of manifesting self-discipline was debilitating both for individuals and for society as a whole. 'Self-indulgence has become a faith. I accept it but ask whether we may not one day miss the strength given by austere self-constraint' (quoted in Macintyre 1991: 127).

Schools were an important means for instilling self-discipline into people. As headmaster of the Presbyterian Ladies' College, Pearson 'gave full support to conventional nineteenth century ideas of mental discipline. Disciplined minds and "the habits of order and precision mathematics and chemistry give" were what girls needed' (Tregenza 1968: 80). As Macintyre (1991: 157) has noted, 'for Pearson education was first and foremost a means of instilling the vital capacity of self-regulation'.

Discipline was important and useful to an individual and a society, but self-discipline was far more important. In a report on proceedings at his college, Pearson wrote that as 'far as mere discipline goes, our calm has been almost unruffled; and the few offences reported … have been easily dealt with. But till that discipline is self-maintained, till our pupils are a law to themselves, not in the highest class only, but through every part of the school, I shall regard our work as only half done' (quoted in Tregenza 1968: 82).

Patriotism

None of the attributes of good character discussed so far necessarily provide the basis on which a stable and lasting society could exist. Each of them contributed to, or was necessary for, the development of good people, but patriotism was the glue that would hold a society of individuals together. The Roman Empire fell, according to Pearson, 'because there was really no sense of national life in the community' (1893: 182.) He hoped that the 'falling off in energy and acquisitiveness, which are fostered by individualism, will be compensated by the growth of what we may call patriotism, as each man identifies himself more and more with the needs and aspirations of his fellow-countrymen' (1893: 27.)

The main problem with excessive individualism was that it would lead individuals to place their interests above a social interest. Pearson rejected forces that might lead individuals to be insensible to a collective interest. For 'unless we regard the State as merely the casual aggregation of persons who find it to their advantage to live in a certain part of the earth, we must assume that there is, or ought to be, a virtue of patriotism, which will bind the Englishman to England, the Frenchman to France in some special and not easily dissoluble way' (1893: 185).

The collective spirit Pearson sought bound people together and drove them to pursue the best for the community as a whole. Patriotism induced people 'to preserve the body politic as it exists, and recover for it what it has lost, or acquire what seems naturally to belong to it. It seeks within the country to procure the establishment of the best possible order. It enjoins the sacrifice of property, liberty, or life for the attainment of these objects' (1893: 187). Individuals choosing to do these things had not sacrificed their individuality but were oriented to their community in a way that induced them to recognise connection and express their commitment to higher causes and ends. It also liberated energies that could not be liberated in any other way.

Good character expressed individuality, not a grasping or petty form of individuality but higher aspects of human nature, a sense of which was acquired and developed through sympathy with other minds. Good character required the capacity to engage in self-discipline and was expressed at a social level in terms of patriotic feelings and actions. For behind the works of humanity, Pearson argued, were 'the indestructible human mind and moral sympathies' (1896: 110), which operated to produce improvement at an individual and a social level.

The various aspects of Pearson's understanding of good character may well contain some tensions. Nevertheless, for the most part they harmonise into the outline of individuals able to choose and bring themselves to pursue personal and socially responsible goals that expressed their commitment to their country. Pearson was not always sure that social trends would produce such individuals but his commitment to this ideal was unwavering. His own practices as politician and as headmaster were intended to exemplify, as far as possible, the traits he valued so highly. 'No one who came under his influence could fail to be the stronger for it. So obviously had he learnt the secret of building up a strong and pure character himself, that those he came into contact with carried away the unshakeable certainty that the higher life of unselfishness is necessarily and always the noblest' (quoted in Stebbing 1900: 208).

Producing Good Character

The elements of good character are the starting-point for an account of Pearson's ideas on character and citizenship. An examination of the social and political institutions that contributed to the formation of good character must be added to this account. While these institutions could not force people to acquire good character, they could be used to create a better society populated by improved individuals. Pearson was convinced that good character was no longer a product of the influences of family and church. He wondered, as a result, 'whether the new forces that are supplanting the churches and the family can so elevate individual character as to give it a new reserve of strength in place of what it is losing' (1893: 279). He looked mainly to schools and a system of small landholdings as crucial factors in the development of good character.

Decline of the family

Pearson believed that families would cease to function as means for inculcating good character because parents would no longer take responsibility for their children and their character. This was a result of the increased demands on parents, especially at work. In the end, he argued, 'the old family feeling, with which self-respect, loyalty to kindred, discipline and sexual purity were intimately associated, must in the course of time disappear from large towns' (1893: 162). Children would be cared for, but with 'incomparably less anxiety to fit them for the moral obligations of life'. This meant that 'the family, as a constituent part of the State, as the matrix in which character is moulded, will lose its importance' (1893: 255–6).

The disappearance of the family would not result in a complete vacuum, as many of the responsibilities previously undertaken by conscientious parents would be taken over by government. The main benefit of this situation was a reduction in the effects of bad parenting.

The main danger with increased governmental responsibility for children's characters was that the individuality that resulted from differences in home environments would be lost.

Increased levels of government action in this and every other sphere would mean greater uniformity among people.

> What the State does … tends almost entirely to make its citizens more perfect parts of the political machine. Its school-training is bound to be more or less automatic or mechanical; the service in the ranks which it enforces will subdue the will even more than it develops the faculties; and if it organises labour, it is likely to do it on conditions of democratic equality that will maintain as far as possible a dead level among employees. (Pearson 1893: 279)

A smoother functioning might be produced at a political level, but the individuality associated with good character might well be lost. Under these conditions, character would be more uniform and some of the richness of life would be lost.

Schooling

Like most liberals, Pearson was convinced of the importance and efficacy of education for forming character. In his view, 'education … increases insight and foresight' (1875: 15), and its 'chief object' is to 'strengthen the faculties' (1878: 89). He believed that 'an educated community is on the whole more moral, more law-abiding, and more capable of work than an uneducated' (1878: 39).

Schools were central to an individual's acquisition of good character. On this basis, Pearson argued that an inspector should reward headmasters of schools in which students demonstrated 'good manners and a sense of honour' (1878: 59). This could be communicated to students via the examples set by their masters: 'any influence for good the master may bring, from the earnestness of a simple and straightforward life, is multiplied indefinitely by the electric sympathies of great masses of students' (1875: 18). He thought that creating a large body of students was important to the development of a sense of belonging to a larger whole. He believed, then, that 'the mixing in large classes, the sense of being attached to a large community, ought … to be an important part of education' (1875: 18).

Schools would also play a major part in reforming, or otherwise redeeming, children with flawed characters. Pearson supported the policy of allowing 'gutter children' to attend the same schools as other children. He argued that 'the chief value of the experiment would be to give a chance of reformation to the better disposed' (1878: 46), for 'half the children in a ragged school are generally such as might easily be made amenable to notions of decency and order … There is every possibility that, if they were forced to attend ordinary schools, they would gradually imbibe notions of order, cleanliness, and good taste' (1878: 9).

Pearson wanted to create a comprehensive education system in Victoria that allowed students to move from primary schools to high schools, industrial schools, and university. These would contribute directly to the creation of a society of resourceful and thoughtful people who could apply knowledge and intellect in their day-to-day lives. He rejected, as a delusion, the view 'that University education is … a costly luxury … which does little to promote the general well-being of the graduate or of his country' (1878: 12).

The benefit of higher schooling and universities was that they improved productivity and enriched people's lives. Thus 'the new high schools and the proposed faculty of Practical Science at the University … will give a higher meaning to the work of the farmer, the miner, and the mechanic, as they find that learning and thought can increase the fruits of the earth or the produce of the factory as well as mellow the mind' (1878: 30).

Women and schooling

Giving women access to all levels of education was an essential element of Pearson's social and political agenda. He supported this for two main reasons: because it improved their character, since 'a woman cannot fail to be the better for the habits of order and precision mathematics and chemistry give' (1875: 14); and because their studies would prevent women from wasting their time and lives on inessential, if not frivolous, activities. Pearson believed that without 'healthy subjects of interest girls and women will catch at those which are trivial, morbid and wrong' (1875: 13).

He had little sympathy for claims that women would be harmed as a result of the nervous tension caused by hard study. Besides, he responded, for every girl injured in such a way 'is it too much to say that fifty are permanently the worse for a thousand forms of fashionable idleness and excitement, for novel-reading and theatre-going, for balls and picnics, and for the consuming *ennui* of a life wasted upon trifles' (1875: 9).

Educating women would not simply improve their characters, however. It would have a beneficial effect on men's characters. Educated women were essential if Australian society was to lose some of its roughness and crudity. Pearson 'had always been deeply interested in the improvement everywhere of female education. For the elevation and refinement of young countries, such as the Australian colonies, he esteemed it of supreme importance' (Stebbing 1900: 209). Educated women, Pearson argued, would 'be better companions; more intelligent, more vivacious, with more character and self-respect' (1875: 12). Australia would remain full of rough-hewn men, but their edges could be softened, even if their attitudes might not be changed, through the influence of educated women.

A system of small landholdings

Pearson believed that an individual's relation to the land was of crucial importance. Possessing a small parcel of land was, in his view, an essential part of the formation of good character. The instant that people bought land in Australia they became 'sober, hard-working, and trustworthy, as one who has a stake in the country and a position to maintain' (1867: 207). 'The Germans and Irish immigrants, who come over often half barbarous, are gradually rising above the English in their own class, simply because the Germans and the Irishmen put their money into land, and the Englishman turns his money into drink for himself and dress for his wife' (1867: 207).

Pearson thought all people had an instinct to own land and that to work one's own land was a superior form of life to most others. Thus he thought 'the position of the man farming his own land ... incomparably better than that of the hired field hand or mechanic' (1880: 528). His experiences in Australia 'persuaded him of the power of free institutions, good wages and the ready availability of land, to give men who worked with their hands an independence and self-respect unknown in England' (Tregenza 1968: 45).

In his view, small-scale farming provided a stable base for a society, for these farmers were 'never likely to commit themselves to abstract declarations of rights or democratic crusades' (1867: 216).

The positive effects of small landholding on individuals would, of course, also benefit the society to which they belonged. Pearson wanted to see Australia occupied in this way because he believed that a system of large estates was 'fraught with every possible evil and danger; bad for production, bad for national strength; and certain to engender a bitter class-feeling in all ranks' (1880: 527). Unfortunately, in Pearson's view, a system of large estates had become the dominant form of land occupation. A society of small landholders who worked their own land, or a yeomanry, was decreasingly likely as government policy tended in the opposite direction. Pearson complained that the Victorian government had 'sold nearly two-thirds, and that the better two-thirds of our available land; and we have not the smallest reason for supposing that we have established a yeomanry' (1880: 525).

> That the family and church were no longer powerful contributors to the formation of good character led Pearson to look to other means to achieve this end. Schooling was a key as it was here that the mind could be strengthened and the impulses to community and morality reinforced. This was particularly true of women. Educated women would not be prone to problems associated with a lack of proper stimulation. In addition, they could bring their influences to bear in softening the unrefined men of Australia. Schooling would also provide an avenue through which blighted characters might be reformed. A system of small landholding was the other important factor in the formation of good character. It contributed directly to the creation of hard-working and responsible people who provided social stability.

Politics and Character

A well-designed, well-supported, and well-monitored school system and occupation of the land via small landholdings were important preconditions for the formation of good character, but they were only preconditions. Opportunities were also required for the expression and extension of good character, and these were provided by political institutions. A well-conceived and organised set of political institutions would bring out the best in individuals and produce sound public polices.

Political institutions contributed to the full realisation of good character in three ways: through the legislation they produced; as forums for the expression and exemplification of good character; and as symbolic expressions of community. Legislation was important because it could be used to promote desirable behaviour. Political institutions could also be organised such that their very operation required and contributed to the formation of sound attitudes and moral actions among citizens; democratic institutions were the best example of these. Finally, political institutions produced and maintained social cohesion by functioning as focal points of patriotic feelings and actions.

Pearson was particularly concerned that Australian society was infected by defects in British society. Poverty in Britain, he argued, was 'due very much to British institutions'. It resulted from large estates, inadequate education, and from 'the fact that the population at large is governed by a few hundred gentlemen who are chosen almost without exception from a class that has no experience of poverty, and that is largely interested in the existing order' (1879: 696–7). Pearson's sense that problems associated with political institutions contributed to the existence of poverty reflects his general belief that politics was a crucial element in the creation of the right social order.

Legislation

Legislation constituted one of the most direct ways though which political institutions affect character. Pearson believed that a variety of recently introduced legislative measures reflected 'certain great advances in morality all over the world … The tendency all the world over is to abolish punishment by death, to stamp out duelling, to punish negligence that ends fatally like a crime' (1896: 101). Legislative interventions to promote good character could take a variety of forms. All involved the creation of an environment within which healthy and provident people existed and functioned.

Pearson believed that the expansion in the role of government represented an inevitable progression in society. He was not overly concerned by this because he thought that 'secular civilisation … is informed with a moral purpose, and is steadily working out what we may call the Christian law of life' (1893: 218). He dismissed those who railed against legislative interventions in social and individual life as advocates of 'individual lawlessness'. These people united 'to denounce as violations of freedom every fresh act of that impassive, ever-dilating power which rends asunder the unrighteous contract between employer and servant, between landlord and tenant, which protects the child from degradation and rescues the woman from misuse' (1893: 219).

Pearson believed that an expanded role for government was in accordance with the general thrust of 'science'. At its simplest level, it reflected the government's responsibility to ensure a healthy social environment. 'Science … is instructing us that it is at our own peril if we allow the conditions of disease to exist anywhere, and that the lives and fortunes of the whole community are at stake if we overlook crowded rooms, bad drainage, foul drinking-water, or diseased food' (1893: 162).

A sound physical environment had to be complemented by sound intellectual and moral environments. Government had to pay careful attention to the incentives and disincentives it created for individual choice if it was to create and maintain these conditions. Taxation was an important element of this system of incentives and disincentives. Pearson argued that among 'the most important questions we have to consider in relation to any tax is how it bears on the morality and well-being of the people'. He supported the abolition of a tax on tea and sugar on the ground that it would make these common indulgences more accessible and would encourage their use in preference to alcohol. It was vitally important, he argued, 'that the cause of temperance should be promoted, with the least possible constraint on the public'. The best means to this end was to give 'the people, in the cheapest possible form, those articles of food which, to a certain extent, take the place of stimulants; of which all partake and which all need' (1877: 7).

Pearson also supported legislation that forced all Australians to 'insure against sickness, old age and death … What I desire is, that every man who cannot show that he has secured himself from becoming chargeable to the State, should be forced to insure with the Government' (1880: 535). Action of this kind would allow the government to single out and punish those who would not take responsibility for their long-term financial security. He wanted to rid society of those who would not provide for their future. 'A community that should rid itself by a tax of its improvident and criminal characters would have purged itself in the first instance of hereditary pauperism', he wrote, 'and would reduce the necessary distress that bad times occasion within the smallest possible limits' (1880: 536–7).

Well-designed institutions

The legislation that governments produced was not the only way in which political institutions could contribute to the development of good character. The very form of political institutions was also important. If they were well-conceived and well-organised, political institutions were important parts of a sound social environment. Pearson marvelled at 'the infinite capabilities of self-respect and generous feeling that show themselves in the English labourer when he lives under free institutions in a new land' (1879: 692). He believed that Tasmania offered a salutary lesson on the beneficial effects of well-designed and well-functioning political institutions. Democratic institutions such as those that existed in Tasmania contributed directly to 'the transformation of a whole people so largely tainted with crime, into one that will compare with most for decency and the absence of grave offence' (quoted in Tregenza 1968: 87).

Democracy

Democratic institutions were particularly conducive, in Pearson's view, to the formation and expression of good character. Well-functioning democracies required citizens who showed responsibility and empathy for those less fortunate. For Pearson, democracy meant self-government 'educated up to a common low level, and trained by the habit of self-government under institutions which secure power to the majority'. People of this sort, he continued, will look 'to the duties of property at least as jealously as to its rights; will sympathise with labour against capital where the two are in apparent antagonism; will wish to see property subdivided; and will be especially careful of whatever secures the independence of the poorer classes, vote by ballot, universal suffrage, and free education' (1879: 688).

Pearson accepted that democratic institutions would not necessarily produce the best policies, but he argued that in a democracy voters 'are bound to interest themselves on all questions of common welfare, bound to form opinions, and bound to give them effect', for while 'a Democratic government will often blunder, and have to retrace its steps … It will not blunder more heavily than its rivals, and … all its experiences will leave it the wiser and the better' (1877: 6).

Plebiscites

Pearson gave strong support to the introduction of plebiscites—what we now call referendums[4]—as a natural part of a democratic system. He believed that this was a logical extension of democratic principles and practices, arguing that the success of democratic institutions in Victoria showed that most of the population was able to deal with more complex issues than those that might be dealt with by plebiscite. Voters had, in Pearson's view, amply demonstrated their ability to take up positions on complex issues. In an election, voters had to choose the best representative as well as 'the best programme, or in some cases to weigh character against opinion, and strike an average' (1880: 540).

Many people, including many politicians, objected to the use of plebiscites to decide major issues of public policy. They argued that these decisions should remain in the hands of those elected to govern. Pearson responded that democracy could not work if people could divest themselves 'of the responsibility of their acts by placing themselves under the control of irresponsible advisers'. He rejected the idea 'that the representative once chosen is to keep the conscience of the constituency for three years' (1880: 540), believing that a democratic system could not function properly if people simply voted and left government to their representatives. Those 'who had looked on with indifference while Parliament was framing bad laws, and who had not cared to understand the purport of the legislation framed, would be absolutely incapable of judging their representatives by their acts' (1880: 540).

Voting in a plebiscite was simply an extension of normal political activity. It was merely an opportunity to express a position about a specific issue that could otherwise constitute part of a general election. In elections voters recorded opinions 'about a Reform Bill, about our State-school system, about Payment of Members, and probably about the institution of State Banks, and to couple these as he best may with the choice of the fittest possible man to represent the district and to aid in devising good laws for the community' (1880: 540–1).

The plebiscite could not be dismissed on the ground that voters were incapable of engaging effectively in democratic processes; they had been satisfying their democratic responsibilities for some time. If the plebiscite had been the first taste of democratic participation that ordinary people would have, it might be treated with some scepticism. Since most people were satisfied that obligations involved in general elections had been 'discharged adequately by the whole community, and that no limitations on manhood suffrage are warranted, I cannot conceive why the infinitely simpler task of deciding for or against a single measure after ample discussion in Parliament, in the press, and at public meetings, should be considered to transcend the limits of national intelligence' (1880: 541).

Well-functioning democratic institutions were important avenues through which individual responsibility and a sense of and concern for community could be evinced and promoted. They also functioned as forums within which exemplary behaviour on the part of leaders of society could be displayed. Pearson rejected attempts by the Victorian Legislative Council to frustrate the will of the Legislative Assembly on the ground that the Council was filled with people who did not deserve their position and could not act with appropriate authority and maturity. While the Legislative Council may have been modelled on the English House of Lords, it was nothing like it. Members of the Legislative Council lacked 'the historic associations, the connection of family names with national life, and, as a consequence of this, the spirit of concession to national wants' (1877: 12).[5] The chief absence in Victorian politics, which this conflict demonstrated, was the lack 'of a habit of constitutional morality' (1880: 539).

The widespread use of democratic institutions was one of the factors that would, in Pearson's view, impede the development of 'political convulsions like the French Revolution'. Pearson made much of 'the remedy for social unrest which the spread of liberal institutions offers' (1893: 322). Who, he wondered, would not support a country that, among other things, provides greater protection for individuals than existed in previous years, 'that adjusts … public burdens so as to be least onerous, that gives … the right to assist in making the laws, that protects him against his own weakness, and offers … the means to start on equal terms in the race for honour or wealth' (1893: 219).

Symbolic unifiers of community

Another important function of political institutions, in Pearson's view, was to provide a focus for patriotism. Political institutions served to bind a community, much in the way that religion had once done. 'The passion for nationality and for free institutions has taken the place of the reforming spirit in religion as a great impulse' (1896: 108). Political institutions that engendered popular support were important contributors to social cohesion. They created an environment in which people felt allegiance to their society and believed that their interests and goals were reflected in public policies.

Revolution, in Pearson's view, would become less likely once 'the State appears to be the best expression of the wishes of the majority' (1893: 27). Everyone would benefit when 'the poorest man in the country … [feels] that he owes inestimable blessings to the political order under which he lives: not only for protection from foreign enemies, but equality before the law, the certainty of employment in bad times, education for his children … and a fair chance of rising out of the ranks if he possesses the requisite ability' (1893: 27–8).

A sense of connection and obligation created by political institutions was intensified through participation in creating a well-functioning community. Participation also fostered a sense of creativity on the part of citizens. Engaging with others in the formation and use of political institutions to further national objectives had 'all the charm of adventure. It is, perhaps, the conscious sense of creative energy, the feeling that we are building up something such as history has never yet recorded, that fascinates us with such a belief in progress as our ancestors have not known even in dreams' (quoted in Stebbing 1900: 252).

> Pearson saw a multifaceted relationship between politics and good character. The laws produced by governments were important for providing an environment that people felt was conducive to their well-being. Democratic institutions allowed and required participation and engagement with the higher responsibilities of community membership. They also allowed people to find connection with political outcomes as an expression of their collective will, which, in turn, enhanced their patriotic feelings.

Conclusion

Pearson's approach to character and citizenship reflects a number of fundamental principles of liberal political thought. The fostering of individuality was central to his thinking. Interaction with people who had more highly developed minds, self-discipline, and patriotism were important to good character because individuality could not be equated with a selfish pursuit of material goods and pleasures and the sacrifice of intellectual and moral development. The chief means through which the basic elements of good character could be communicated and promoted were schools and a system of small landholdings. Political institutions were particularly important for the promotion of good character and effective citizenship through the legislation they produced, the forms of participation they encouraged, and as focal points for patriotic feelings.

Citizenship was important to him, but Pearson's main concern, and the focus of his efforts, was the formation of good character. Goldstein and Murdoch tended to give greater attention to citizenship.

A concern with the formation of good character represents something of an 'old-fashioned' preoccupation. While all liberals desire to promote characteristics associated with good character, contemporary liberals do not evince the same preoccupation that Pearson did. The closest that contemporary discourse comes to a concern with self-development may well be found in the plethora of 'self-help' advice provided in books, magazines, and newspapers. Much of this advice seems to reflect a liberal concern with individuality and self-actualisation; some of it indirectly calls for discipline and self-discipline. It tends to neglect, however, the social dimension of good character that Pearson and other Australian liberals, including Goldstein and Murdoch, sought to promote. Further, this advice rarely outlines a role for governments in the formation of good character and often places the entire responsibility for self-development on the individual (rarely understood as functioning within a political context). The lack of a political dimension to self-help is also manifested in a failure to promote communal feelings such as patriotism. This lack of a political dimension to self-help, combined with a tendency to focus on economic rewards as the primary rewards for successful self-actualisation, results in a failure to consider the positive effects on character of effective participation in political processes. Thus Pearson's approach to and understanding of good character seems markedly different from anything that can be found in contemporary Australian society.

---

1   'I suppose if we had to describe the political work of the last forty years, in the briefest possible way, we might describe it as the carrying out by Englishmen, Scotchmen, and Irishmen, on virgin soil, of the reforms they had dreamed of at home. Grote's vote by ballot; the manhood suffrage, which was an article in the charter of 1848; Fox and Miall's ideal separation of Church and State; O'Connell's Home Rule; the Birmingham League's free and secular education; John Mill's yeoman proprietorship, have all become realities here, while they are for the most part still nothing more than aspirations in England' (Pearson 1896: 220).

2   Some care needs to be taken here. One of Pearson's major works, *National Life and Character*, is a sometimes pessimistic prediction about the future of society and individual character. The factors that shape character may just as well produce undesirable forms of character as desirable forms. However, as Stebbing (1900: 262) has suggested, 'the Liberalism [Pearson] preached pointed rather to the gradual advance of all mankind to a higher state and happier conditions under unerring laws of development.'.

3   My failure to remove sexist language from this book is not intended as implicit or explicit support of the use of sexist language. I found it impossible to remove alleged universals such as 'man', 'he', 'his', etc. because they were used so extensively by many of the authors studied here. I believe that it is no longer necessary to use these

words, as a variety of substitutes exist. I also believe that it is no longer available to people to allege a conventional use that is supposed to legitimise the use of sexist language. I apologise to, and sympathise with, those readers who find it offensive.

4   'The plebiscite was not an intellectual's "impractical enthusiasm". Under its new name of referendum it now has a permanent place in Australia's political system, and if anyone has a claim to be its foster-father, that person is Charles Henry Pearson' (Tregenza 1968: 158).

5   'Their antecedents and talents do not fit them in any eminent degree for the critical work which the English Peers perform. They have been successful as money-makers, not as thinkers or debaters, as administrators, or, for the most part, as professional men. They are conscious that if they claimed, like English Peers, to sit in their own right only, they would fall immeasurably short of the power which they can claim as representatives of a class, no matter how limited' (Pearson 1879: 710).

3

VIDA GOLDSTEIN
(1869–1949)

Philosophers, poets, and statesmen have rhapsodised about the beauty and the blessings of representative government, but few have pictured women as co-partners in such a form of government. America was the birthplace of modern democracy, but America has never dreamt in its philosophy of applying the fundamental principles of the Declaration of Independence to American women. No, it has been left to the newest of nations to admit that as 'men are created equal … endowed by their Creator with certain inalienable rights … [and] to secure those rights governments are instituted, deriving their just powers from the consent of the governed,' so shall women be endowed with the rights that are considered the just due of sane, law-abiding, naturalised men. (Goldstein 1904b: 105)

Vida Goldstein was born in Portland, Victoria, in July 1869. She operated a school for girls in East St Kilda, which she closed in 1899 in order to give all her time to the campaign to secure equal rights for women. Between 1899 and 1905 she was owner and manager of the journal *Woman's Sphere*. In 1902 she went to the Conference of the International Women's Suffrage Society in the USA where she was secretary and a speaker. Goldstein formed the Women's Federal Political Association in 1903. She also stood for the Senate in 1903, which made her one of the first women to stand for election to a national legislature.[1] She stood again in 1911. Despite the fact that she was unsuccessful on both occasions, she showed outstanding political skills. In 1911 she also went to Britain to meet the members of the women's suffrage movement. While she was there, she formed the

Australian and New Zealand Woman's Voters Association (London) to safeguard the interests of Australian and New Zealand Women in the Imperial Parliament. Goldstein was a member and officer of the Criminology Society, which sought to secure better conditions for prisoners. Between 1914 and 1919 she chaired the Peace Alliance and in 1915 formed the Women's Peace Army. She was organiser of the Women's Unemployment Bureau, which operated in 1915 and 1916.

Vida Goldstein dedicated most of her life to the struggle to secure greater opportunities for women in Australian society. She had a leading role in the struggles for women's suffrage that occurred around the turn of the twentieth century. In Searle's view (1988: 61), Goldstein's 'impact on the first wave women's movement in Australia is a legend as she is considered one of the most distinguished suffragists in the history of Western female suffrage movements'.

Her attempts to gain both the vote for women and the right to stand as candidates in elections reflected her general concern with the stultifying effects of an environment in which full participation was not available to all individuals. She campaigned most strongly for female suffrage, the most pressing issue of her time. The denial of the vote to women was a potent sign of the failure to recognise women's individuality and their rights. But it was only one of the signs. Women were excluded from many activities, and the cumulative effect of this was a reduction in the opportunities for women to participate and develop their characters.

The only real difference, in this context, between Goldstein's concerns and those of many male liberals of her time was that she sought to extend the rights and privileges associated with male individuals to women. As is suggested in the quotation with which this chapter began, Goldstein's project was to provide women with access to the same social, political, and economic opportunities as men. Many male liberals had denied opportunities to women, in effect, by denying that they were individuals. They were construed as irrational and otherwise incapable of acting effectively in public forums, which meant they did not have to be accorded the same rights as men. The project of extending the rights of individuals to female individuals required fundamental change to Australian society. This project does not take it outside a liberal political agenda, however. Indeed, it mirrors earlier forms of liberalism as a (radical) rejection of the failure to promote and provide for individual freedom that resulted from the domination of a social elite (whether this elite was the landed nobility of feudal England or colonial administrators in Australia). Goldstein's liberalism, however, shared more with later liberals, such as J. S. Mill, than it did with earlier ones. This was mainly a result of her view that social context was significant for the formation of individuality. Goldstein's liberalism, then, is entirely consistent with the radical dimension of early liberal political thought and the cognition of the significance of the social environment for individuality of later liberal political thought. Indeed, her political project relied on the basic principles of liberal political thought for their meaning and force.

The following discussion of Goldstein's political approach to character and citizenship is presented in two sections. The first is an examination of her views on the stunting effects on women's character, and following that on children and on society, that resulted from their exclusion from social life. One of the most important ways these effects could be counteracted was by allowing women to engage in political processes, in short, by granting them full rights as citizens, and this is looked at in the second section.

Women's Character

Like many other liberals, Goldstein was convinced that environmental factors were crucial in the formation of character. On this basis she argued that social conditions had meant that women were unable to develop their characters fully. This created a number of problems for women as individuals, as members of society, and, most importantly, as mothers. Goldstein argued that one of the more immediate problems caused by socially induced deficiencies in women's character concerned their capacity to fulfil their roles as mothers. She accepted that there were some natural differences in the social roles of men and women but rejected the multitude of artificial devices through which characters were stunted and their life opportunities constrained.

Constraints

Australian women of Goldstein's era were subject to a variety of constraints that precluded them from full participation in social and political life. Discrimination operated at both an official and an unofficial level to deny women opportunities to develop and flourish as full members of society.[2] They were discriminated against as workers and as parents. Thus the initial policies of the Women's Political Association, of which Goldstein was founder and principal representative, included 'equal pay, a Federal divorce law, equal parental authority over children and equal power for husband and wife over the distribution of the accumulation of property in marriage' (Searle 1988: 66).

Women as mothers

Discrimination was harmful for society as a whole because it denied women the opportunity to bring their particular capacities and perspectives fully to bear in the running of society and the family. Goldstein did not attack the view that the primary role of most women was as wife and mother. She simply contended that to deny women both full participation in society and equal authority within the home was to diminish their capacities as mothers.[3]

Central to Goldstein's campaign to improve the status of women was her sense that the role of mother required a much stronger figure who commanded a respect that women did not receive. Freedom was not sought to avoid familial responsibilities but to carry them out effectively. As Bacchi has suggested, 'emancipated women were not trying to avoid maternity. On the contrary, they were awakening to a truer sense of their maternal responsibility'. They would not use artificial means of avoiding motherhood. 'True, the women were in revolt against "enforced maternity" but they would never use methods which they regarded as "nothing less than criminal". Truly emancipated women in her view appealed to reason and self-control' (Bacchi 1980: 149). The idea that emancipation had to do with reason and self-control returns us to the concern with individual development that is part of the explanation for a liberal's general concern with character.

Limited characters

The task of improving the status and life chances for women in Australia had to be carried out in the face of well-entrenched opposition. It required education of both men, who felt that their position was threatened by any improvement in the position of women, and women, who resisted change. Each of the freedoms they won was gained by 'women suffragists, who faced obloquy and the cruellest ridicule in carrying on the educational work in order to rouse the public from its opposition to women's complete social, political, and economic emancipation' (Bomford 1993: 206).

In Goldstein's view, their existence left many women without a full sense of themselves, their social position, and their capabilities. She believed that women lived, for the most part, as adjuncts of men. Thus she sought a society in which 'no longer will woman be relegated to the boudoir as the plaything of the wealthy man, or to the kitchen as the slave of the poor man' (quoted in Bomford 1993: 133). She saw herself as a representative of 'those who are pioneering the way for the women of the future, the women who will be free in the spirit as well as in the letter' (quoted in Bomford 1993: 127). Goldstein's sense of the importance of the English suffragette movement, according to Gowland (1980: 227), was in 'teaching the world that women were not merely weak creatures of sentiment and sex but were strong, self-reliant, self-respecting human beings'.

Women were not born weak and lacking in self-reliance and self-respect; they were made this way. Their social environment had to be altered in fundamental respects if they were to be allowed to achieve strength, self-reliance, and self-respect. Goldstein's sense of the stultifying effects of a poor environment was reflected in her estimation of the quality of the floats produced for the 1920 Labour Day march in London. She wrote that the workers' 'feeble, methodical machine like efforts at decoration on the carts and cars were the only striving after beauty and joy of expression that life and education had hitherto offered them' (quoted in Bomford 1993: 201). In her view, the 'most abandoned men were the victims of wrong education, of low ideals, of no ideals' (quoted in Bomford 1993: 131).

If male workers were victims, then their female counterparts were even worse off. Working-class women 'suffered *both* because of their class position and because they were women. All women, regardless of class, in her opinion, suffered discrimination because of their sex' (Searle 1988: 76). The conditions in which all women found themselves limited the scope of their interests and understanding. They were, consequently, unable to engage fully with many important issues of the day. In a letter to Edith Martyn, an English suffragette, Goldstein expressed her longing for the company of women who engaged with issues of the scale with which they dealt. She wrote that there were no women 'with whom I can discuss the questions in which you and I are interested. No woman at all to whom the moral and legal status of women, their spiritual value in human affairs, the welfare and rights of the so-called "common man", and the interdependence of nations, is really vital' (quoted in Bomford 1993: 212).

Society was replete with forms of discrimination against women. A failure to respect women was an important element in the high incidence of venereal disease in Australia at that time; or so found a committee investigating the control of venereal disease on behalf of the Women's Political Association. The first cause the committee identified as contributing to venereal disease was:

> *Wrong education*, which begins in babyhood owing to the neglect of parents to teach their children to control their restless dispositions, their tempers, and their inclinations to please themselves regardless of others; which refrains from teaching children self respect, respect for each other, respect for their parents and elders; which, by joke and innuendo, treats lightly the natural attraction between youths and girls, and laughs at the disrespect for womanhood expressed in books, in the Press and in the theatre; which inculcates a double standard of morality by teaching boys that they must sow their wild oats, and that chastity and continence are injurious; which fails to teach that marriage is merely legalised prostitution unless it is based upon a love that ennobles both the man and the woman; which fails to teach that the sex function is for one purpose only—that of procreation. (Women's Political Association 1916: 2–3)

Women could not help being diminished when they were subjected to disrespect and double standards.

Nor could they help being diminished as individuals when they were construed as mere objects to be used to satisfy men's needs for sex and progeny. The eighth cause of venereal disease the committee nominated was that 'woman has been considered merely as a creature of sex, to minister to men's physical gratification, and to bring children into the world. Enforced motherhood and unwanted children have made many a woman's life one long, silent tragedy' (Women's Political Association 1916: 3).

That any inadequacy that might be found in women was artificial rather than natural was a central part of Goldstein's attack on the unequal treatment of women. As we have seen, their diminished characters were a result of their social environment and were not some essential problem. Everyone may have been victims of socially induced false consciousness, but women suffered most. Those women who showed no interest in the Women's Political Association tent at the Royal Melbourne Show, for example, 'have been so long in bondage to tradition and custom that their poor enslaved minds cannot grasp the meaning of freedom and justice for themselves, let alone others' (quoted in Bomford 1993: 103).

Granting women full political and social rights would give them the freedom and opportunity to enrich their lives. It would also lead to a more equal society in which women were allowed to enjoy fully what Goldstein took to be the bare necessities of life. No women of her time could claim complete access to these necessities, which included 'good housing, good food, good clothing, good education, choice of occupation, recreation, amusement, books, holidays, and a competency for old age' (quoted in Bomford 1993: 156).

According to Goldstein's reasoning, an improvement in women's position would manifest itself most immediately in an improvement in their capacity as mothers. This improvement would be substantial and could be achieved only through a complete recognition of the contribution that women could make to society. Not all women would take full advantage of the opportunities they might gain, but they had to be seen to be equal to men and worthy of respect if they were to be able to be good mothers and fully realised human beings. Further, they had to be seen to be people endowed with rights and opportunities if their individuality was to be respected and promoted. This could only happen if the social environment in which women found themselves was fundamentally altered. So Goldstein was demanding a complete cycle of reform in which women's social standing and their womanly capacities echoed each other.

Women's Representation

The denial of voting rights was one of the main obstacles to women achieving the freedom to develop their characters. A consequence of denying women full rights as citizens was that their interests were not represented in parliament. Another problem was that women were discouraged from seeing themselves as having a significant role to play in public spheres. While Goldstein committed much of her energies in early life to improving the position of women more generally, in her middle and later years she devoted herself fully to seeking enfranchisement for women. As Kirsten Lees (1995: 123) observed: 'In 1899 she closed the St Kilda coeducational school that she had started with her sisters, and dedicated herself full-time to winning votes for women. (Perhaps she asked herself what was the point in educating girls to be responsible adults if they weren't given a say in the way they were governed.).'

Striving for and gaining the vote were important to women and society for three reasons. First, exclusion from full citizenship reflected a perception that women were incapable of performing public roles; this meant they were not encouraged to develop a broader sense of political issues and to acquire the capacity to engage in public debates and political movements. Gaining the vote was also important because it would provide opportunities to educate women about both their civic duties and the public roles available to them. Finally, allowing women to vote and to enter parliament would lead to the adequate representation of women's interests and would result in a new form of politics, of a higher kind than had previously been possible (see below, pp. 56–8).

Exclusion

Refusing them voting rights was a logical extension of the view that women could not understand issues of substance and were unable to contribute to debates on these issues. Women were perceived, and not just by men, to be inferior in ways that meant they did not deserve either the vote or a place in parliament or cabinet. Goldstein claimed the right to vote as an essential aspect of human nature; *ergo*, that women were human beings required that they be given voting rights. She contended that 'the abstract right of women to the vote need no longer be argued. In these days, in democratic countries, it is not for the voteless to prove their claim, but for those who would exclude any human being from citizenship to make good some special reason for that exclusion' (1901a: 7).

Goldstein may have erred in her presumption that all men, and even all women, saw women as 'human beings'. That many men saw women as inadequate versions of themselves allowed them to believe that women were not fit to participate in politics. Another, and possibly more pernicious, form of the argument for the exclusion of women was that women's characters would be corrupted or somehow besmirched through inclusion in representative processes and assemblies. Goldstein argued that such views were of fairly recent creation. In arguing that women should enter parliament, Goldstein denied that this was a novel proposal. 'Before the long ebb began in the curtailment of women's legal rights and privileges, early in the seventeenth century, women had taken their seats in Parliament on the same terms of men' (1903b: 135).[4]

Women's 'inadequacy'

The views that women were unsuited to political activity and would be tainted by inclusion were pervasive. They were so prevalent that, in Goldstein's view, it required the success of Queen Victoria's reign to destroy 'the old shibboleth that a woman cannot understand politics; she has proved that a woman can participate in the nation's affairs without the slightest sacrifice of her womanly worth and dignity' (1901b: 1). Women could be effective in politics without becoming like men. Queen Victoria was a 'mistress of statecraft,' Goldstein wrote, 'and yet her domestic virtues, her womanly dignity, never suffered for an instant because she played a leading part in politics' (1903b: 135).

While women would not be made worse by politics, politics, in Goldstein's opinion, would be improved through women's participation, for, among other things, women would bring a clearer and more balanced sense of many social issues, especially domestic matters; they would also engage in political activity with a far less combative attitude than men would. Once they appreciated and understood the problems facing society, Goldstein argued, women would see that their participation in politics was vital to the health of their society. Those women who 'came face to face with the adverse conditions of human existence, with social, industrial, and moral problems … saw the urgent need for women taking part in public affairs' (1948:117).

Goldstein regularly encountered resistance from women to their involvement in politics. Her interpretation of this was that those women who would not sign petitions calling for the vote for women were 'those whose interests ended at the garden gate'. These women saw little of their society. Women whose interests extended beyond the garden gate, on the other hand, would realise that the social, industrial, and moral problems that afflicted Australian society were a direct result of women not being given the opportunity and encouraged to participate in politics and public life.

Confining women to the domestic sphere was therefore disastrous because it prevented them from making major contributions to society. It also represented a false division between public and private spheres.

> It is suicidal to divorce the home and the State, and that is what we have done in the past, in insisting on man-governed institutions. The State is only an aggregation of families, and as the best-governed family is that where husband and wife work loyally together in the highest interests of their children, so the best-governed State will be that where men and women work together in the highest interests of the people, the country, the race. (Goldstein 1903b: 136)

Another consequence of their exclusion was that the community was denied the services of a number of able and, indeed, highly talented people. Women were unable to enter public life, but some were particularly suited to contributing in this sphere. Goldstein did not argue that all women were suited to parliament, just as all men were not so suited, 'but once get the right woman, or women, there, and the people will ask themselves "Why on earth didn't we try this experiment before?"'. Queen Victoria's success in public office was merely a foretaste of what was possible. She 'was not a brainy, intellectual, broad-minded woman … [and] shone as a ruler merely through good common-sense and a conscientious appreciation of the great responsibilities laid upon her; but let a woman of great mental capacity, combined with executive ability, enter Parliament, become, perhaps, a Minister, and she will "make surrounding nations stare"' (1903b: 136).

Goldstein further challenged orthodoxy by arguing that excluding men from domestic responsibilities had rendered them less able to organise politics. Men, she argued, lacked a sense of tidiness. 'Untidy at home', she wrote, 'untidy in business, so is he untidy in the nation'. Because of his failure to appreciate 'the first principles of household management, he gets the national household into a terrible state of muddle. He is so busy looking after the big things, that he forgets all about the little things that make the big things a success, instead of a failure' (1904b: 106).

Motherhood, citizenship, and exclusion

The way society treated women created problems in politics and in society. An unbalanced relationship between men and women, in which the latter were denied opportunities available to the former, resulted in maladjusted children. Goldstein believed that 'well-adjusted children were the product of happy, secure parenting in a situation where men and women operated as equals and had the same chances to develop and be educated' (Bomford 1993: 225).

Children raised in families in which both parents were active citizens were much more likely to be good citizens. Only when women were full citizens, Goldstein argued, could they give children a true sense of what citizenship required from them, for 'women cannot train their sons and daughters in the varied, complex, and sacred duties of citizenship unless they possess a first-hand knowledge of what citizenship means'. One of the problems with politics was that 'those who conduct them have been trained by women who have no conception of public duty, who knew not the meaning of public spirit, who, consequently, could not be expected to equip their sons properly for the public arena' (1904b: 106).

War

Goldstein attributed a number of undesirable characteristics of society to the exclusion of women from the public sphere. She argued that war was a direct result of the absence of women's input and an inevitable result of 'the existing commercial and industrial system, the antiquated ideas governing secret diplomacy and foreign affairs, the predatory instincts of financiers, armament firms, newspapers, the Militarism of Germany, the Navalism of Great Britain, and the consequent fear of other nations' (1916: 2). There could be little doubt that men contributed most to this predisposition to war.

Goldstein thought it 'a fearful reflection on 2000 years of Christianity that men have rushed into war before using every combined effort to prevent this appalling conflict. It is my earnest hope that women in all parts of the world will stand together, demanding a more reasonable and civilised way of dealing within international disputes' (quoted in Bomford 1993: 143). Thus Goldstein called on Australian women to reject conscription: 'And so we ask you to be true to your womanhood, and, with your vote, bring to the State the same gifts that you bring to your homes, the gifts of order, of beauty, of forbearance, of harmony, of love. The nations are dying for lack of these gifts from women' (1916: 2).

Education

The quest for representation was much more than simply a struggle to gain the vote. It was also a way to highlight both the problems associated with male-dominated politics and women's capacity to contribute to political debates and forums. It was, in short, a means of educating people, especially women. For gaining the vote of women was as much a matter of changing women's sense of themselves as it was of changing men's views on women. Women's suffrage movements demonstrated that women were capable of organising and campaigning effectively. They showed everyone what women were capable of and gave women a clearer sense of their shared interests.

One of the main reasons that many women did not demand the vote, in Goldstein's view, was that they had not been exposed to the ideas that underpinned such claims. Women who failed to recognise the necessity of their enfranchisement 'only need to hear the *raison d'être* of the woman movement explained to them to range themselves on the side of progress and justice'. It was for this reason that 'the chief value of the suffrage at present is its educational value' (1904a: 49). Women's suffrage movements encouraged and allowed women to see themselves as able to contribute to political debates and in the public sphere more generally.

Goldstein supported all forms of political organisation among women, as they were indicators of increasing engagement with public issues. 'For organisation means education and enlarged interests, and I would sooner see women educated in views diametrically opposed to mine than not educated at all, and displaying the too prevalent apathy and indifference to important social and political questions' (1904a: 49). Of course, the vote would provide women with the greatest incentive to engage with and understand the issues involved in political life, for 'by giving women political power you give them incentive to study, or at least to interest themselves in public questions' (1904b: 106).

Political efficacy

One of Goldstein's main objectives was to increase women's sense of their ability to participate in politics. Encouraging them to engage with major political questions and to pursue voting rights was also a means through which women could be brought to recognise their inherent worth and encouraged to take responsibility for, and exert control over, their lives. Increasing women's self-confidence was a central objective. Increased self-confidence would allow them to resist and reject their treatment at the hands of men.

If nothing else, the struggle for participation was confirmation of the idea that women were both necessary to and could cope in the political sphere. Goldstein believed 'that the only way to teach the world that women were not weak creatures of sentiment and sex was to go out and prove it' (Gowland 1980: 222–3). Women, rather than men, were the primary targets of this message, for many women still had to be convinced of the need for women parliamentarians. Goldstein wrote that 'the prejudice against women entering Parliament is more pronounced amongst women than it is among men. It took about twenty years to educate the women of Australia up to the point of asking for the franchise, and they are going to stick there for some time before they go any further' (1904b: 105–6).

Women's suffrage movements also provided forums within which women could come together to experience and reinforce their sense of community as women. In a parting speech to English suffragists, Goldstein said: 'I have addressed three Albert Hall meetings. Each one has had its own special characteristic, but each has had for centre and circumference an exalted sense of the sisterhood of women, a conception of liberty and justice that the world does not yet understand.' She then told the audience that she left for Australia 'to carry on our work. For it is *our* work. We suffragists are one all the world over. The principles for which we stand, and of which the vote is only a small symbol, have to be woven into the national life everywhere' (quoted in Bomford 1993: 114).

Inclusion
Goldstein based her argument that women had something particular to contribute to representative politics on two main grounds. First, she argued that only women could adequately represent women's interests; this required women's suffrage and female parliamentarians. Second, she contended that the inclusion of women in politics provided the basis for a reconstruction of the political that would move it away from the petty selfishness of the politics of her day and towards a higher form of politics.

Representation of women's interests
As to the first of these, Goldstein took the view that having the vote was only the first step in achieving true justice for women and adequate representation of women's interests. She saw the vote 'as a lever by which it would be possible to introduce into government the representation of matters which were peculiarly women's concern, and about which they were entitled to demand a hearing' (1930: 17).

Getting women into parliament was the next step. 'The vote in itself is a powerful weapon for good', she wrote, but 'direct parliamentary representation is essential if full effect is to be given to the vote' (1904b: 106). Her view that women needed to be represented by women is summed up in her 1910 Senate campaign slogan: '*All the Men* in Parliament cannot represent *One Women* as adequately as *One Woman* can represent *All Women*' (quoted in Bomford 1993: 94).

According to Goldstein, 'Wherever there are women's and children's interests to be considered, women should be there to consider them; because, owing to the differences in sex, men cannot understand such questions from the woman's point of view, and injustices creep in, in spite of their most earnest efforts to prevent them' (1903b: 136). Goldstein thought that men's attempts to deal with women's interests were either pathetic or laughable. Men foundered, whereas 'women, from their personal experience and intimate knowledge of what touches their lives at a hundred points, could steer a straight course' (1903b: 136).

Goldstein ran for the Senate because she believed 'that women should enter Parliament as representatives of the home, and to voice the opinions of women on important domestic and social affairs' (1903a: 360). She was unsuccessful. If she had received greater support from women voters, she would have been elected. However, 'she understood that they were so ignorant politically that they had not yet learned that it was impossible to get the necessary reforms from men, not because men were unjust but because they did not know how to be just to women' (Bomford 1993: 99).

The immediate consequence of women's entry into parliament was that they would bring a special expertise to the handling of matters that affected women. This would enable parliament to address their interests more effectively. Women voters had to understand that when male parliamentarians dealt with issues that affected women and children, 'they cannot do it effectively, because they cannot see such matters from a woman's point of view'. The result was that 'the interests of women are misunderstood or neglected' (Goldstein 1903a: 360). Representation of women by women would provide a means for addressing the interests of women and children. A system in which women could neither vote nor run for Parliament would not.

Goldstein argued that 'some women have a special contribution to make to purely social and domestic politics, in the same way that the mining, pastoral, farming, commercial and industrial interests bring their special knowledge to bear on politics as they affect their particular domain' (1930: 17). Goldstein's 'Woman Suffrage in Australia' contains an extensive list of the sorts of measures she believed were introduced because women were in parliament representing women's interests. These included laws requiring equal pay for equal work in the Public Service; equality of naturalisation laws between men and women; protection of women and children from cruelty, neglect, desertion and infidelity; laws dealing with drunkenness and gambling; controls on publication of indecent literature; and laws regulating children's work hours (1948: 7–8).

A new politics

Including women as voters and representatives in Australian parliaments would do more than simply introduce women's interests in political debates and public policies. It would also provide for a new form of politics in which voters and parliamentarians moved from a narrow concern with personal welfare to a more inclusive sense of national welfare. In short, it would introduce a 'public spirit' into Australian politics.

This would not happen overnight. Goldstein looked to the next generation as the bearers of this new spirit. This generation would be born to women who were active citizens and who could teach them to adopt a different perspective from those who had previously engaged in political activities.

> Ever since I have taken an active part in social and political affairs I have had reason to deplore the lack of public spirit amongst the Australian people. Lacking public spirit, they lack also the true national spirit. The people as a whole have not grasped even the faintest idea of the principle of nationhood … I am not surprised. It is only emphatic proof of what I have always maintained, what all woman suffragists have maintained, in the struggle to secure the right of suffrage, that public-spirited citizens are not born of unpublic-spirited mothers. The people of a country are just what the mothers make them, and mothers who have no civic responsibilities cannot be expected to teach the political idea … Not knowing the duties of citizenship how can they teach them to others? We have only just sown the seed of a true Australian public spirit, we must wait many years before we see the fruit. Politics at present are more or less personal. Most men are in politics not for their country's welfare, but for their own, and the mothers of Australia have a huge task ahead of them in endeavouring to teach their children, the citizens of the future, that national welfare means individual welfare, and is a nobler idea than personal welfare. (1904a: 48)

That women were not prone to the narrow selfishness typical of men meant, in Goldstein's view, that their inclusion in parliaments would introduce a spiritual dimension to politics. 'The great social need is a spiritual sense amongst individuals. What earthly use is the best legislative lever unless it is worked by people with a lofty sense of personal and public duty? … In these days of legislative storm and stress, the need for an ethical motive power is often lost sight of' (1905: 2). This explains something of Goldstein's refusal to join a political party. 'I am unwilling to identify myself with any party', she wrote, 'because my experience of party organisations is that they place their party and the particular measures it supports before every other consideration, moral or national. "Give us measures," they cry, "never mind about the men." "Give us measures," I say, "supported by men whose moral character, whose public spirit, whose devotion to principle, are above suspicion'" (1903a: 6).

Goldstein was convinced that including women in politics and parliament would result in this new approach to politics. This was, in her view, the main contribution women could make to the tenor of public life. It was 'only by stirring the national spirit toward idealism, toward those intangible things that cannot be valued in money, that women may best demonstrate their influence in the nation's life. They are peculiarly fitted to do this, for at all times women have been looked to provide a brake on mere materialism' (1930: 17). In her view, 'selfishness, competition, lust, which gives us a world of suffering and hideousness, must make way for love, co-operation, and purity, which make way for happiness and beauty' (Women's Political Association 1916: 3).

The exclusion of women from parliaments and the refusal to grant them a vote were negations of their rights as individuals and limited their horizons and being in an unacceptable manner. The struggle for inclusion was one means of re-educating women and men about women's true rights and capabilities. It was also a means of overcoming the debilitating effects of prejudices against women among both sexes. Including women would result in their interests being more adequately addressed, produce a new form of politics, and result in a greater capacity for citizenship among all members of society.

Conclusion

Goldstein saw environmental factors as crucial to the formation of character. The constraints and discriminations to which women were subjected meant that their characters were tragically underdeveloped. The result was a negation of their potential as individuals, as mothers, and as citizens. The struggle for enfranchisement and representation of women by women were crucial elements in the reformation of women's character, in achieving social justice for women, and in creating a healthy and more spiritual society.

The most important effect of acknowledging that women had the same social and political rights as men was on Australian children. They would be changed forever once they saw their mothers as active citizens, with a full range of career options, and equal status in the community and family. They would appreciate that women were capable of participating in public life and that they brought special qualities to public life. They would learn the rights and responsibilities of citizenship from people who understood them properly because they practised them. The result was that women, men, and society as a whole would be transformed. Character would be improved throughout society. Citizenship would be fully realised and a new form of society ushered in. While all of this would take time, giving women the vote was the first step along this path.

Goldstein was undoubtedly more optimistic than Pearson. While he was less sure about the sources for the improvement of people's character, she was more certain. Allowing women full rights as citizens would produce transformation, in and of itself. Pearson saw great value in improving women's character and granting them full rights as citizens, but he did not think it would have the impact that Goldstein thought it would have. Another important difference between Pearson's and Goldstein's views was that the former had less explicit political objectives. Goldstein had a clear political agenda and was more certain of the results of the changes she advocated.

Murdoch was more like Pearson in this regard. They shared a commitment to improving character, but the means by which this was to be achieved were far less clear to them than they were to Goldstein. Women had already been granted the vote when Murdoch wrote, and some had even become members of parliament. No immediate political reform was obvious to Murdoch. He still sought improvement, but in less direct ways. Goldstein could see that something important was missing from the political picture and that a new and improving element could be introduced to politics and society. Creating opportunities for women to engage at all levels of society and politics would have an important effect in allowing women to fully develop their capacities, including the capacity for citizenship. This would have an immediate and positive effect for all.

---

[1] According to Mackenzie (1960: 190), she was 'the first woman in the English-speaking world to stand as a candidate for a constituted national legislature'.

[2] 'Her Women's Programme included a federal equal marriage and divorce law; equal custody and guardianship of children; raising the age of marriage (at that time, twelve for girls with parental consent); equal pay for equal work; equal opportunities in the Commonwealth Public Service; amendment of the Naturalisation Act to enable women to retain their nationality and civil rights if they married non-Australians; protection for deserted wives and children

and protection of women and girls from the White Slave Traffic (prostitution)' (Bomford 1993: 123).

3 'Her beliefs comprised elements of the two great contradictory streams within the Western women's movement: one the "Enlightenment" and the other ... an emerging middle class familial ideology and Goldstein saw Australian women in the context of both these ideologies. She urged equality for women as individual (the Enlightenment stream); and measures of reform which related to women's familial role. Yet Goldstein's ideology implicitly envisaged woman's role ultimately in familial terms. Goldstein ... agreed that to raise the status of woman was to raise the status of the family and hence, they thought, eventually to morally elevate society as a whole. But if Goldstein's ideology envisaged woman as the nurturant core of a "private" collective—the family[—]her own life was a testimony to the Enlightenment ideal of woman as an autonomous and publicly active individual' (Searle 1988: 61).

4 An indirect problem caused by their exclusion was that women had to spend far more time and energy in influencing debates in parliament than inclusion would have required. 'Through not having women in Parliament, the energy and valuable time of individual women and women's organisations outside has to be spent on the often Herculean task of educating members up to the point of seeing the injustices in certain measures affecting women' (Goldstein 1903b: 136).

4

WALTER MURDOCH
(1874–1970)

I want a country of free men and women—free to be the persons that they were meant to be, along their own individual lines; for no two of us are alike, and a country that tries to force its citizens into one mould is a poor sort of country to live in. I want a country where opportunities are equal for all, so that all may have a fair chance of finding their true place in society and the work for which they are best fitted … I want a country which gives its children the very best education that human wisdom has devised, and which gives all its children, rich and poor, the opportunity of getting the best education they are capable of benefiting by. I want a country so educated that its citizens are capable of choosing the best and wisest to govern them. I want a country whose children are trained from the earliest age, not for competition with one another as at present, but for living together a friendly and helpful life—trained in social sympathy … I want a country which is entirely tolerant of all religions and of all eccentricities of thought and speech … I want a country in which there are no classes as we use that term now, in which character counts for everything and possessions for nothing. I want a country that cares greatly for books, for music, for painting, for science, for philosophy, for all those higher activities of the human spirit which have raised man above the brutes and clothed life with pleasure. (Murdoch 1935: 22–3)

Walter Murdoch[1] was born in 1874 in Scotland and spent his childhood in Scotland, England and France. He came to Australia in 1885. He graduated with a Bachelor of Arts, with honours in Logic and Philosophy, from the University of Melbourne. He was an assistant lecturer at that university in 1903. He spent 1912 as a member of the literary staff of the *Argus* newspaper. In 1913 he became professor of English at the University of Western Australia, where he remained until 1939. He served as Pro-chancellor at the university between 1941 and 1943, and from 1943 to 1948 as Chancellor. Between 1920 and 1936 he was president of the local League of Nations Union and was president of the Kindergarten Union over the same period. Throughout his career he was a regular newspaper columnist whose works were syndicated across a number of Australian newspapers. He also contributed programs for ABC Radio.

Individuals who thought for themselves, but who appreciated and respected others' interests, peopled Walter Murdoch's ideal society. In this society, well-developed citizens understood and willingly took up their social responsibilities. Fostering the development of civic individuals, as these people will be called, was at the core of his political project. Civic individuals did not happen naturally; they did not emerge from the womb fully formed. To foster their development required a carefully designed system of education and an environment in which they could flourish.

Civic individuals were, above all else, individuals. The first step in forming civic individuals, therefore, was forming individuals. The next step was to provide these individuals with an education that gave them a sense of their civic roles and the attributes they needed to fulfil those roles. Finally, civic individuals had to be situated in a political system in which citizenship could be engaged with actively. Each of these elements of Murdoch's approach to the formation of civic individuals will be dealt with in separate sections. Together they give some insight into Murdoch's views on character and citizenship.

Civic Individuals

Murdoch's conception of civic individuals begins with his commitment to the view that a life that expressed true individuality was the best life possible. Such a life was the only way though which people could fulfil their inner potential. Individuality did not require or imply isolation; indeed, people needed others if they were to achieve individuality, because individuality was only possible in a social environment. They also required the assistance of good teachers and, beyond school, the input of people who could provide wise counsel.

Individuality

Any account of Murdoch's views on individuality must begin with his sense of the isolation at the very core of human nature. Individuality was a necessary consequence of the fundamental separation of human beings. For Murdoch 'the fundamental thing about human beings is their loneliness'. While people might be able to put this out of their minds, in those moments when they acknowledged their 'solitary fastness', they realised that between them and those they loved 'best in all the world is a gap which all the love in the world cannot bridge' (1932a: 103).

The separation between human beings explained their gregariousness: gregarious behaviour was each person's attempt to overcome their solitude, 'to break out of the prison of [their] own soul, to find, somehow and somewhere in the vast universe, companionship' (1932a: 104). Murdoch believed that 'we are all prisoners condemned to solitary confinement; and something in the core of our common nature drives us to try … to communicate with our fellow-prisoners, and so to mitigate the horrors of our own captivity' (1932a: 104–5).

There were dangers, however, in this natural tendency to overcome isolation through immersion in the company of others. It was one thing to be part of a group, and yet another to be a follower of that group. Murdoch rejected any tendency to subsume oneself in society. He was 'an individualist to the core' and was convinced that 'the only life worth living is the life you live standing on your own feet and maintaining your own integrity' (1934: 132).

Inner potential

The main problem associated with a failure to stand on one's own feet was that it prevented a person from fully realising his or her inner potential. Both the individual and society as a whole were responsible for ensuring that individuals realised their potential. Above all, individuals had to be given freedom to pursue their own course. Liberty, however, was not mere licence. It was not 'freedom from this or that restraint, but freedom to do this or that thing that is worth doing. Not freedom to do whatever one pleases … But freedom to do what our best self tells us we ought to do—freedom to live the very finest kind of life possible to our nature—that is liberty' (Murdoch 1912: 208).

Society was essential for the realisation of inner potential. Society, through the mechanism of government, provided the conditions under which individuals could live according to their higher natures. For governments assisted 'every individual member to realise his highest possibilities ... The work of the state is to remove from every person's path the obstacles which would prevent him from living this best life; to secure certain essential conditions, without which this best life is for ever impossible' (Murdoch 1912: 14).

Government could not do everything, however, and should not satisfy all the demands people might make of it. Individuals had to be encouraged, perhaps even forced, to take responsibility for their own fortunes. In Murdoch's view, people should avoid becoming dependent on government. Thus 'it is better that we should throw ourselves whole-heartedly into all our enterprises, feeling that success depends on ourselves, and that the State will neither help us nor hinder us'. Becoming too used to government support would 'lead us to a weakening of the national character, and ultimately to national decay' (1911: 217, 218).

Producing individuals

The importance of self-reliance and strong character for national success created something of an obligation on the part of the nation to promote individuality. The most important means by which this could be achieved was through the provision of a sound educational system. Such a system would 'train children for the real duty of life, which is to think for oneself and to act for oneself, and not to be one of the lifeless automata which make up the serried ranks of respectability' (1934: 126). A good education, Murdoch argued, was 'a training of the will. In a word, the muscles and sinews of the mind need training' (1939: 109).

Murdoch lamented the fact that much of the education provided in schools at his time did not promote individuality and did not equip children with the capacity to choose for themselves. In Murdoch's view, a good education was an 'education which teaches you to think for yourself instead of swallowing whatever the fashion of the moment may prescribe' (1947: 84). A proper education was certainly not one through which educators sought to replicate themselves. Indeed, for an educator to aim 'deliberately to mould the character of another can only mean trying to make the other resemble oneself' (1934: 185). Teachers who approached their task with this intention were 'not fit to be put in charge of innocent youth. If I were a headmaster, I should dismiss any assistant whom I suspected of dabbling in character-building' (1934: 185–6). The only question a teacher needed to address was 'Can you honestly say that many boys and girls who leave your schools have been trained to think? (1939: 109).

Intellectuals and civic individuals

Civic individuals may have been responsible for themselves, but they nonetheless required assistance or guidance if they were to develop fully. The difficulty of delimiting the relationship between civic individuals and those responsible for facilitating this process is evinced in a variety of forms in Murdoch's work. Indeed, this is an ever-present problem for those who adopt a liberal preoccupation with individuality combined with a sense that good character cannot be achieved in isolation. Others had an important role to play in an individual's self-formation, but they had to be careful not to overplay their role.

Murdoch's conception of the proper relationship between an intellectual and a developing individual can be inferred from the essays he contributed to daily newspapers. They were intended for a general audience and designed to promote independent and critical thinking. In Murdoch's view, 'a good essay is the best substitute that literature has to offer us for a good talk' (1932b: 210). This conversational aspect of an essay obliged essayists to resist the temptation to instruct in a direct and forceful manner. An essay, and a conversation between an intellectual and a developing civic individual, was not an opportunity for indoctrination, even when the intellectual's positions were more carefully and clearly developed and when 'the real progress of humanity has been due to ideas in the heads of certain "star-begotten" persons … who could think clearlier and see trulier than their fellows' (1939: 129).

The most important aspect of a good essay was that it was not a sermon. For 'a real essay is never didactic … [and] an essayist never holds forth' (1932b: 210). A good essayist, like all good teachers, had to bear in mind that they were 'talking to the reader, not instructing', for in the instant an essayist 'becomes heavy or pompous or pontifical, the charm is snapped, the spell dissolved' (1932b: 211). The art of the essay would be lost if the essayist deliberately sought to form the opinions or character of others. An essayist or intellectual who adopted such an attitude would have forgotten the requirement that each individual participates in her or his own formation and would have practised another form of education, as control.

This attitude led Murdoch to deny responsibility for what readers did upon reading his essays. Detractors might accuse Murdoch of false modesty, but this refusal to see himself as responsible for others expresses an important part of his approach to the intellectual's role in the formation of good character. Murdoch began an essay entitled 'A new Charity' with the following:

> The other day a man stopped me in the street and told me that my last article had done him good. Making a desperate effort to remember what my last article had been about, and not succeeding, I could only murmur that he must surely be mistaken; it was somebody else's article he was thinking of. But no, he said, it was mine, and it had done him good. There was, of course, only one honourable thing to do, and I did it: I offered him my profuse apologies, assured him that it had been quite unintentional, and promised to be more careful in the future. (1947: 101)

Murdoch reported that the meeting ended without violence. This he attributed to the restraint shown by the other party, 'for we are all driven to thoughts of dark deeds when we meet somebody whom we suspect of deliberately trying to do us good' (1947: 101).

Murdoch evinced considerable resistance, if not downright hostility, towards 'social reformers' and anyone who tried to mould others. It was not that he doubted the importance of intellectuals for social progress; he simply rejected the view that better educated, more knowledgeable, and otherwise better thinkers ought to impede others' capacity to think for themselves.

Good essayists, like all good teachers, had to promote independence, not dependence. Civic individuals required individuality more than anything else. This could not be achieved under conditions in which they were denied opportunities for self-formation. Only when they were self-forming would individuals fulfil their potential. Certainly they required education and quiet talks, but neither of these implied indoctrination or manipulation.

A Civic Education

The aim of my book [*The Australian Citizen*] is to strengthen the civic fibre of our children by presenting in lucid and attractive form the essential constitutional facts of the Commonwealth, the salient points of our history, & the qualities of a good citizen. (quoted in La Nauze and Nurser 1974: 14)

The importance of a well-designed and readily available education for individuality in general has already been noted. Education was particularly important for the formation of civic individuals. The particular attributes of civic individuals necessitated particular inputs from an education system and the social environment that supported it. Only a well-constituted education system supported by an appropriate public culture would produce such individuals. This was a function of the particular attributes Murdoch associated with civic individuals.

In short, a civic education encouraged and enabled individuals to display responsibility, thoughtfulness, and an ongoing capacity for self-culture. In Murdoch's view, a good education was 'a training of the character as well as the intellect' (1912: 76). Encouraging responsibility meant equipping individuals with the capacity to empathise and sympathise with others, which in turn resulted in a propensity to assist others in furthering their projects. Thoughtful individuals needed the ability to think carefully and deeply. They also had to recognise the importance of ideas as tools for controlling and manipulating the world. That human development was an ongoing process meant that a civic education had to provide individuals with the capacity for self-development, or self-culture. This was important for individuals and for society as it would result in a dynamic and open society.

Responsibility

Developing each individual's sense of responsibility and, in particular, responsibility for others was an important part of a civic education. Murdoch believed that human beings were inhabited by two basic instincts. The first was a social instinct. Society, in Murdoch's view, was 'simply the expression of the *social instinct*' (1911: 5). The other instinct was 'the instinct for *freedom*. We feel the need of order, laws, of government; but we feel just as strongly, and sometimes far more strongly, the need of freedom' (1911: 5–6).

This was not the only duality that Murdoch found in human nature. He argued that capacities and predispositions to do both good and evil inhabited people. In his view, humanity 'is deceitful, and desperately wicked; there is no need to be sentimental, and ignore the fact of human depravity'. But depravity was not the only source of human motivation and action. Murdoch insisted that people did not forget 'the other side of human nature—the nobility of it, the passion for truth, the devotion to duty, the sense of justice, the comradeship, the readiness to die for a cause' (1941: 12).

While neither aspect of human nature could be denied, it was the social instinct, or capacity for concern for others, that allowed society to survive and improve. A civic education would promote the positive in human beings and provide them with the means to constrain, if not reduce, their negative impulses. Murdoch relied, in this context, on the work of 'a famous biologist' who 'pointed out that the species which have survived have been the species that have given free play to the instinct, not of mutual destructiveness, but of mutual helpfulness; and the human species is the crowning example of this' (1941: 160). Facilitating the social instinct and releasing positive attributes of human nature were essential to improving society. Indeed, in Murdoch's view, 'civilization may be defined as the gradual process of eliminating cruelty from human relations and putting mutual helpfulness in its place' (1941: 188).

Thoughtfulness

A sense of responsibility for others needed to be complemented, for Murdoch, with a general thoughtfulness about life and society. The best sort of society was peopled by individuals who thought carefully and clearly about the problems that faced them in their personal and social lives. This was particularly true of democracies. 'The supreme need of a self-governing state', Murdoch wrote, 'is the need of a body of enlightened and thoughtful citizens; men and women trained to reflect, to reason, and to observe' (1912: 75). Only a thoughtful nation was capable of setting goals and pursuing them with any likelihood of success. For 'thinking is what we are desperately in need of if we are to control our own destinies' (1941: 91).

Murdoch accused Australians of 'the vice of not thinking, or not thinking hard enough' (1941: 90). This resulted in 'an incapacity for seeing life steadily; a jumpiness in the public mind. In the face of great world problems, we find ourselves incapable of thinking calmly and dispassionately. We think in spasms and hysterically' (1939: 43–4). Murdoch was, as he put it, 'a university bloke'. This sort of person wanted Australia to become 'a kind of university, with everybody in it trained to regard the truth and "the sovereign good of human nature."

He thinks that therein lies the hope of the world—in the application of trained intelligence to the problems of life' (1941: 148).

The right kind of thinking produced ideals, which allowed countries to survive and progress. For 'it is by its ideals that a country is saved; without them, it can only drift along—perhaps to perdition' (Murdoch 1945: 48–9). Australians were apathetic, in Murdoch's view, simply because they were not presented with ideals. 'But show us an ideal, and we will fight for it … Show us the way to a better Australia, saner and sweeter than the Australia we know, the home of a finer justice and a kindlier comradeship and a nobler democracy—and you will not need to complain of our apathy' (1945: 49).

Thoughtful people did not crave material possessions. They wanted a higher form of life, which no amount of material goods could provide. Murdoch wrote passionately about what he called the fallacy of thinking that the phrase 'standard of living' referred simply to material comfort or economic prosperity. A certain amount of material goods were necessary, but these provided only the basis for a standard of living. They did not constitute or necessarily produce a higher standard of living. Murdoch extolled the virtues of the Italian nationalist Mazzini who, 'throwing aside his chance of a prosperous career, and living an exile in a squalid London boarding-house devising means of serving his country and the world, reached a higher standard of living than any multi-millionaire known to history' (1935: 13).

Self-culture
Maintaining an ability to think and to think deeply required continuous effort. Individuals had to be conscious of the need to reinforce, if not extend, this ability. This necessitated a willingness on their part to expose themselves to new stimuli in order to deepen and extend their thinking. In short, civic individuals had to see themselves as ongoing projects, which required renewal and expansion. They needed a capacity for self-culture.

Murdoch's views on self-culture are best explained through reference to his two great passions: travelling and sitting still. This was no paradox. Developing oneself, or self-culture, had to include exposing oneself to the stimulation and broader horizons that travel provided. Constant movement would not be beneficial, however, so periods of travel had to be complemented by quieter times. In these quieter moments, reflection and introspection would allow individuals to capitalise fully on their experiences and generally acquire greater depth of thought and fullness of character.

Travel

Murdoch was a firm believer in what he called 'spiritual adventures'. These adventures did not have to involve travel, but they were almost impossible for those living in the suburbs. For most people, 'the suburban atmosphere is heavy and oppressive; if we breathe it too long, we degenerate into poor spiritless conforming creatures ... I advise every young person to travel, and not by tourists' routes' (1947: iii). Those who wanted to develop their character fully had to expose themselves to enlivening and uplifting influences. This was why tourist routes would not do. Murdoch's advice to young people, then, was to expose themselves to 'strange lands and seas, strange peoples and strange ideas. Be a vagabond, for a time at least. Escape from the suburban villa, and save your soul' (1947: iii).

Sitting still

One reason that Murdoch advised against using tourist routes was that they were more likely to result in simple activity and therefore were not sufficient for spiritual adventures. Activity was not conducive to thought and was often a mask for its absence. Thinking was, in Murdoch's view, 'the hardest work in the world' and most people avoided it. Most people preferred a 'Strenuous Life, which means being busy and fussy ... and imagining that we are doing a great deal of good in the world, and blinding ourselves to the fact that we are all suffering from ... a disease which we can cure only by shaking off our laziness and acquiring the difficult art of sitting still' (1947: 19).

When reviewing his travels, Murdoch thought that the most valuable hours were 'spent at various open-air cafes, sipping black coffee, keeping eyes and ears open, watching the ceaseless flow of life in the city square, and trying in a humble spirit to practise the noble, the dignified, the philosophic art of sitting about' (1947: 39). Sitting about involved great effort rather than relentless movement.

Obviously, Murdoch was not arguing for just any sort of passivity. He would have been horrified by the extent to which television has promoted a culture of vegetative inactivity. Vegetables could not achieve self-culture. Self-culture involved individuals using experiences they had gained from spiritual adventures to deepen and improve their characters. Resisting movement was just as important as travelling.

A proper education provided individuals with the ability to generate these moments of sitting still.

A civic education stimulated an individual's sense of responsibility. It built on the higher social instincts in human beings. Civic individuals were thoughtful people. A country of thoughtful people was a country alive to possibilities and growing through the pursuit of collective ideals. For social improvement was an ongoing process, and depended on each individual's ability to improve. Self-culture was a product of both travel and quiet reflection. Individuals could not develop each of these abilities without the assistance provided by a civic education.

Citizenship

Little point would be served in producing civic individuals, however, if they were not given the opportunity to exercise their rights and responsibilities as citizens. They could not extend and develop their capacities without the opportunity to act as citizens. In short, civic individuals needed a system of government that took advantage of and extended the attributes they had acquired through a civic education.

If good citizens needed a good political system, then the reverse was also true. For a 'good system of government is useless without good citizens' (Murdoch 1911: 232). A democratic system was, in Murdoch's view, a good system, and a system that required good citizens. Indeed, democracies were in particular need of good citizens. Murdoch considered it 'dangerous to give power to people too ignorant to know what to do with it'. In his view, therefore, 'a national system of education must precede a national system of government' (1911: 161.) A civic education laid the foundations for a civic individual to emerge; participation in a democracy gave civic individuals the opportunity to express and improve on those foundations. Above all, civic individuals who participated in a democracy needed a clear sense of their duties and responsibilities.

Citizenship and democracy

Murdoch was reluctant to posit a necessary relationship between a democratic system and civic individuals participating fully in citizenship. The relationship seems so close, however, that this necessary relationship might be assumed. Democracies required active individuals who were able to formulate and act on their own opinions. A successful democracy requires 'that a sufficient number of persons should do a little thinking for themselves' (1934: 55). Democracies could work properly only when people were open to other points of view. They needed people who were both critical and self-critical, people willing to seek change whenever they were persuaded that it was necessary. 'The glory of democracy is that it is not sure that it is right; it is friendly to criticism, to the demand for change. It believes in educating all its people; which means, producing a generation of critics and reformers' (1941: 14.)

This communicative dimension was an important element of a democracy. People had to be willing to discuss issues openly and thoughtfully. Democracy could 'only succeed when it becomes government by enlightened public opinion; and enlightenment can only come by hearing all sides' (1935: 8). For all sides to be heard, all individuals needed the ability to articulate and defend their point of view. Just as, if not more, importantly, they needed to be able to listen and carefully evaluate the positions of those who held to other points of view. Only then would democracy reflect enlightened public opinion. For 'how is public opinion formed but by communication of ideas? ... We should have a truer democracy in Australia today if we were better able to get hold of one another's ideas' (1939: 97).

Active participation on the part of citizens was essential to democracy. This was simply an extension of the requirement that individuals be allowed to act freely. For Murdoch, 'liberty is itself an indispensable part of the general well-being, an essential condition of the best kind of life' (1912: 209). Democracy promoted freedom because 'the right to vote ... is yet a part of liberty; it is a gateway by which we enter into the larger life of our country; it is an opportunity for playing a part, however humble, in public affairs' (1912: 209–10).

Thoughtful individuals, open to other opinions and able to consider them fully, were essential to democracy, and democratic societies had to produce these people. Democracy provided people with the greatest amount of freedom. When properly conducted, it created opportunities for expression and participation not available in most other political systems. Having these opportunities meant that individuals could continue to develop. Expression and participation were essential elements of continued growth.

Citizens in a democracy were not perfect and would make mistakes, but they could and would learn from their mistakes. Murdoch's faith in democracy was 'not a blind faith; it is not a shutting of the eyes to the shortcomings of men and women as they now are; but it is a faith in the possibility of improvement. Democracy ... believes in education' (1941: 13).

Citizenship, duties, and responsibilities

While freedom was important to a well-functioning democracy, so too were duties or responsibilities. Citizens had to accept and seek to satisfy three main duties. The first was to seek to attune themselves to a collective interest when they participated in public life. The second was to vote thoughtfully. The third was to understand their political system. These duties overlapped and intertwined. Indeed, they could even be subsumed under the rubric of a duty to adopt a public spirit. Murdoch believed that democracies could only work when 'the majority of citizens ... are animated by *public spirit*. The term, public spirit, covers the whole duty of a citizen' (1911: 227).

Attuning to a collective interest

Murdoch devoted much of his energies to outlining the duties of citizenship. He felt it important to make the point that in democracies people had to make decisions with the interests of the community in mind. Murdoch believed that good citizens obeyed the following rule: '*Act in such a way as, upon mature consideration, you think it would be good for the State that all the citizens should act*' (1911: 229). The ability to conceive of a collective interest reflects the sense of responsibility inculcated in civic individuals. To become a good citizen was to learn 'the great lessons of love and kindness, of obedience and truthfulness, of courtesy and consideration for others' (1912: 233). This ability to consider the interests of others and of society as a whole reflected 'the unity of a democratic people, a unity springing spontaneously from within, not imposed from without' (1941: 54).

One manifestation of this sense of solidarity or shared interests was a commitment to achieving social justice. Good citizens wanted everyone to be treated fairly and provided with the opportunities that were their right. They would act to change political and social structures in order to secure justice for all.

> So long as any injustice is done anywhere in our land, so long as the wealth of the land is unjustly distributed, so long as any man or woman through no fault of their own suffers a degrading poverty, so

long as a single child is denied any of the opportunities which ought to be the common birthright of all, there is … a field for the active exercise of good citizenship. (Murdoch 1912: 236)

Voting thoughtfully

Recognising the interests of others and ensuring that these interests were reflected in their public acts was only possible if citizens had the capacity to reflect carefully on policies and their outcomes. Citizens in a democracy had to accept the duty of thinking. For Murdoch 'it is hardly possible to speak too emphatically of the duty of thinking—especially when we grow old enough to have votes' (1911: 235). Failing to vote may be 'a gross neglect of our duty as citizens; but it is better not to vote at all than to vote thoughtlessly' (1911: 235).

Thoughtful voters gave careful consideration to the interests of the community as a whole and to the means by which these interests could be furthered. In voting, 'it is the duty of every citizen … to consult the interests of the whole State' (1911: 235). A good citizen had to accept responsibility for the consequences that his or her actions, including voting, had for the collective interests of the people and for the institutions on which all relied. 'We said that the first duty of the citizen was to learn to govern. We may now put the same thing another way: we may say that a citizen's first duty is to get into the way of forming right opinions on matters that concern the welfare of the State' (1911: 233–4).

Understanding the political system

As was suggested in the preceding quotation, Murdoch believed that citizens had to learn to govern. To do this they had to understand the political system in which they participated. Citizens had to know how their society was governed. They needed to understand the mechanics of democracy, 'for it is another curious thing about this extraordinary machine, that it will never work really well until its parts understand what they are doing' (1912: 18).

Murdoch's understanding of the duties of a citizen was a reflection of his view that a properly functioning democracy relied on an active, thoughtful and educated citizenry. Citizens needed to accept that they were part of a community that deserved consideration, respect, and sympathy. Democracy required an educated and enlightened citizenry who understood the mechanics and the spirit that were essential to democracy. These attitudes manifested themselves primarily in voting but applied generally in the life of a citizen.

Conclusion

Citizenship, then, was simply a manifestation of the attributes acquired as a result of a civic education. While additional skills and capacities were certainly required for citizenship, each of these was either an extension or a product of the attributes of responsibility, thoughtfulness, and self-culture that were part of a civic education. A civic education reflected respect for individuality, a sense that civic individuals were not self-forming, and required intellectuals to provide the wise 'quiet talk'. It was an integral part of facilitating the development of good citizens who could participate fully in a good society.

Forming good character was undoubtedly essential to an individual being able to fulfil the obligations Murdoch thought were involved in citizenship. The relationship was not unidirectional, however, as citizenship could be understood to promote and allow for the development of good character. All three liberals whose works were dealt with in Part I acknowledged a close relationship between character and citizenship. Their emphases differed depending, in part, on their perception of the immediate needs of Australian society.

Pearson saw a particular need for the development of a system of education that would generally raise the quality of Australian society and politics. Character, therefore, received greater attention in his works than citizenship. Goldstein, who believed that the various forms in which women were excluded from public life contributed to the debasement of their characters, confronted issues of character and citizenship. Her campaign for women's suffrage and entry into parliaments represented a multifaceted struggle to improve women's position in society and to improve society as a result; developing a conception of citizenship that made women's participation both necessary and beneficial was one part of a broader agenda. When Murdoch wrote, a comprehensive education system and women's suffrage were both part of Australian society. His goal was to raise the quality of Australian people. This would result in a good society based on a sound political system.

Each thinker's commitment to improving character and promoting good citizenship was a reflection of deeper commitments and principles. Each believed that individuals needed freedom and support in order to express and improve themselves. All thought that the lack of commitment to and provision of resources for education in all its forms debilitated society. Each engaged, in various ways, in providing formal and informal education. This was merely one manifestation of their commitment to promoting good character and citizenship in Australia.

---

[1] I am not sure what Murdoch would have made of his inclusion in this book. He may have been hostile to it. 'In the name of common sense', he wrote, 'let us try to judge measures, and men, on their merits, and not by some half-understood label that some nebulous-minded person has stuck on them' (1932: 50). Then again, he might not have cared. 'I am sick of labels and doctrines; and I don't care in the least whether you style me Fascist or Bolshevist or democrat or aristocrat or plutocrat or anything else your fertile imagination might suggest' (1939: 5).

Part II

SOCIAL
STRATIFICATION

Social stratification is an important issue for liberals because of their commitment to promoting individual development and fostering social improvement. Liberals reject artificial barriers that prevent people realising their full potential and diminish their freedom to pursue their goals. A stratified society is one in which some individuals do not have the same life chances and opportunities to express themselves that others have. That the inequality stems from a form of social organisation and is not a naturally occurring phenomenon is what makes social stratification a problem for liberals. They accept difference among individuals and unequal capacities on the parts of individuals, but they do not accept inequalities that are artificially created or maintained.

Social stratification is a term used mostly by sociologists. Studies of social stratification are 'studies of structured social inequality: that is, studies of any systematic inequalities between groups of people, which arise as the unintended consequences of social processes and relationships'. Such studies document 'inequalities of condition, opportunities and outcomes, and the ways in which groups maintain class or status boundaries' (Marshall 1996: 512). The final important aspect of social stratification, at least for the purposes of Part II, is that this inequality is ongoing. Sociologists appropriated the term 'stratification' from geology in order to imply that social strata are enduring features of social life. 'As in geology, the term refers to a layered structuring or strata, but in sociology the layers consist of social groups, and the emphasis is on the ways in which inequalities between groups are structured and persist over time' (Jary and Jary 1995: 621).

Individual life chances

The existence of social strata is a clear indication, for most liberals, that individuals do not share similar life chances. The centrality of the individual to liberal political thinking makes this a significant problem because it violates a liberal's commitment to equal opportunities among people. It also represents a dampener on individual motivation. If individuals approach their lives, as some liberals think, in terms of the satisfaction of material needs, then they may lose motivation to act when they realise that some people are better positioned to satisfy their needs. If individuals approach their lives in terms of the realisation of the highest form of self, as other liberals believe, then they need to know that they will be given an opportunity to do so. They need to know that resources will be available for their pursuits and will not be monopolised by others who have not earned that monopoly.

The best sort of society is one in which people are free and motivated to act and are increasingly able to achieve their goals (so long as they are not anti-social goals). A society in which some groups have a monopoly over access to essential resources and are otherwise advantaged in their ability to pursue their goals is not, for a liberal, a good society. It offends against fundamental principles of liberal philosophy and, at a practical level, it is much less likely to maximise and facilitate individual motivation. The existence of social stratification, in short, is an indicator that there are problems at the heart of Australian society.

Natural inequality

An important point to note in this context is that most liberals accept the existence of inequalities in society. They believe that individuals are different and that these differences will have an effect on their abilities to acquire the goods they want and occupy the social position they desire. Natural differences between people produce inequality and this inequality is not objectionable. Indeed, most liberals would encourage the existence of inequalities that register natural difference. They would argue that greater social rewards ought to flow to those individuals who, because of particular innate characteristics, are more productive, efficient, or more generally capable. Some liberals may place a limit on the level of tolerable inequality, but all accept some degree of inequality. They do so as a reflection of differing abilities among people and as a means of providing incentives to greater effort on the part of those with abilities that they may not otherwise maximise.

None of this is intended to deny a very complex relationship between natural difference and social inequality. Only some natural differences will be significant in allowing individuals to maximise their life chances and fully benefit from their abilities. The particular field individuals choose to pursue as careers will tend to reward those with particular attributes. Agility may be important in the making of a great tennis player, but it does not seem to have much to do with what makes a great politician. Height may be an asset in basketball, but not in Formula One car racing. Greater intelligence may be an advantage in most fields, but being more attractive seems to count for a great deal more in many occupations.

Artificial inequality

Rather than desensitising liberals to non-natural inequality, however, their acceptance of natural inequalities heightens their concerns about non-natural or artificial inequalities. While they may lack the will to take on entrenched interests who occupy dominant positions in society, liberals are worried about the effects of this domination. Their ideal society is one in which rewards are distributed according to merit in an environment where all people are free to acquire the skills they need to pursue their goals. Equality of opportunity is an essential part of a liberal political program.

Social stratification is a clear indicator that equality of opportunity does not exist. It indicates that some people are being denied their basic rights to capitalise on their natural differences or to overcome a lack of natural abilities through willpower and hard work. Social stratification also indicates that some individuals are being prevented from making their full contribution to society. It may also indicate the existence of major disincentives to individual effort, since those in disadvantaged circumstances may be prone to simply surrender to structured inequality.

Wentworth, Higgins, Menzies, and Dowse

The following chapters deal with the ways in which four liberals have understood and dealt with the problem of social stratification in Australia. William Charles Wentworth (1793–1872) found himself in opposition to a variety of powerful people in the developing colony of New South Wales. As a leading figure among former convicts and their children, sometimes referred to as the 'emancipists', Wentworth challenged the power of a group known as the 'exclusives', something akin to an Australian aristocracy, who derived their position from land ownership and their relationship to the colonial authorities. Wentworth protested against the dominance of a group of people who had not earned their dominance. He believed that the structured inequality of his time was both philosophically objectionable and debilitating for colonial society. He did not reject inequality, he simply rejected the artificially induced inequality of his society.

Henry Bournes Higgins (1851–1929) served as a judge on the first Court of Industrial Relations and on the High Court of Australia. His landmark decision in the Harvester Case established principles of industrial relations that endured through most of this century. Higgins was a judge who was concerned with the achievement of a fair economic order in Australia. He believed that workers had to be protected from exploitation and other forms of mistreatment that resulted from the political and social advantages held by employers. He thought that a system of industrial arbitration was an important mechanism for addressing social inequalities. In itself this would not produce a truly free and open society, but the lack of such a system was producing profound inequalities that reflected and resulted in a highly stratified society.

Robert Gordon Menzies (1894–1978) was an important figure in the formation of the Liberal Party of Australia. He thought that two main groups dominated Australian society: the rich and organised labour. He believed that the economic and political resources of the rich and the organisational and political resources of workers gave them an advantage in Australian society. He argued that a 'forgotten' middle class was being denied opportunities to participate in society and that their contributions to economic and social life were neither adequately recognised nor properly rewarded.

Sara Dowse (1938–) made an important contribution to the articulation of an Australian liberal feminism. The form of social stratification she addressed was the structured inequality that women experienced. Women suffered from discrimination in almost every aspect of their lives. They were less able to participate as workers because of a variety of official and unofficial constraints. They were exposed to sexual harassment and other forms of intimidation that precluded their full development as human beings. Most importantly, they were denied the support from governments that would have given them an approximation of equality of opportunity. The effects of discrimination were to produce a structured inequality that denied women their rights and so restricted their ability to pursue their goals effectively. The result was that they could not fully realise their potential and could not live a life of their choosing.

Each of these thinkers responded to a particular manifestation or form of social stratification. An examination of their works provides a way of understanding the concerns all liberals have about structured, or artificial, social inequality. The political will required to eliminate these near permanent forms of inequality is not always to be found among liberals, but all liberals object to these forms of inequality because of their commitment to individuality, to freedom, and to maximising the opportunities available to people to realise their full potential.

5

WILLIAM CHARLES WENTWORTH

(1790–1872)

Arbitrary governments … impair the moral and physical energies of a people … Whoever is convinced that he has no rights, no possessions that are sacred and inviolable, is a slave, and devoid of that noble feeling of independence which is essential to the dignity of his nature, and the due discharge of his functions. (Wentworth 1978: 164)

William Charles Wentworth was born on 26 October 1791 on Norfolk Island (he was one of the first persons of European descent to be born in Australia). In 1813 Wentworth, William Lawson, and Gregory Blaxland were the first Europeans to cross the Blue Mountains. In 1819 he published *A Statistical, Historical and Political Description of the Colony of New South Wales*, the first book written by a 'native-born' Australian. He was admitted to the bar of the Supreme Court of New South Wales in 1822. In 1824 he became editor of the *Australian* newspaper (he sold his shares in the newspaper in 1828, in order to defend himself against a libel charge). He entered the Legislative Council of New South Wales in 1843. In 1848 he and Robert Lowe established a State Primary Education system, and between 1848 and 1852 he was a leading figure in the movement that resulted in the creation of the University of Sydney. In 1852 and 1853 he played an important part in efforts to secure responsible government for New South Wales. In 1853 he chaired the select committee that drafted the NSW Constitution, which was enacted in 1855.

Wentworth was deeply critical of the state of society in the colony of New South Wales. He believed that the colony was hampered in its development as a result of the domination of those some people referred to as 'exclusives' or 'exclusionists'. While the derivation of either word is unclear,[1] its meaning is not. 'The exclusionists were the well-to-do minority who had come free to the colony, the officers of the regiment, ex-officer, the higher civil officials, the merchants, the privileged' (Barnard 1978: 106).

Exclusives dominated society in New South Wales and sought to exclude their main rivals, the emancipists, from public office and 'polite' society.

> Society in New South Wales was a highly stratified thing in which the normal economic divisions between rich and poor were complicated by another set of divisions between those who had come free to the colony and those who had come out as convicts. The free settlers regarded themselves as socially superior to those who had arrived in New South Wales as felons, and gloried in the sobriquet of 'pure merinos' or 'exclusives' in order to distinguish themselves from the criminally tainted 'emancipists'. It was perfectly acceptable for exclusives to conduct business with emancipists, but it was decidedly unacceptable for there to be any social intercourse outside of business. Former convicts, irrespective of their economic status, were not considered people fit to hold office or with whom a gentleman could associate. (Clarke 1992: 64–5)

Wentworth's mother was a convict and his father was not included by the exclusives, so Wentworth had common ground with the emancipists. He became one of their chief spokespeople.

Wentworth's objection to the state of society in New South Wales was that emancipists were not being given the respect due to a group that was making a significant contribution to prosperity in the community. Social and political positions in the colony were not accorded to those who demonstrated their worth, but went to those whose past was unblemished by criminal conviction, even though their present might be blemished in many other ways. Wentworth was neither an autocrat nor a democrat. He believed that political power should be concentrated in the hands of those who, through their efforts, demonstrated a worth that justified possession of political power.

When he observed the social structure in New South Wales, he encountered, and objected to, a form of social organisation that was based on systems of patronage. This form of social organisation did not reflect the worth of those who benefited from this system, nor did it encourage the development of political maturity within the colony. Rule by governors and their appointees, whose powers were largely unchecked and who served only one section of society, created a form of social stratification that prevented the colony from developing economically and politically.

Wentworth championed political reforms that he thought would lead to New South Wales emerging as a mature and productive part of the British Empire. These reforms were designed, above all else, to provide a degree of openness within New South Wales society that would encourage and support the development of a colony and would make the most of the available resources.

This chapter is divided into two sections. The first outlines Wentworth's views on human nature and social stratification; the second presents his views on the reforms necessary to create a healthy and prosperous society in New South Wales. Wentworth's intention was not to prevent the emergence of inequality but to make sure that the inequalities that did exist reflected differences in ability and in people's capacity to serve the interests of the colony. When it came to politics, Wentworth wanted rule by an elite whose membership was earned through effort and initiative and not, as was the case in his time, through a perverse system of patronage and discriminatory practices.

Human Nature and Society

Like many liberals, Wentworth believed that people were naturally unequal. Some of them were conscientious, hard-working, and imaginative; others were not. Some people, in short, were simply superior to others in important respects. These people deserved to play a greater role in society, since they were better equipped to serve the collective interest and often had a greater stake in social progress.

One of the most important issues that Wentworth's society faced was the treatment of former convicts and their offspring. Some people, possibly because it was in their interests to do so, believed that convicts and their children shared a genetically deficient character, that natural inequality was correlated with criminal conviction. Wentworth denied this and believed that these people were not naturally inferior. He argued that they deserved to be given the opportunity to prove their worth and that some of them would do so. One of the best indicators of superiority of ability, in Wentworth's view, was ownership of property that had been gained through personal effort and was used productively (cf. Pearson's view of the ennobling qualities of small landholding). Property of this sort was both an indicator of worth and a qualification to play a leading role in domestic politics.

Human nature

An account of Wentworth's views on human nature must begin with his sense of human fallibility. No one, in his opinion, was immune from corruption, but some people were more corruptible than others. Thus while all people might pursue lower forms of behaviour, this potential was not as evident in some as in others. 'So great, indeed, is the fallibility of human nature', he wrote, 'that the very best of us are apt to deviate from that just mean, in the adherence to which consists virtue' (1978: 173). The social environment was the most important determinant of deviation. Virtuous habits might be formed under the right conditions; under the wrong conditions, many people would acquire habits of the opposite kind.

The question of whether reform was possible for those who had been convicted of criminal offences is an important one. It was particularly important in a penal colony. Wentworth believed that all who had fallen were capable of redemption—if, that is, they could be removed permanently from the conditions that had promoted their criminal behaviour. He believed that a return to lives of crime among former convicts who went back to England was a result of their return to conditions in which their old habits re-emerged, whereas 'if sufficient encouragement and protection had been afforded them in the first instance, they would have gladly remained, and have continued good and useful members of society' (1978: 217).

Ironically, the prosperity of the colony in New South Wales created problems for the reformation of character. Wentworth believed that habits of thrift and responsibility could not easily be overlaid on criminal habits under prosperous conditions. These old habits died hard and, in those in whom they had taken firm root, might readily re-emerge. Many convicts had achieved some measure of reformation. 'Already but too much inclined by their early habits of irregularity to licentious indulgence, the prosperous state of their affairs during the first fifteen years after the foundation of the settlement, presented the strongest inducements to revival of their ancient propensities, which had been repressed, but not subdued' (1978: 197).

Former convicts needed encouragement in their attempts to improve themselves and the removal of inducements to maintain their blighted state. Wentworth argued that care needed to be taken to ensure that 'every incentive to the renewal of their ancient disorderly and profligate habits should be withdrawn' (1978: 395). Incentives to orderly and productive habits were also necessary. Those in positions of authority had to ensure that former convicts were properly rewarded for increased productivity in the colony: 'A certainty of reaping the fruit of their exertions, is indeed an indispensable preliminary to the resumption of those active habits which have been so long paralyzed, and a recurrence to which all *shoots* of future retrenchment must be engrafted' (1978: 389).

Wentworth acknowledged that reform was unlikely among a significant proportion of those who had fallen into lives of criminality. This was not the result of some essential depravity on their part. Indeed, Wentworth did not accept that people had essential characteristics. Those with permanently blemished characters had them because of the length of time they had practised their undesirable habits. 'For his part he disbelieved men came into the world with any innate feeling whatever. Conscience was acquired as all other habits were from long association' (Clark 1973: 2).

Most of those who had been transported as convicts were beyond redemption, in Wentworth's view. They would 'always be more or less addicted to the pernicious habits contracted in their early days of riot and debauchery' (1978: 261). Their offspring, however, were not so addicted. Creating conditions under which these children acquired desirable habits offered the only real hope of raising the quality of society in New South Wales. For the children of convicts would 'necessarily soon form the majority of this colony'; thus it was their 'amelioration or reformation [that] all legislative measures should have principally in view' (1978: 261).

Parents did not pass on genetically determined attributes; they simply contributed to an environment in which desirable habits, or character traits, were acquired. Birth was no indicator of superiority or inferiority. Real worth was determined by the habits people formed. Good habits would be formed if society was organised to reward desirable behaviour and to punish undesirable behaviour. Once this system of incentives and disincentives was in place, it was up to individuals to prove their worth.

Social position

If society in New South Wales was well organised it would divide into those who had taken advantage of the opportunities provided to demonstrate good character and those who did not. The latter were not to be dismissed as worthless, but neither were they to be treated with particular kindness or allowed to take up leading roles in society. According to Clark (1978: 42), Wentworth thought it was up to each individual 'to survive nature's never-ending war without any regrets for the fate of the weak or those who could not manage life at all'.

Those people who demonstrated their worth and showed they could manage themselves had proved their fitness for leadership. Their achievements also showed a commitment to the colony and resulted in a direct interest in its development. Wentworth looked forward to a time when the colony would be dominated by 'a powerful body ... formed of men of wealth, property, and education—men not raised from any particular section of the community, but from every class that has the energy to aspire to rank and honour' (Clark 1955: 338). Wentworth 'took no account of social boundaries. He stipulated industry, intelligence and an acceptable material status for those participating in civil duties and responsibilities' (Fifer 1984: 161).

Because of the nature of the Australian colonies, owning productive property was an important indicator of worth. The central role of agriculture and animal husbandry for the survival and prosperity of the colony meant that the measures of success and fitness for command were strongly related to the acquisition and productive use of land. This was true of all societies that were organised around agriculture and animal husbandry. A dominant landed class was, according to Wentworth, a feature of all societies of this type. This 'class which has been great and powerful in all ages and in all countries where it has existed ... must continue to be great and powerful here as long as the great interior wilds of this country can be applied to no other purpose than the sustentation of sheep and cattle' (quoted in Clark 1955: 339).

Society in New South Wales could only improve if those who possessed capital directed its energies. Labour was important, but it added little if it was not properly organised and directed. Labour could only lead to public and private advantage when it was organised by 'a directing intelligence, which can combine its energies, and render them subservient to the attainment of some single end', because the 'necessary combination of labour can only be maintained by the help of capital; and where such capital does not exist ... the main source of prosperity ... cannot be immediately organised and established' (Wentworth 1978: 381–2).

Men—Wentworth thought solely in terms of men—who acquired property had demonstrated their merit and gained a direct interest in the welfare and improvement of the colony. Wentworth did not deny 'the right of the intelligent poor to aspire to seats of government but they must first become "men of substance", participating in one of the great interests on which the welfare of the community depended. Preeminent among those was the landed interest' (Persse 1972: 23).

Wentworth believed that New South Wales offered so many opportunities to acquire wealth that a failure to do so was a clear indicator of a lack of intelligence and application.[2] Those who had inherited property might be considered for leading roles because of the environment in which they were raised. They would confirm their worth by using their land productively and increasing their wealth. As Melbourne (1972: 109–10) has noted, 'to merely wealthy people, he would give no political power; but to the owners of wide estates who were engaged in producing wealth, he would entrust the government of the colony'.

He was a trenchant critic of land grants to military officers and former officers, a practice that produced a group of landholders who had not earned their property. The main problem was that 'it rarely happens that those, who emerge suddenly into power … without that due preparation, which grows up with ascending rank and seniority, the usual and natural stepping stone to greatness, know how to confine themselves within the strict limits of moderation and propriety' (Wentworth, date unknown: 2).

Social organisation and stratification

Wentworth's understanding of the determinants of personal superiority was complex. He regularly referred to 'birth' as a qualification for superior positions. Yet he could not have meant genetic inheritance, as he rejected notions of genetic predetermination (he did not seem to acknowledge even genetic predisposition). He seems rather to have meant the domestic environment provided by parents and siblings as well as the education and opportunities for travel that parents could afford. Domestic and environmental conditions were important in whether an individual formed good or bad habits. Like all liberals, Wentworth could not treat these factors as final determinants. Thus he believed that each individual remained the final cause of her or his being and social position; or, at least, this was what Wentworth contended in his struggles with the exclusives.

Birth

When Wentworth wrote or spoke of 'birth' as significant for an individual's fitness of positions of leadership, the birth he referred to was usually his own. That is, he felt that he had been fitted by birth for high social status and political position. His intention to pursue a legal training in England did not reflect a desire, he wrote, 'to abandon the country that gave me birth. I am sensible of the sacred claims which it has upon me ... In withdrawing myself, therefore, for a time from that country I am actuated by a desire of better qualifying myself for the performance of those duties that my birth has imposed' (quoted in Fifer 1984: 149).

His reference to birth seems therefore to be a reference to his own familial environment. The Wentworths had come to occupy a position of social significance in New South Wales, but because they could not claim an untainted lineage they were still being prevented from occupying a position at the very peak of society and politics. They were, rather, leaders on the second rung of the social ladder.

The exclusives

The exclusives represented a major threat to society in New South Wales in that they tried to maintain their social position by excluding members of all other groups as contenders for positions of significance and influence. Understanding birth purely as genetic heritage, they denied political and social rights to anyone not born to their rank. This gave them a justification for denying rights to others without having to do anything that showed that they themselves deserved to be in control.

The following quotation is a reasonable summary of Wentworth's opinion of the exclusives.

> The covert aim of these men is to convert the ignominy of the great body of the people into an hereditary deformity. They would hand it down from father to son, and raise an eternal barrier of separation between their offspring, and the offspring of the unfortunate convict. They would establish distinctions which may serve hereafter to divide the colonists into *castes*; and although none among them dares publicly to avow that future generations should be punished for the crimes of their progenitors, yet such are their private sentiments; and they would have the present race branded with disqualifications, not more for the sake of pampering their own vanity, than with a view to reflect disgrace on the offspring of the disenfranchised parent, and

thus cast their own children and descendants into that future splendor and importance, which they consider to be their present peculiar and distinguishing characteristics. (1978: 349)

Wentworth's confrontation with the exclusives was focused mainly around demands for political rights. Liberal theory requires that rights be equally available to all; to deny them to some individuals was to deny them an essential resource through which they could improve their lives and social position. In the context of society in New South Wales, rights would also provide a means through which the position of the exclusives could be challenged.

Since he eschewed notions of essential inequality, Wentworth was committed to the idea that social positions should be open to all. Birth might provide an initial indicator of fitness for higher activities because of the environment that wealthy parents might provide, but it was not a final indicator. Those who had not been born to the ranks of the well-to-do could not be denied higher aspirations and the rights to which they were entitled. Wentworth's elitism was not one of impenetrable divisions. Superior and inferior individuals were suited to different roles in society, but there was nothing eternal about those divisions. The abilities associated with the productive use of property, responsibility, and a right to exercise political authority were not acquired as part of some genetic inheritance. That these abilities tended to be transmitted through families was more a function of the environment that families created than of an innate superiority.

Political Reform

Wentworth was convinced that society in New South Wales was divided on unacceptable grounds. An autocratic governor, supported by a military elite, created social divisions that had more to do with who was and was not in the governor's favour than they did any qualities in the people themselves. Whether they were free settlers, emancipists, or the children of emancipists, those who were not exclusives could enjoy none of their privileges. More importantly, they could not avail themselves of the rights normally available to British subjects. Wentworth believed that the means by which inequality was produced in New South Wales were pernicious and degrading for his society.

Political reform was necessary because the progress of the colony had been impeded through these artificial social divisions. The dominant interests in New South Wales had made it impossible for that society and its economy to develop in ways that reflected the real needs and interests of colonists.

This section deals with two elements of Wentworth's view on political reform in New South Wales. The social problems that derived from corrupt political processes are examined first. The problems chosen for discussion are not the only ones Wentworth identified; they nevertheless give some sense of his understanding of the detrimental effects of the social divisions that had developed in the colony. The reforms he championed in his attempts to create a positive, or progressive, form of social stratification are dealt with next. For the most part, reform involved the creation of essential political institutions that would result in the proper management of the colony.

Problems
The exclusives and civil rights
Wentworth railed against the exclusives. He accused them of being 'a set of *interlopers* … [who sought] to monopolize all the respectable offices of the government, all the functions of emolument, power, and dignity to themselves … [with] no object in view, but their own personal aggrandizement, and the maintenance of a self-assumed aristocratic importance' (1978: 353–4). This resulted in mismanagement of the colony. Those with most to contribute to progress within the colony were least likely to hold positions they could use to maximise progress.

Current and former military officers dominated the colony and organised it to preserve their positions of power and privilege; they were not interested in improving society (except where this benefited them). Wentworth objected to 'the pretensions of the military faction which seemed to him to be inimical to the interests of the colony. He held the opinion that the future of the colony depended on the efforts of those free settlers who were engaged in developmental work, and he believed that they should enjoy the influence which the military faction had usurped' (Melbourne 1972: 14).

A lack of rights
One of the factors that contributed to the mismanagement of the colony was the lack of protection from arbitrary rule normally available to British subjects. Those who had most to contribute to development

were not merely marginalised, they were diminished through being subjected to arbitrary authority and denied basic human rights. As Deer and Barr (date unknown: 50, 67) have pointed out, 'At that time there was in New South Wales no Parliament, no trial by jury, no freedom of the press, and little true education.' '"What has caused the people of the country to degenerate," [Wentworth] asked, "but the slavish system of begging for rights, which, as British subjects, we ought to possess?"'.

Full participation in society was only possible when people felt certain of their rights and knew they would be protected by legal institutions that could enforce those rights. The 'noble assurance that he is in the path of duty and security, so long as he refrain from the violation of … laws … is the main spring of all industry and improvement. But this dignified feeling cannot exist in any society which is subject to the arbitrary will of an individual' (Wentworth 1978: 164).

It was possible to make a complaint about abuses of power by governors. At least, they were if the complainant was willing, and could afford, to travel to seek remedies in British courts or from the British government. Appealing to British courts and governments to uphold their rights was of course no real option for most people. To suggest to people with limited funds that they might 'obtain redress in the court of King's Bench', Wentworth wrote, 'is … but a cruel mockery, calculated to render the pang more poignant, which it would pretend to alleviate' (1978: 165).

Reforms
Rights and progress
Making civil rights generally available was an important step in creating conditions that were conducive to social progress. Incentives to greater effort would be given to those who had a real interest in the colony and its improvement. These rights could be protected by local institutions, and the people would feel free to invest their energies in the colony.

One of the most important effects of granting civil rights to the people in New South Wales was that the prospect of acquiring those rights would speed the reform of convicts. Wentworth could think of no other initiative that would promote good behaviour on the part of convicts. No other measure 'would prove so efficacious as the prospect of regaining, after years of unimpeachable integrity, all those civil rights which they had forfeited, of becoming once more privileged to act as jurymen, magistrates, and legislators'. The possibility of convicts being granted rights they had lost 'would quickly revive the latent sparks of virtue wherever they were not quite extinct, and electrify the mind when all other applications would fail to rouse it from its despondence and lethargy' (1978: 353–4).

Wentworth accepted that this ought not to be the case in Britain, where entirely different circumstances obtained. He thought it a sensible policy, in that the prospect of losing one's rights if convicted of criminal offences served 'to promote virtue and discountenance vice' (1978: 351). In New South Wales, however, the very opposite was true.

> The very same grounds of policy require that such disqualifications should not exist in New South Wales. There the great mass of the people are composed of persons who have been under the operation of the law, and who were transported with the avowed intention of the legislature to effect their reformation. How then is this great philanthropic end to be best attained? Is it by holding out no inducements to good conduct, no distinction between repentant vice and incorrigible enormity? (Wentworth 1978: 351–2)

Responsible government

Any attempt at political reform in New South Wales, in Wentworth's view, had to address the way in which political authority was created and deployed. He believed it was necessary to create institutions that reflected the key interests within the colony and protected those interests from interference from either above or below.[3] Political institutions that promoted the interests of the colony were an important element in the achievement of a sound and prosperous community.

Wentworth contended that the ability to control its own destiny was crucial to the success of any society. He argued that 'the prosperity of nations has kept pace with the degree of freedom enjoyed by their citizens' (1978: 327). Freedom created an atmosphere in which the members of a society felt that their lives and property were protected. In Wentworth's view, a society without 'a free government, is devoid of that security of person and property which has been found to be the chief stimulus to individual exertion, and the only basis on which the social edifice can repose in a solid and durable tranquillity'. That the people of New South Wales were not truly free meant that society did 'not rest on this foundation stone of private right and public prosperity' (1978: 327).

Responsible government would also result in public policies better suited to the conditions that existed in the colony. In a speech in the Legislative Council, Wentworth spoke of 'the plenary power of legislation so long contended for by the Council, and the want of which has so often impeded the passing into law of measures which were essential to the welfare of the country' (quoted in Clark 1955: 335).

Wentworth argued that significant improvement in New South Wales would 'inevitably follow the establishment of a free representative government'. Only a properly constituted local legislature, he concluded, would fill owners of capital with the 'confidence which is essential to the free unimpeded extension of industry, [and] … provide an instant relief for those growing wants, which spring out of the progress of advancement, and are contingent on those changes of circumstances and situation, to which incipient communities are so peculiarly liable' (1978: 333–4).

At a minimum, the idea of responsible government means that a government, or Cabinet, is responsible to a legislature. Wentworth's conception of responsible government, though, was not that of a government responsible to a legislature elected by the whole community, but one where the executive was held accountable to a legislature voted for and peopled by property-owners (Persse 1972: 22). While Wentworth 'was anxious to raise the Legislative Council to a position whence it would be able to control administrative work … he was anxious also to protect [it] from popular opinion' (Melbourne 1972: 74).

Representative government?

Wentworth supported responsible government, but not what we think of as representative government. People had no right to be represented in parliament; at least they had no such right until they showed they were worthy of having it. Voting rights had to be earned, especially by former convicts; they were not to be given away. No one was to be denied voting rights because of their past, but they had to demonstrate clearly their entitlement to these rights.

This was even more important in the context of determining who was eligible to offer himself for election to parliament. Wentworth did not want to be taken as arguing that 'the doors of the legislative assembly should be thrown open to *all indiscriminately* who may *happen* to be *free … None* should be able to arrive at that dignity, but those whose conduct during their abode in the colony shall have been *absolutely unimpeachable* (1978: 354–5).

Wentworth's resistance to an extended suffrage was reinforced by the influx of immigrants attracted by the discovery of gold. This immigration had changed the composition of society in New South

Wales, and the issues that went to who should be granted voting rights had also changed. Wentworth's elitism became more obvious when it was no longer a matter of determining whether emancipated convicts and their children were eligible for voting rights. The discovery of gold, in his view, had resulted in an immigration into New South Wales of a large number of people from different countries and with different political principles. Among these, Wentworth wrote, were 'a very thick sprinkling of Democrats, Chartists, Socialists, Red Republicans ... forming altogether a transitory and most undesirable addition to the population of the Colony'. He was not about 'to transfer the government of the Colony into the hands of the very scum of the colonial population' (1855: 5).

Wentworth's rejection of popular suffrage was construed, both by his contemporaries and by later commentators, as a retreat from democratic sentiments he was thought to have espoused in his early years. In reply, Wentworth asserted that he had never been a democrat and had always believed in a restricted franchise (but had had little reason to articulate the nature of these restrictions). To those who criticised him for resiling from democratic principles, he responded:

> The belief has grown among the deluded and ignorant mass that ... it was being a squatter which had caused the dereliction from what were termed the liberal and constitutional predilections of my former years, and which made me a leading member in what it is called the squattocratic oligarchy. I hope that I shall at least show ... that I am neither going to desert the squatters, nor the opinions I have previously formed ... I am firm in the conviction that the representation of the country should be based on, or proportioned to, not the mere population, but the great interests of the country; and it should be so proportioned that no one interest shall have a preponderating influence over any other. (quoted in Melbourne 1972: 89)

Parliament

Wentworth applied an even stricter property test when it came to deciding who was eligible to stand for election to a lower house of parliament, or Legislative Assembly.[4] The restrictions he suggested would result in a small number of electors choosing from candidates who came from an even more restricted pool. This did not concern Wentworth. The issue in his mind was not about numbers. The real test was whether a Legislative Assembly would do 'its utmost to promote its own interests, *or what would have been the same thing,* the welfare of the community which it represented' (1978: 341, emphasis added).

Constituting an upper house was a pressing issue in Wentworth's time. He applied different principles, in this case, and argued that the upper house ought to be a nominated one, and that its members should be chosen from among those who held the largest estates in the colony. He believed that a house constituted in this way would give the colony the greatest degree of protection from maladministration.

Wentworth believed that the interests of the colony were likely to be threatened from two directions. The immediate threat was from the governor of the colony. A nominated upper house, in Wentworth's view, would provide

> a remedy for the inexperience or ignorance of governors; and it is a sort of nucleus, round which all new bodies may easily agglomerate. Like a handful of veterans in a newly raised regiment, it will be capable of setting in motion the whole machinery of the government, and establishing with the greatest celerity that organization and discipline which are as requisite in administration as in war. (1978: 362–3)

The other threat would come when an elected lower house was introduced, even one organised along the lines he suggested. A nominated upper house constituted 'an element which, though antagonistic at times, and necessarily antagonistic, because it exercises, and has a right to exercise, a veto on the legislation of the Lower House, contains within it a principle without which … there is no safety-valve, and can be none' (quoted in Clark 1955: 339)[5]

When it came to a choice between the protection of property and the promotion of democratic principles, the latter was to be sacrificed. In Wentworth's view, 'an Upper House, nominated or elected (for, after all, nomination and election mean the same thing), by the foremost talent and judgement of the country … [would] be composed of better men than would be elected by any constituencies, whether their franchise be high or low' (1855: 15).

Wentworth sincerely believed that democracy would introduce a form of government that was not in the colony's interests. He wanted New South Wales to be governed by men of property because he believed that this would provide a more enlightened and effective government.

He 'consistently associated power with service. He wished to rule because he thought he could rule best. He wished to establish the influence of his own class because he thought democracy would destroy the colony' (Melbourne 1972: 112).

If New South Wales was to become a progressive and flourishing society its members had to be given responsibility for governing themselves. This required the creation of responsible government. Responsible government, however, may allow for a variety of institutional arrangements. Wentworth advocated houses of parliament that were governed by those who held productive property because he believed them to be most likely to have the interests of the colony at heart. The threats posed by an ineffective or corrupt governor and an exuberant lower house prompted Wentworth to advocate an upper house, which would protect the interests of those with productive property and consequently the colony as a whole.

Conclusion

To understand Wentworth's liberalism requires a sense of his views on human nature and the significance of property ownership as an indicator of worth and fitness for leadership. These views led Wentworth to support a system of responsible government in which those with property played a central role. He believed that, because of differing circumstances in which differing habits were developed, people formed different characters. This did not preclude a change in their situation, including reformation from a criminal past, but it meant that a demonstration of personal worth was necessary. Possession of productive property was an indicator of both personal worth and a commitment to the progressive development of the colony. Wentworth was a liberal, but he was not a democrat.

Certainly he was less of a democrat than the other liberals whose works are dealt with in Part II. He also comes closest to advocating an alternative form of social stratification, rather than an end to social stratification. He can be defended from the charge of actually advocating a form of social stratification on the ground that he did not advocate a system in which some individuals could neither improve their situation nor occupy dominant positions in society. His struggle was to gain social and political rights for those who proved their worth, irrespective of their initial status in the colony. Like all liberals, he believed that some people were more able than others. The problem, as it is for all liberals, was to develop a system in which they would prove their greater ability and be rewarded for doing so.

---

[1] Chisholm (1963: 385) has suggested that Wentworth may have coined the term.

[2] 'He believed that only the foolish and the ignorant would fail to accumulate a certain amount of wealth in New South Wales, and that, for this reason, government should be controlled by people having a sufficient property qualification' (Melbourne 1972: 55–6).

[3] 'He was wedded, however, at least for much of his life, to the Whig tradition which had displayed such a prominent role in the conduct of British affairs in the eighteenth century. The Whigs favoured constitutional government along the lines embodied in the political settlement after the Glorious Revolution of 1688. In this scheme the legislature was the ultimate authority in government. The Whigs supported strongly such civil liberties as trial by jury and the imposition of taxation only under Parliamentary authorisation. Their thinking was influenced by John Locke on the working of constitutional government and on the need for religious toleration. Many Whigs, however, drew the line at opening up legislative institutions to reflect mass opinion. Wentworth was one of these … [He] favoured a society in which the rich, the intelligent and the powerful naturally provided leadership for the masses' (Castles 1982: 126).

[4] 'With respect to the nature and extent of the property to be possessed by the members of the legislative assembly, I am of opinion, that a freehold estate of five hundred acres in any part of the territory of New South Wales, or its dependent settlements on Van Dieman's Land, should be considered a sufficient qualification, and that in the case of electors twenty acres of freehold should give the right of voting at election for the districts in which such freehold property may be situated; and that either a leasehold of the value of £5 a year, or paying a house rent of £10 a year, that of voting at elections for towns' (Wentworth 1978: 356).

[5] Wentworth went so far as to support the creation of hereditary titles, 'leaving it to the option of the Crown to annex to the title a seat for life in the Legislative Council. Such hereditary titles would lay the foundations of an aristocracy, and the formation of an upper house modelled, as far as circumstances would admit, upon the analogies of the British Constitution' (Clark 1978: 36). The seats that accompanied those titles could not be passed on to future generations. The goal was simply to recognise the existence of superior individuals who were of greater worth to the colony and who were most likely to act responsibly when in positions of power. Thus 'as talent and ability are not naturally hereditary, it could not for a moment be proposed that the seats of those upon whom hereditary titles might be conferred should descend to those who come after them … An Upper House formed on this principle, whilst it should be free from the objections which have been urged against the House of Lords, on the ground of the hereditary right of legislation which they exercise, would lay the foundation of an aristocracy which from their fortune, birth, leisure, and the superior education which these advantages would superinduce, would soon supply elements for the formation of an Upper House, modelled, as far as circumstances will admit, upon the analogies of the British Constitution' (quoted in Clark 1955: 337–8).

6

HENRY BOURNES HIGGINS
(1851-1929)

So, free men everywhere condemn the social arrangements which create inequalities on unreasonable grounds, which create inequalities of opportunity, which doom the bulk of humanity to excessive toil, to insufficient sustenance, insufficient rest, insufficient recreation—to dependence on others for opportunity to work and live, to perpetual anxiety as to the means of subsistence. No one can estimate the gains to science, to art, to literature, to national and social life, if every child reared to manhood or womanhood had equal, or even approximately equal opportunities for culture—opportunities for leading a sane, healthy existence, in which there is scope for the exercise of all the vital powers. (Higgins 1902: 17)

Henry Bournes Higgins was born in Ireland in June 1851 and came to Australia in 1870. He graduated from the University of Melbourne with a Master of Arts and a Bachelor of Law. He served on the council of that university between 1887 and 1923. He was elected to the Victorian parliament in 1894 and remained there until 1901. He participated in the series of conventions, held between 1897 and 1898, that framed the Commonwealth Constitution. He was elected to the first federal parliament as the Member for North Melbourne and was re-elected in 1903. In 1904 he became federal Attorney-General. He was appointed to the High Court of Australia in 1906 and remained on the bench until 1929. He was appointed the first president of the Commonwealth Court of Conciliation in 1907 and stepped down from this position in 1920.

Henry Bournes Higgins may be seen as a humanitarian visionary or, in terms of his economic theory, as 'a nut who, to the great detriment of his country, found himself able to give legal form and substance to his fantasies' (Evans 1985: 31). Both views reflect Higgins' centrality in the development of a system of industrial arbitration that shaped, for better or worse, Australian industrial relations and, as a result, society for most of the twentieth century.

Higgins' liberalism was deeply affected by his view that the existence of social stratification in Australia should be redressed through intervention from governments and their agencies. He believed that human beings needed to have their individuality facilitated and protected. The advantaged could not be left free to exploit, or otherwise deal improperly with, the disadvantaged. Individuals might be unequal by nature,[1] but this did not explain all the sources of inequality in society, or preclude attempts to reduce the detrimental effects of this inequality. The creation of a healthy society, in his view, required the reconciliation of competing interests of existing social strata, or, as Higgins might have written it, 'class'. This reconciliation was largely a political problem. Higgins directed much of his energy to political institutions he saw as central to the resolution of tensions produced by the social strata.

This examination of Higgins' views on social stratification begins with a discussion of human nature and society. Higgins took the view that society was divided into groups, or classes, of people with opposed or divergent interests and different capacities to promote or protect those interests. That society contained divisions, however, did not preclude a collective or communal interest. The form of social organisation through which this could be achieved is examined in the second section. The best form of social organisation, in Higgins' view, was that which maximised each individual's ability to pursue his or her interests while preventing inequalities and antagonisms that threatened the very existence of society. That people were governed by interests that produced both antagonism and empathy provided political institutions with the wherewithal to promote individuality and community. This was not a simple task, however, and required a well-conceived set of political institutions.

Human Nature and Society

Higgins' society was dominated by antagonism between employers and workers. Most of his public life was spent trying to deal with this antagonism. The antagonism was produced, in his view, because of the way that economic, or material, interests diverged along class lines. He accepted that material interests were important, but he thought that non-material (i.e. spiritual, moral, and cultural) interests were also important. These interests were particularly significant for a society because they did not produce conflict. Indeed, in Higgins' view, they could provide a basis for overcoming conflict, or ameliorating its effects. Higgins thought that society continued two potentials that reflected these two forms of interest. One was towards division or class conflict. The other was towards cooperation or community.

Economic interests

For Higgins, the satisfaction of material wants constituted the primary motivation to action on the part of human beings. While he thought that people were capable of more than simple selfishness, he assumed that material interests were central to all people. He adopted a narrow view of individual motivation when it came to his work on the Court of Conciliation and Arbitration. The employer 'was simply to be regarded as a citizen carrying on a certain business for personal profit; the employee was, in a position of less advantage, doing the same thing' (Palmer 1931: 209).

The particular interests that derived from their economic positions meant that employers and employees had markedly divergent perspectives on questions concerning wages and conditions. This manifested itself in very different attitudes to decisions handed down by the Court of Conciliation and Arbitration. 'The employer ... looks at money results, at profits, at expenses. The union looks at the results to the human instrument' (Higgins 1968: 51–2). Employers and employees had much to gain and lose in their economic interactions. They did not have the same things to gain and lose, however. 'The capitalist has his capital at stake; the employee has his life at stake. I do not mean by his life merely his food, clothing, shelter; I include the whole mass of his life's powers and activities' (Higgins 1968: 156).

Higgins did not assume that either employer or employee would be able or willing to consider the interests of the other: 'The members of each class have neither the knowledge nor the imagination nor the sympathy necessary to enable them to understand how facts present themselves to the other class.' Even when people had connections with both classes, 'every one tends to hold the opinion of the class in which his interests and his associations chiefly lie' (1919: 4)

The main source of the lack of understanding between employers and employees was a result of their separate existences. That they interacted very little and had no experience of how the other lived left them standing firmly in their opposing camps. Higgins argued that a lack of contact between employer and employee was one source of the tension within society. He thought that employers needed to develop a sense of those in the alternative camp. 'If employers could only see more of their employees at work and in their homes—if they could see the other side of life—their humanity would generally assert itself' (1919: 5). The same went for employees. Higgins felt that when workers made demands about wages and conditions they did 'not concern themselves as to the frequent difficulties of the employer in carrying on the business at all—as to his competition with rivals, as to the effect on prices, as to the incidental consequences of the demands (1919: 5).

Non-economic interests

That Higgins took economic interests as fundamental to human beings and social classes did not mean that he felt people had no other interests, even if those other interests tended to be secondary. Material interests would predominate when material needs were not being met. People, in Higgins' view, would focus almost exclusively on their material interests as long as they were uncertain about their future capacity to maintain themselves with some degree of material comfort. 'Give them relief from their materialistic anxiety', he wrote, 'give them reasonable certainty that their essential material needs will be met by honest work, and you release infinite stores of human energy for higher efforts, for noble ideals' (1968: 37–8).

Higgins was convinced that too little recognition was given to non-material interests. He thought that people had not considered the issue of 'how much energy is being diverted from the higher and more spiritual activities while men are so obsessed by the never-ceasing struggle for a due distribution of material things' (1919: 3). If people could broaden their conception of human interests, they would realise that 'man does not live by bread alone, that he has a higher nature to be satisfied' (1902: 13).

The development of this higher nature and cultivation of non-material interests constituted, for Higgins, the achievement of true humanity.

A man who seeks his own personal comfort only is selfish; a man who seeks the comfort of his family is less selfish—his sympathies are broader, if he seeks also the good of his town, his district, his country, he attains a higher level with each step. But the man who works for the good of others, for human beings who have not done, and who will not do, anything for him; the man who aims at doing justice to all with whom he comes in contact, without distinction of creed or country, breathes a still higher and purer air' (quoted in Callaghan 1983: 61).

The level of compassion to be found in a community was a measure of the level of civilisation it had achieved, for 'the more civilized a race is, the more it wards off the cruelty of nature toward the weakly members' (Higgins 1896: 15).

Interdependence

Higgins' rejection of simple egoistic accounts of human nature was central to his understanding of human nature and society. He may have believed that people tended to be selfish and that only a few could conceive of a collective interest, but thought that a trend was developing in which people rejected those things that isolated them from each other. In Higgins' view, 'the most advanced philosophy is discarding what used to be regarded as the fundamental distinction between the *ego* and the *non ego*. The "I," it is said, has no fixed limits—it blends with all the other constituents of the universe' (1896: 9). Higgins saw various indications that people were abandoning narrow egoism and recognising their interdependence: 'It would seem as if extreme individualism in religion were losing in public favour at the same time as extreme individualism in economics and philosophy' (1896: 16).

This did not mean, however, that individual self-actualisation was not important. Human beings, in Higgins' view, needed 'an adequate opportunity for self-expression, for realising [themselves] and [their] powers' (1919: 9). Rickard's account of this aspect of Higgins' political philosophy connects changes in his private political beliefs with his public practices:

Autonomy was always to be important for Higgins ... But as he moved into an active political career, Higgins sensed that autonomy was not enough. Human beings had to relate to each other—they married and had children. Similarly, society was not simply a set of autonomous human beings: it was ... characterised by *interdependence*. As his own career waxed, the assertion of autonomy could be relaxed, and the need for reconciliation, whether between individuals or social classes, emphasised. Factory legislation provided a suitable means for working out his political ideas in these terms, and it launched a personal development which was to culminate in his new province for law and order. (Rickard 1984: 90)

The interdependence of human beings meant that society was a means for, and not an impediment to, individual self-realisation.

Autonomy itself was a reflection of membership of society and not its repudiation. The bonds of society enhanced freedom; they did not prevent it. For Higgins 'the greatest liberty is obtained where there is the greatest law—that where there is the greatest restraint in the common interest, there is to be found the greatest liberty for the individual and for individual action' (quoted in Callaghan 1983: 60), for human beings never achieve their highest level of development outside society. Thus every person 'has more real freedom if all are bound, in links of common interests. For this purpose, more freedom, it is one's duty to subordinate one's personal will to the collective will' (Higgins 1915: 5).

Views of this sort created enormous problems for Higgins in the context of the First World War, for the Germans could be taken to have adopted the principles Higgins outlined. His response was to develop a moral hierarchy in which obedience to essential human principles was the highest moral position. The German people had stopped short of achieving true humanity. According to Higgins, the war 'could not have happened but for the mad theory that there is no end higher than the State and that ... the particular State to which we happen to belong, has a claim on our obedience which is paramount to all claims. There is surely a higher claim—the claim of humanity, of justice' (1915: 13). The 'spirit' that Higgins desired was 'the spirit which, while it puts our nation's interests above our personal and family interests, puts humanity above even our nation' (1917: 2).

Class and community

How people understood themselves and their interests was an important determinant of their approach to society. Those who were absorbed by the pursuit of economic or material interests tended to focus on division. Many saw their interests in terms of class interests, and their society as containing opposing classes. Those who focused on non-material interests saw society in terms of communal interests and the pursuit of higher ends. Class and community constituted competing tendencies for Higgins. He sought to promote community by dealing with the tensions caused by class.

Higgins was optimistic about the future. He believed that the potential for overcoming the tension between economic self-interest and community had increased significantly in his time. Up to his time, 'settled law as to individual rights, and that kind consideration for our neighbour, which is so intimately associated with Christianity, have never yet been satisfactorily fused and amalgamated' (1896: 22). Yet he saw various signs that people were becoming better able to overcome the specific interests resulting from their economic position in order to take on general interests. He detected 'hopeful indications of a growing feeling of common interest on the part of the antagonistic forces of employers and employed; a tendency, by means of co-operation and otherwise, to fuse the two classes into one' (1896: 10).

Unfortunately, in Higgins' view, community was not the dominant tendency in his society, and division remained its most obvious feature. Conflict between holders of divergent economic interests filled many aspects of Higgins' society, life, and politics. This conflict produced antagonisms that sometimes erupted into violence. Higgins entered the Victorian parliament in 1894 in the wake of major social disruption and class antagonism. 'Optimism and confidence had little place in the 1890s, the times of collapse, depression and constriction. The prospect of harmony and co-operation was tried by conflict among employer and employed, and the forces of fear and suspicion divided one man from another. Recognition of common interests was thwarted by self-interest and provincialism' (Callaghan 1983: 59–60).

Antagonism increased as these economic relations became increasingly entrenched, through concentrations of ownership and increases in worker organisation and union membership. The result was that the community as a whole suffered. In Higgins' view, 'the war between the profit-maker and the wage-earner is always with us; and, although not so dramatic or catastrophic as the present war in Europe, it probably produces in the long run as much loss and suffering, not only to the actual combatants, but also to the public' (1968: 1).

Great care was required in this regard. Communal interests could not be allowed to fully displace economic interests. While Higgins believed in the need to maintain 'a vigilant watch and a strong controlling hand in the interests of the community', he also believed that 'great care has to be taken not to hinder the free play and flexibility of the forces which have tended so much hitherto to progress and improvement, under the system of unrestrained competition' (1896: 22).

Human beings would always have interests that derived from their specific economic locations and that would divide them from each other. Ameliorating the effects of these divisions was an essential element of creating a productive and healthy society. Class and community had to be reconciled. In the first instance, this required overcoming the divisiveness produced by separate economic interests in order to produce recognition of a shared interest in society. Community was to be pursued diligently in the face of the tensions caused by class. Community, however, could not fully supplant the stimulus to action and innovation that economic interests provided.

Managing Economic Relations in the Social Interest

Higgins' solution to the problem of reconciling class and community was fundamentally political. He looked to political institutions to bring people to recognise a collective social interest that operated alongside those that derived from the socio-economic strata to which they belonged. His immediate goal was to ensure that the collective interest was defended against the divisive effects of the struggle around individual, strata-producing, economic interests. He sought to create and adapt political institutions to promote a sense of collective interests among the combatants in the class struggle.

Higgins saw the main threat to social harmony as the conflict that resulted from the pursuit of economic interests. This conflict militated against recognition of a collective interest and was becoming more prevalent and more destructive. The divergent interests that produced it were also tending to ossify into irredeemable cleavages. This conflict would also lead away from, rather than towards a rational and just society.[2] Higgins looked to political institutions to produce the reason and justice that were required in troubled times.

> Much can yet be done by liberalising institutions, by giving a fair hearing to all theories, by applying wholesome criticism, by getting theorists to face the responsibility of actual legislation and government, by gaining a clear apprehension of, and holding with a tenacious grip, that which our civilization has of solid good, by bringing severed classes together and making them appreciate one another's difficulties. In the general dislocation of industries, in the conflicts of employers and employed, in the bitter rivalry of nations, in the difficulties of obtaining remunerative work, in the complicated interplay of interests, much distress can be avoided by the exercise of the modest virtues of patience and caution, combined with a sympathetic regard for, and attention to, the reasonable wants of others.'
> (1896: 23)

He did not promote a direct attack on the processes that produced social stratification. His solution was to develop institutions capable of encouraging a cooperative, and even empathetic, attitude on the part of the combatants in economic conflicts.

Political institutions

Higgins' faith that individuals had the capacity to recognise a collective interest meant that he believed that, through reason, they could resolve the conflicts between them. Political institutions were central to the employment, perhaps deployment, of reason. Higgins believed it was possible, as Callaghan (1983: 57) put it, 'to better order social relations and behaviour to achieve moral ends by means of rational development of society's own laws. Through earnest rational effort on the part of law makers, parliamentary or judicial, equality of power and opportunity, that is social justice, might be established and the potential for human greatness enabled to be realized'.

Higgins believed that the time had come for political institutions to become active in the regulation of economic conflicts. 'As slavery passed into serfdom, the rights of the lord [became] limited by law or custom; as serfdom passed into the contractual relation ... so the contract of employment is being gradually regulated by or under the State in the interests of the community' (1968: 149–50). In other words, political institutions had a responsibility to encourage the use of reason in the resolution of conflicts and to discourage the use of violence. As government had, in the past stopped 'the duel, and the private wars of barons, displacing the use of physical force by the application of reason, so it seeks to substitute the use of reason for the use of economic force' (1924: 15).

No matter how extensive state intervention in the free market became, however, it could never amount to an overthrow of a capitalist system. He considered those who advocated worker control of industries to be impractical. Even though he had read many books on the subject, Higgins could not 'find any coherent statement showing how these thinkers propose to attain their object, or how ... the system can be worked' (1919: 10). He could see no viable alternative to a system of wage-labour, even if he could recognise that it had problems. 'It may be that the wage-system is but a parasite on society, and a baleful parasite; but if we recklessly pull down ivy, we may pull down the wall also. It is no simple matter to uproot a system which has become embedded in society for hundreds of years, and which has grown extraordinarily with the development of power machinery' (1919: 11). His approach was to accept that economic structures would tend to produce social stratification, and then work to moderate and modify their effects.

Parliament

Parliament was to be the central element of the management of economic conflict in the collective interest: first, because of its role as a producer of policies that created the environment within which all other agencies operated; second, because it was a leading institution in Australian society; third, because it had the power to create and direct specific institutions designed to deal with economic conflicts. These institutions could be designed so that they encouraged productive and cooperative relations between the combatants in economic struggles.

The second aspect of parliament's role was particularly important to Higgins because he felt that parliaments of his time were not providing the sort of leadership that was required. He looked first to parliament as a source of social guidance and as a means of encouraging the replacement of force with reason in the resolution of economic conflicts. He saw it as a forum that produced leaders equipped to lead parliament and country.

Tribunals

Parliament was not the only source of the direction and social structure through which tensions caused by social stratification could be managed. Courts and tribunals could contribute to the creation of a legal system that served a collective interest by promoting social justice and greater productivity. Central to this legal system were courts and tribunals of conciliation and arbitration. Higgins saw such a system as particularly significant in times of economic recession, for 'the Court and the tribunals are the chief barrier against the return to the old anarchy in wages, against the lowering of the standard of life for the workers, against the cruelties and stupidities of industrial warfare' (1922: 8).[3]

Higgins approached conciliation and arbitration with the intention of creating an environment in which representatives of employers and employees could meet that was not one of the normal points at which those strata met. His court could be counted a success if it merely promoted 'the meeting of representatives of the unions with representatives of the employers. Such meetings produce a good effect, even when the employers adhere to their methods, giving their reasons' (1968: 49).

Judicial leadership was important for creating an environment in which social harmony, justice, and progress could be achieved. Through it, all parties could be brought to develop a lasting commitment to the process, even if they were not always satisfied with the outcomes it might produce on any particular occasion. Higgins believed that 'the Commonwealth Court had a chance of laying down a tradition of deep-seated justice … And once the tradition had been created the Court would be a power for industrial peace, compelling the loyalties even of parties who were dissatisfied by a particular award' (Palmer 1931: 213–14).

The system of arbitration and conciliation was an important device for removing force as a means for resolving disputes within society. 'The arbitration system is devised to provide a substitute for strikes and stoppages, to secure the reign of justice as against violence, of right as against might' (Higgins 1968: 61). It was also designed to promote the sort of social responsibility that Higgins believed was essential for social progress and individual freedom. If this was to be achieved, all people had to develop a 'higher conception of duty … a clearer grasp of duty to society, to humanity, as being paramount to the interest, or supposed interest, of any narrower class. It is ultimately a matter of morals' (1919: 6).

Curbing the power of employers

The conflict between employer and employee was not one between equals. Employers had a decided advantage when it came to the struggle over wages that was often at the centre of the conflict between employer and employee. Higgins argued that 'freedom of contract is a misnomer as applied to the contract between an employer and an ordinary individual employee. The strategic position of the employer in contests as to wages is much stronger than that of the individual employee' (1968: 19).

> As a rule, the economic position of the individual employee is too weak for him to hold his own in the unequal contest. He is unable to insist on the 'fair thing.' The power of the employer to withhold bread is a much more effective weapon than the power of the employee to refuse to labour. Freedom of contract, under such circumstances, is surely misnamed; it should rather be called despotism in contract; and this Court is empowered to fix a minimum wage as a check on the despotic power. (Higgins 1911: 27)

While wages were usually at the centre of contests between employer and employee, Higgins detected an 'increasing demand of employees for some voice as to the conditions of working, the uneasy feeling that the employers, or rather their foremen, have an autocratic power which is too absolute' (1968: 49).

Higgins did not assume, therefore, that the Court of Conciliation and Arbitration dealt with equal parties. Curbing the power of employers was central to the task of creating industrial harmony. That they were more likely to feel they had been hard done by through the Court's decisions was, in Higgins' view, simply a result of the superiority of their position in the industrial struggle. 'The ideal of the Court is a collective agreement settled, not by the measurement of economic resource, but on lines of fair play. The stronger economic position is usually held ... by employers. This is the reason why the awards necessarily operate more frequently as a restraint upon employers than as a restraint on employees' (1968: 40). Higgins' intention was to leave 'every employer free to carry on the business on his own system, so long as he does not perpetuate industrial trouble or endanger industrial peace' (1968: 13).

An inequality of power with respect to wages or conditions was only one manifestation of the unequal relationship between employers and employees. Employers were advantaged in terms of their ability to influence politics, as they had a greater standing in society and more resources. Thus 'the man who has wealth, education and position has a power in politics which far exceeds his voting power' (quoted in Rickard 1984: 77).

Improving productivity

A judicial system organised for the purposes of resolving industrial disputes was not simply a device for compensating for the power of employers who were in dispute with their workers. Higgins thought that the system could also serve the interests of employers, for he believed that the system of arbitration and conciliation would promote the most effective and efficient use of human labour power. Arbitration and conciliation could, in his view, be used to promote both better management practices and greater productivity. This would result, in part, from the creation of rules and guidelines for employment in industry. Higgins argued that anyone familiar with the problems of production would 'recognize the immense advantage it is to the working of the industries to have definite rules laid down by some constituted authority for guidance ... always provided that the authority does not interfere with the discretion of the management rashly or stupidly' (1968: 93). The efforts of the Court of Conciliation and Arbitration had to be considered from three aspects: '(1) How far continuity of industrial operation is secured; (2) how far the conditions of the workers have been improved; and (3) how far the use of human life for industrial processes has been reduced to system and standardization' (Higgins 1968: 78).

A more effective use of labour power would also result from involving workers in decision-making within enterprises. Higgins thought that workers were unhappy with their conditions because they were 'being treated as cogs in a huge machine, and that there would be far more interest in the work and the results, and even valuable suggestions made for improvement, if the workers were taken into account' (1968: 156).

Beside these indirect contributions, the court might make its own contribution to the achievement of greater productivity. Higgins based his decisions with respect to conditions of employment on 'recent scientific studies ... as to fatigue and efficiency' (1968: 125). His interest in scientific management had been fostered by a visit to the USA and friendships with Louis Brandeis and Felix Frankfurter. All three sat on the bench of the highest court in their country. They were also, according to Nyland (1987: 24), 'liberals who believed that social justice could be achieved by peaceful means and that the judiciary needed to play a role in this process. All three ... believed in the need for industry to achieve greater system and rationality and this had led the two Americans to collaborate with the scientific management movement'.

Higgins wanted to apply scientific principles in his own decision-making. He believed that his court had 'largely reduced to system and standardized the use of human life for industrial purposes' (1968: 121). He often bemoaned the fact, however, that there were not enough statistics on issues crucial to measuring the effect of differing working conditions on productivity, with the consequence that he had little objective information to assist him in making his decisions. He also lacked sufficient information to help him determine the level of the basic wage that would not threaten industry and would allow workers to live decent lives and provide for their families. 'The Court has repeatedly invited full enquiry on scientific lines as to the cost of living', he wrote, 'but neither the Government nor the parties have yet responded. Preferably the enquiry should be made by expert statisticians and on the basis of distinct regimens' (1968: 53).

A 'socially responsible' wage

Higgins' most famous contribution to the creation of industrial peace and social cohesion was the determination and enforcement of a 'basic wage'. To his chagrin, for he expected greater leadership from parliament, he had been left with the task of determining whether wages in industries over which he had authority were 'fair and reasonable'. Higgins interpreted this as bestowing upon him the primary responsibility of political institutions, which was to foster economic harmony and social progress. It indicated an obligation to ensure that justice was provided for all workers. Providing justice for workers meant treating them as human beings and thereby ensuring that they could maintain their productive capacities.

In Higgins' view, being left to determine a basic wage meant that the court had been given the responsibility of protecting essential human rights. This was suggested by the fact that it had to determine a basic wage, for 'the very expression "basic wage," [pointed]... to the fundamental human rights as distinguished from secondary rights' (1922: 8). In protecting these rights, the court promoted economic justice and a civilised community.

Determining a basic wage allowed the court to protect a stratum of society that was generally less able to promote its interests. Workers were no longer to be left in a situation in which they were engaged in 'the usual, but unequal, contest, the "higgling of the market" for labour, with the pressure for bread on one side, and the pressure for profits on the other'. To determine a basic wage required considering 'the normal needs of the average employee, regarded as a human being living in a civilized community' (Higgins 1906: 3).

Providing justice for workers, Higgins assumed, also involved recognising that the worker was the head of a household.[4] A sound family life was central to a civilised community. This could not be maintained in impoverished or otherwise under-resourced conditions. The needs of the workers 'included the needs of the family. Sobriety, health, efficiency, the proper rearing of the young, morality, humanity, all depend greatly on family life, and family life cannot be maintained without suitable economic conditions' (1968: 37).

Respecting workers

Its defence of the basic rights of workers and their families did not exhaust the work of the court. It could also encourage employers to respect workers as human beings. If workers were treated with respect,

Higgins hoped, this would be conducive to the creation of a sense of community. It also facilitated the creation of a productive workforce.

> By presenting the unskilled worker as a human being in a civilised community, entitled to marry and raise a family, Higgins placed the onus on employers and critics to either accept this standard or justify a lesser one. By quantifying 'fair and reasonable', he forced others to calculate the realities of human survival. This approach was more cogent at a time when there was a new concern about what was called 'national efficiency', including the extent to which a nation made efficient use of its human resources. (Rickard 1984: 174)

Higgins' goals were not simply economic. They were also fundamentally social. Economic cooperation, productivity, and social cohesion produced a civilised community that all could enjoy. It was not just a matter of setting wages. 'The end to be jealously guarded and preserved is the actual standard of life—not the money which is merely a means to that end' (1922: 9). Work, in Higgins' view, was more than merely a means to satisfy material needs. It conditioned people's being, so that a sound working environment would produce a healthy individual who could, in turn, contribute to the creation of a healthy society.

> The pale and overworked, underpaid, and underfed makers of shirts or boots, not merely are stunted and miserable in their own lives, but their offspring also suffer; and our society suffers. The most precious treasure which any nation has is its human beings; and we must guard that treasure jealously. Labour is good for us all; but it is good only when it draws out and develops our powers, not when it dwarfs or crushes them. (Higgins 1902: 13–14)

The role of the Court of Conciliation and Arbitration in overcoming the division between worker and owner and in making for a more efficient and productive working environment is indicative of Higgins' view of the main task of all political institutions. These had to assist in the creation of a sense of a collective interest and promote mutual respect on the part of members of all social strata. Political institutions, then, represented the prime means of dealing with the problems caused by divisions around divergent economic interests, for only these institutions could manage social conflict in such a way that it was not socially destructive. Only they could create an environment in which people of all social strata could be persuaded to overcome their narrow interests in order to recognise and contribute to the successful pursuit of a collective interest. Parliaments were important because they could create a sound policy environment for cooperation and could otherwise provide the leadership necessary for cooperation. Most of all, only parliaments were capable of creating those tribunals which, like the Court of Conciliation and Arbitration, could intervene in social conflicts to achieve a just and socially progressive outcome.

Conclusion

Higgins approached his role as president of the Court of Conciliation and Arbitration in the same manner as he approached all his political goals: first, with a sense of the fundamental problems that economic conflict could cause; second, with a sense of the possibility for creating a community that derived from each individual's capacity to identify with a collective interest and to feel empathy toward others; third, with a sense of the role of political institutions in reducing industrial conflict, ensuring productive efficiency, and promoting a sense of community. In his various political roles, but particularly in this one, Higgins acted out his commitment to these fundamental principles.

He spent much of public life attempting to deal with the effects of social stratification. His primary political ambition was to promote community among competing classes. He did not attempt to fundamentally change the economic system and seemed, as a result, to accept the existence of social strata as an inescapable part of social life. He did not promote the existence of social strata as Wentworth did. Nor did he assume, unlike Wentworth, that it was an easy matter for individuals to overcome the effects of social stratification. His sense of social stratification involved a competition between two groups: workers and employers. Menzies, on the other hand, believed that a middle class was being crushed in the struggle between the workers and employers. Indeed, the system of industrial relations to which Higgins contributed may be thought of as providing workers with the power that Menzies attributed to them. Unlike Dowse, Higgins did not focus his attention on issues relating to the treatment of women. In fact his Harvester judgment may be understood as a manifestation of men's ability to exclude or marginalise women's interests.

1   'It is not by leaving wheat to drop its seeds, and sow itself, that we get the rich and waving crops; it is by taking the seed and scattering it on prepared ground, and at intervals. Some seeds will fail, whatever you do; some lives will fail, whatever you do. But it is simply following out the guidance of this Dame Nature to seek the best conditions of sustenance for your seeds; as it is also to seek out the best conditions of life for the human being' (Higgins 1902: 14).

2   As Crisp has observed, Higgins 'believed in a compassionate, radical-liberal, socio-political order which set equal store by civil rights and liberties and by basic social justice for all Australians without geographical or other distinctions' (1990: 164).

3   Higgins believed that the Court of Conciliation and Arbitration could measure its success by the amount of enmity directed towards it by extremists of both employer and employee groups. With respect to the hatred that emanated from these groups Higgins claimed that 'the chief object of the hatred is the Commonwealth Court; for that Court has led the attack on the autocratic power of employers to dictate the terms of employment, to do what they like with their own business (as they call it); and it has tended to spoil the gospel of the revolutionary—the gospel that there is no remedy except in force' (Higgins 1922: 8).

4   The patriarchal implications of this are obvious and have been dealt with by a number of commentators. McNeil, Jackson and Morrigan (1986: 23) argued that 'the sexual division of labour was enshrined in the wage fixing system in Australia through the concept of the family wage'. In Cass's (1995: 62) view, 'women's position was rendered essentially different from men's by this judgement'. One of the most important aspects of the difference created by the decision, she suggested, was that it contributed directly to a policy environment that eliminated 'the necessity for the employment of married women in the labour market'. There can be little doubt that the Harvester judgment created real problems for women such as Sara Dowse, who sought to achieve social justice for women. That women workers could be treated as fundamentally different from male workers meant that their rights to fair wages, including equal pay for equal work, were seriously infringed. The judgment also reflected the (patriarchal) implication that the normal woman was a married woman who depended on her husband for her survival.

7

ROBERT MENZIES
(1894–1978)

If our motto is to be, 'Each for himself and the devil take the hind-most', then want will be the portion of the least active or the least fortunate, and our civilization will be disfigured by those extremes of wealth and poverty, of comfort and despondency, which have defaced our history ... and which any proper understanding of human dignity will roundly condemn. (Menzies 1943: 26)

Robert Gordon Menzies was born in Jeparit, Victoria, in 1894. He practised as a barrister before becoming a member of the Victorian parliament in 1928. He served as Deputy Premier of that state between 1932 and 1934. In 1934 he was elected to the House of Representatives for the United Australia Party, and was federal Attorney-General from 1935 to 1939. He served as Prime Minister from 1939 to 1941. After the collapse of the UAP, he played a leading role in the formation of the Liberal Party of Australia, which he led from 1943 to 1966. He was Leader of the Opposition between 1943 and 1949 and Prime Minister from 1949 to 1966 (he remains the longest-serving Prime Minister of Australia). He was knighted in 1963 as the first Knight of the Order of Australia.

Like many Australian liberals, Menzies went beyond a simple 'economic' understanding of individuals (in which people are understood to be motivated solely by material interests, ameliorated only slightly by secondary attachments to immediate family and, possibly, very good friends). Menzies understood individuals to be motivated by a sense of community and a basic morality that allowed them to rise above the particular interests of their social stratum and to recognise a general interest. Thus while he was an individualist, he believed that individuals were members of communities that contained traditions, moralities, and other bonds that exceeded those taken into account in narrower liberal conceptions of human nature.[1]

Menzies' view that people were governed by a variety of interests or motivations was reflected in his belief that different types of spirit animated people. Certainly they demonstrated initiative and enterprise in economic matters, but intellectual forces and cultural pursuits also enlivened them—or at least they were so enlivened when these pursuits were available to them. Spirit, in any of its forms, was not evenly distributed throughout society, however, and people were essentially unequal. The role of politics was to ensure that everyone was given the opportunity to express their capacity for spirited animation. Menzies was particularly concerned at the denial of opportunity to those he referred to as the 'forgotten people', whose opportunities for expression were restricted in a society dominated by big business and big unions.

In defending these forgotten people, Menzies sought to create an Australian community that maximised people's capacities to satisfy their economic and non-economic interests and in which the varied forms of spirit could emerge. This examination of Menzies' liberalism in the context of his approach to social stratification is divided into two sections. The first is an examination of his conception of human nature; the second deals with his views on the nature and function of politics, particularly as these relate to social stratification.

Individuality, Community and Inequality

As has been intimated, Menzies adopted what may be described as an expanded conception of the individual. People sought to express their individuality, but they also recognised their membership of a community. They were individuals who were capable of identifying with a community and of empathising with other individuals. They were also individuals who sought to satisfy material, or economic, interests while being able to express other forms of spirit. A corollary of these views was Menzies' belief that society was more than simply an arrangement that suited an individual's self-interest. It was also a community that expressed an individual's being and constituted the grounds through which they could pursue connections with others and other noble ends that reflected their higher natures. Societies were, however, communities of the unequal in which some people were more important for social progress.

The expanded individual

Protecting and promoting opportunities for individuals to pursue their personal goals was central to Menzies' political philosophy. He rejected a narrow view of those goals, however, and went beyond a minimal liberal construction of human nature as materially oriented self-centred entities. People pursued economic rewards, but they also acted through an essential connection with other members of a community and evinced a sociability and interdependence that created a real sense of belonging. Menzies thought that people were also inhabited by a 'spirit' which produced enterprise and energy while driving them to seek intellectual and cultural satisfactions. He sought to liberate these drives to pursue intellectual and cultural activities in order to realise the highest form of human nature.

Individuality

None of these points should be taken to suggest that Menzies did not see the individual as central to social development and progress. Individual initiative was one of the main driving forces of human history. Menzies valued the strong-willed individual. He believed that those who relied only on themselves, and needed little in the way of support in their pursuit of their goals, were extremely valuable members of society. He rejected socialism because 'human beings were individuals, and not statistics. And I was an individual, with my own ambitions' (1967: 281). In his view 'the greatest element in a strong people is a fierce independence of spirit. This is the only *real* freedom, and it has as its corollary a brave acceptance of unclouded individual responsibility' (1943: 5).

Material needs

Like all liberals, Menzies began with the view that human motivation started with the drive to satisfy physical, material needs. People are bodies which have basic requirements that must be satisfied for them to live. This concern with satisfying material needs often led to a degree of self-centredness. Most people were prone to consider their immediate material advantage in any social interaction. Menzies thought that the pursuit of material satisfactions was an important expression of a person's individuality and was enlivening and generally improving. 'The great race of men is that one in which each individual develops his fullest individuality, in which ambition is encouraged, in which there are rewards for the courageous and enterprising' (1943: 115). One of the rewards of enterprise was a home of one's own. For Menzies, 'one of the best instincts in us is that which induces us to have our little piece of earth with a house and garden which is ours' (1943: 3–4).

But the pursuit of material satisfactions was only a limited pursuit. It could not provide full and true human satisfaction. In Menzies' view, Australians did 'not yet adequately understand that making money, though some people have elevated it to a science, is as a rule the lowest of all the arts' (1943: 74). He believed that Australians measured 'the success of people by what they can earn, the achievement of scientists by what they can add to national power, the merit of governments by the current standard of living and social services'. The consequence of this was that Australians were 'so little concerned with the things that really make life worth living that we half starve our clergy and expect many of our best writers and artists to live in a sort of eccentric penury' (1967: 234).

Community

Individuals were not only self-centred and materialistic, in Menzies' view. They were also interdependent and consequently concerned about their fellow human beings. Other people were not simply means to ends and objects to be manipulated to serve individual interest; they were people with whom an individual could identify and even empathise. Menzies praised the British, who, unlike Australians, had achieved a society within which there was a 'real willingness to allow the other man to live his own life and willingness to understand the other man's point of view'; he stood 'for honesty and fair-dealing and friendliness, for neighbourliness' (1941: 74).

Others members of society were central to the process of self-formation and the expression of identity. The family was a site in which this concern for and identification with others grew. People might acquire a house, but this was not enough to fully satisfy them. For a house was not a home. A house needed a family if it was to be a home. 'My home is where my wife and children are. The instinct to be with them is the greatest instinct of civilized man; the instinct to give them a chance in life—to make them not leaners but lifters—is a noble instinct' (Menzies 1943: 4).

Beyond the family was the community. Individuals belonged to communities, which provided them with a sense of belonging and responsibility. In Menzies' view, 'the sense of historical continuity is, in any people, a powerful instrument for the production of sanity and responsibility'. People who lacked a sense of being members of a continuous whole would have no thought for others and for future generations. 'So the scramble for individual wealth and prosperity will go on, with all its accompaniments of selfishness. The short view, the demand for immediate and increasing personal benefits, will place great obstacles in the way of statesmanship and the steady march of civilization' (1967: 2–3).

While he wanted people to take the interests of others into account, he was 'not asking for or expecting a community of archangels or of martyrs … [or] asking for an orgy of self-destruction. There is no necessary antithesis between our own interests and desires and the good of our neighbour'. Seeking to further a collective interest was a vital element in good voting. For 'if, as a voter, I am concerned only with my own advantage and am indifferent to the cost to others, I am simply corrupt. I am selling my vote for an individual mess of potage' (1943: 173). Communities represented higher elements of an individual's being and conduced to personal stability and responsibility. They were also necessary for personal development and the increasing civilisation of human societies.

Spirit

Menzies' rejection of selfishness was only one manifestation of his expanded conception of human nature. He also alluded to an almost mystical or divine element in human nature, which he often referred to as the human spirit. He believed that the human spirit was often unrecognised and under-emphasised. People spoke 'of "man power" as if it were a mere matter of arithmetic: as if it were made up of a multiplication of men and muscles without spirit' (1943: 5). In a similar vein, he argued that Australians had thought of democracy 'in mechanical terms', as simply a means for organising government. They had failed to recognise it 'as a spirit, a moving force; not a vehicle for the expression of the human mind alone, but a challenge to the human spirit' (1943: 171).

Displaying spirit and living a spirited existence were central to people's well-being and personal development. Spirit could not be manifested if individuals were hampered by excessive restrictions. They had to be allowed to express their initiative and individuality in all aspects of their lives. 'The real freedoms are to worship, to think, to speak, to choose, to be ambitious, to be independent, to be industrious, to acquire skill, to seek reward. These are the *real* freedoms, for these are of the essence of the nature of man' (quoted in Joske 1978: 183).

The intellect

Freedom was particularly important if individuals were to increase their intellectual capabilities. Intellectual development was a necessary part of the full acquisition or development of spirit. For Menzies, 'pure learning, the freeing of the mind from the inhibitions of ignorance, is one of those great moving forces that distinguish the civilized world from the uncivilized world'. He was keen to promote the development of universities in Australia, since he believed that 'the scholarship for which universities stand, is an essential ingredient in the freedom not only of the human mind but of the human spirit' (1941: 79, 80).

In one sense, intellectual development could be understood to constitute an increase in the avenues for self-expression. It enhanced the capacity for identification with others and was also a source of pleasure in itself; it gave individuals the opportunity to create their own rich worlds of the imagination. Intellectual development was also a means by which people could improve their financial situation. 'The Scottish farmer ponders upon the future of his son, and sees it most assured not by the inheritance of money but by the acquisition of that knowledge which will give him power' (Menzies 1943: 4).

Culture

Another important manifestation of spirit was the pursuit of cultural activities. Like intellectual development, an appreciation of 'culture' gave people the means to develop themselves and to broaden their horizons. Menzies feared that his legal studies might make him more proficient at law but would diminish his humanity. His contemporaries seemed to him to be preoccupied with their legal studies and to read no more widely than their studies required. The result was that 'no other civilizing influence had any place in their lives. I began to fear that if my mind grew more technically acute it would cut a more and more narrow groove; make me a more skilled practitioner, but detach me from a broad and humane life' (1967: 318). Culture, in short, was a source of width of vision and of depth of feeling. People could not be understood to display true spirit if their minds were closed to cultural influences.

Living a spirited existence put people in touch with higher aspects of their being and provided forms of connection with others that were not otherwise available. Recognising and providing for the expression of the human spirit was not only important for individual well-being; it was also crucial to social cohesion and the ability of a society to organise effectively. Menzies believed that the Allies would achieve victory in the Second World War because of their ability to unite around higher principles. 'It is only a faith in something that goes beyond … purely physical matters which can really inspire a nation to honest self-sacrifice' (1943: 163).

That everyone was capable of displaying spirit in these diverse forms required that conditions be created in which spirit could be manifested. The war was, in Menzies' view, a struggle to defend 'the right of every human soul—which is also an immortal soul—to reach its full development' (1943: 140). All people had a place in society and to that extent were of equal worth to society; all deserved to be treated with respect and governed fairly and responsibly. Democracy was 'based upon the Christian conception that there is in every human soul a spark of the divine; that with all their inequalities of mind and body, the souls of men stand equal in the eyes of God' (1943: 172). And, in an echo of Vida Goldstein, it included women, whom Menzies believed had also suffered through the creation of artificial inequalities: 'In the long run, will our community not be a stronger, better balanced and more intelligent community when the last artificial disabilities imposed upon women by centuries of custom have been removed?' (1943: 89).

Inequality

An equality of souls, however, was not actual equality. Menzies supported equality of opportunity, and as we have seen he deplored artificial inequality, but he had no quarrel with what other liberals called 'natural inequality' and he did not believe in any necessary equality of outcome. People deserved different rewards based on differences in effort and ability. That they had equal value as human souls was undeniable, in Menzies' view, and that all people should given a chance to pursue their personal goals 'must be the great objective of political and social policy. But to say that the industrious and intelligent son of self-sacrificing and saving and forward-looking parents has the same social deserts and even material needs as the dull offspring of stupid and improvident parents is absurd' (1943: 8–9). Menzies entertained 'no foolish doctrine of equality between the active and the idle; the intelligent and the dull; the frugal and the improvident' (quoted in Seth 1960: 110). For him 'there is no uniformity among personalities, or talents, or energy' (1967: 282). 'The basic philosophy of Australian Liberalism is that the prime duty of government is to encourage enterprise, to provide a climate favourable to its growth, to remember that it is individuals whose energies produce progress, and that all social benefits derive from his efforts' (1970: 35–6).

That individuals were not uniform in their characters and abilities meant that all individuals had to be allowed to pursue their goals free from interference. This was good for individuals and for society, for 'true rising standards of living are the product of progressive enterprise, the acceptance of risks, the encouragement of adventure, the prospect of rewards. These are all individual matters' (1967: 282). Menzies rejected public policies designed to create 'a dull equality on the fantastic idea that all men are equal in mind and needs and deserts' (1943: 7). He thought that 'great reliance must be made on the creative genius of the individual, assisted, and sometimes controlled by the government in the general social interest, but encouraged and rewarded' (1967: 283).

Leaders

One of the most important fields in which inequality had to be recognised was that of political leadership. Only some people were equipped and able to take up positions of political power. To Menzies 'the world's progress depends in the first instance not on the average man, but on what Confucius called the "superior man". The great movements of human history have sprung from a few uncommon men' (1943: 175). Great leaders, in Menzies' view, were not merely good representatives; they had a sense of their people and an ability to appeal to their higher instincts. He judged Stanley Baldwin to be among the great leaders, mainly because Baldwin did not resort to appeals to people's lower instincts. 'He aims higher than that. He knows … that in a British country the appeal to the best in man, his unselfishness, his chivalry, his sense of obligation for the destiny of his race, his instinct for beauty and harmony and justice, is never made in vain' (1967: 98).

Baldwin was great also because of his sense or responsibility to and for others. 'For the better the individual, the more conscious will he be of his responsibilities to his neighbour and to society' (Menzies 1961b: 5). In Menzies' view, 'the prime art of politics is that of persuasion which cuts deep into the popular mind and heart, which convinces and satisfies the human spirit' (1967: 8–9). A leader 'must not condescend. He must seek to instruct, to explain, and to inspire' (1961b: 9).

Menzies' conception of human nature begins with an attribution of essential individuality. Individuality played itself out first in terms of the satisfaction of economic interests. But people were more than simply economic beings: they had a sense of connection; they also had a capacity, mainly through enhanced intellect and feel for their culture, to become broader and more civilised beings. Some would be more successful than others in the fields of endeavour open to them; some, for instance, would make better leaders.

Menzies' sense of individual inequality meant that he saw society as divided into those who developed their capacities and spirit and those who did not. While he thought of people as having the same basic rights, he did not expect that all had the ability to take up important positions in society. A healthy and progressive society required the efforts of superior people. Such a society allowed the maximum opportunity for self-development without sacrificing the communal interest. Society was a site within which initiative and enterprise could be encouraged and in which other aspects of the human spirit such as intellect and culture could also be given full rein.

Politics

This section elaborates Menzies' analysis of the politics of his time and his views on the ideal form of political organisation in Australia. The first section is an examination of his views on the domination of Australian politics by unions and business groups; the second is a discussion of his ideal political organisation. His position on these issues directly reflects his conception of and response to social stratification. Economic processes were central to social stratification, but rather than focus on employers and employees, Menzies looked to defend the forgotten middle class that had economic interests but were also animated by a broader spirit that was not being accommodated in Australian politics.

Politics of the powerful

Menzies was critical of politics in Australia. He believed it was dominated by powerful interests, which meant that political processes and public policies tended to reflect these interests and not the collective interest. The 'forgotten people' had been forgotten because they had few political resources. Unlike the wealthy, they lacked the financial resources and status that gave them a significant influence over politics and society; unlike members of unions, they had no organisation that would provide political and economic power and influence. Menzies argued that politics had become corrupted or perverted by the conflict between powerful business interests and powerful unions. As a consequence, it no longer fulfilled its proper function of generating directions for the community.

Unions

Menzies had no problem with workers organising to defend themselves against unscrupulous or callous employers.

> The trades union movement has meant a great deal in our industrial history. It has represented collective bargaining. It has given strength to workers as a group which no worker as an individual could have possessed. It has been an effective weapon against the obdurate or short-sighted employer. It has had supreme value in the working of the characteristically Australian system of compulsory industrial arbitration. As a servant of the wage-earner, unionism has done an extraordinarily good job of work. (1943: 125)

However, he rejected moves by unions that went beyond this limited role and resulted in their becoming a powerful force in politics. The expansion of union power had produced an industrial and political framework in which their interests were too well protected. In defining the forgotten people, Menzies excluded 'the mass of unskilled people, almost invariably well-organized, and with their wages and conditions safeguarded by popular law' (1943: 3). He was sympathetic to their use of industrial action to achieve their goals with respect to wages and conditions. But he believed that the influence of organised labour in politics more generally had become so great that society did not operate in the general interest but served this as one of the dominant interests. In his view, 'trades unionism is rapidly becoming a great vested interest in Australia—a vested interest just as powerful as that of any manufacturing cartel' (1943: 127).

The rich

Domination by organised labour was not the only problem for politics in Australia. Menzies also felt that those he called 'the rich' had excessive influence. Their wealth and social influence gave them the ability to promote their interests over the interests of people in all other strata of Australian society. Menzies' forgotten people were not 'the rich and powerful: those who control great funds and enterprises, and are as a rule able to protect themselves' (1943: 2). These he excluded 'because, in most material difficulties, the rich can look after themselves' (1943: 3). Through their status ownership of important industries, of which the media were the jewel in the crown, they were able to extend their influence far beyond industrial matters. The result was that they had a greater ability to ensure that politics operated to their benefit and that competing interests were excluded from the political process.

Control over the mass media gave the rich considerable power over Australian politics. It also meant that the media tended to reflect the interests of the rich and not of the people as a whole. The contest to interpret and influence public opinion was between 'Parliament, freely elected ... and representative of the people ... [and] the press, self-elected, anonymous, and in some cases representative only of the wealth and whims of a few' (quoted in Joske 1978: 220). Menzies even suggested that there was a deliberate attempt on the part of the media to undermine the power of parliament. This was done, he believed, in order to make the media the dominant 'voice' of the people. He alleged a 'great campaign to lower the prestige of Parliament, and correspondingly to increase the authority of the press' (quoted in Joske 1978: 222).

Domination of the political process by unions and the rich meant that political debates and public policies reflected the struggle between labour and the wealthy. While Menzies accepted that these were important interests, he believed that their control over the political agenda precluded others from action and influence. One effect of their dominance was that politics tended to be concentrated around economic and industrial issues. Another was that the collective interest hardly figured in public debates. Values associated with that interest were rarely articulated and defended and did not shape public policies.

The 'forgotten people'

The main effect of the domination of Australian politics by those with wealth and those who were well organised was that those Australians who were not members of these social strata were simply ignored in politics. Apart from the implications this had for democracy in Australia, the problem with it, Menzies thought, was that these people were carriers of values and lifestyles that were more likely to reveal a collective interest and less likely to reflect a narrow material orientation. The result was that a type of person who was essential to Australian society and its progress was forgotten in Australian politics.

The forgotten people were not organised. They did not belong to unions and were not predisposed to join these sorts of organisations. They were independent people who sought to rely only on their own efforts to better their life. They did not rely on organisation to protect their interests, in the way that many workers were required to do. 'They are for the most part unorganized and unself-conscious … They are not rich enough to have individual power … They are not sufficiently lacking in individualism to be organized for what in these days we call "pressure politics". And yet … they are the backbone of the nation' (1943: 2).

The forgotten people were not rich. They did not have the resources to be free from the struggle to make a living, nor were they able to buy political influence. They had material interests that they pursued through economic activity, but their interests were not simply in material possessions. According to Brett (1992: 41), the forgotten people were 'not just an economic class but a moral category whose members are defined by their political values, social attitudes and moral qualities as much by their social and economic position'. Menzies included women in this: 'Prima facie the forgotten people Menzies was addressing were the middle class, but they were also women whose particular interests and problems had generally been forgotten by a politics organised around the conflicts of the economy and the work place' (Brett 1992: 56).

The forgotten people had interests in educational and cultural pursuits, access to which they could not take for granted (as the rich could). They provided, in Menzies' view, 'more than perhaps any other the intellectual life which marks us off from the beast: the life which finds room for literature, for the arts, for science, for medicine and the law' (1943: 6). The forgotten people had to make sacrifices to afford cultural pursuits. This gave them a clear sense of the real importance of these pursuits. The forgotten people had to sacrifice to provide an education for their children. This made them more aware of the value of education and intellectual development.

The most important feature of the forgotten people, though, was that they were forgotten. They were not taken into account in the political process; their values were not defended and their concerns not addressed. They were 'constantly in danger of being ground between the upper and the nether millstone of the false class war' (Menzies 1943: 1). The result was that those people whose values and interests should have been central in the definition of a collective Australian interest were excluded from the processes through which a collective interest was defined.

They may have voted at the elections, but this was the full extent of their political power. One consequence of this, Menzies maintained, was that despite the length of his engagement in Australian politics, he could not recall a policy 'which was designed to help the thrifty, to encourage independence, to recognize the divine and valuable variations of men's minds' (1943: 8). The forgotten people could not look to parliament for recognition and assistance in achieving the way of life they wanted. Menzies wrote of 'the ordinary middle range of people in this country—those who are not rich and yet, urged on by a spirit of independence, endeavour in spite of every parliamentary discouragement, to provide for their own future' (1943: 107).

Menzies' acceptance of difference and inequality meant that he did not seek to make everyone alike or to end social stratification. His goal was to use the values and attitudes of the forgotten people to give a more complete shape to Australian politics. His plan was not radical. He did not wish to end the power possessed by either labour or capital. Like Deakin, he 'believed the Australian dream could be achieved without any change in the ownership or distribution of wealth' (Clark 1987: 10). But he did want to see politics shifted from its almost exclusively material focus to a broader one that was more likely to result in the definition and pursuit of a truly collective interest.

An ideal politics

Menzies' ideal form of politics in Australia included people of all social strata. It was a politics of nation-building, and required leadership through which the people were organised and shown how to pursue a collective interest. This was not to be done in such a way as to damage the economic system, which relied on individuals promoting their material interests. The interests of capital and labour were also important, but they were not to be allowed to dominate. Menzies wanted politics to 'once more become a noble and glorious vocation' (1943: 187). The ideal role of political institutions was to manage divergent interests to create a good society for all.

Community

True politics, for Menzies, was a politics of community-building, not simply one of selfishness and material ambition. As we have seen, he saw politics as a means for the release and expansion of the human spirit, not a vehicle for class warfare. In his view, 'our democratic system cannot continue if its motive power is to be a mixture of class selfishness, materialism, disregard of minorities, and a somewhat lazy regard for the future' (1943: 157). 'Capitalism cannot rebuild the world aright except on the basis of human and enlightened responsibility to the community' (1943: 162).

Menzies' belief in the need to develop community did not conflict with his commitment to the freedom of individuals. Individuals required community to pursue their interests and to gain an appreciation of their true interests. Social progress relied on individuals seeking to express themselves and realise their ambitions. It also relied on a reconciliation of individual self-expression and the communal interest. Menzies believed, as Joske (1978: 184) has put it, that 'an essential element in the liberal outlook was harmonising the full development of individual talents and aspirations with the desires and needs of the whole community. There must be social consciousness, an understanding of duties and responsibilities and a seeking after social justice'.

The need to harmonise individual and collective interests was the basis on which Menzies rejected simple *laissez-faire* approaches to government. He thought that government had an important role to play in ensuring that competition did not have damaging effects on society. Individual effort and initiative would remain an important social driving force, but this did not mean a 'return to the old and selfish notions of laissez-faire. The functions of the State will be much more than merely keeping the ring within which the competitors will fight. Our social and industrial obligations will be increased. There will be more law, not less; more control, not less' (1943: 10). The best form of politics for Australia promoted a concern for others, within a system in which individual initiative was valued.

Individual initiative

The pursuit of economic interests was not to be dismissed, however, as it 'is the dynamic force of social progress and is of the essence of what we call private or individual enterprise' (quoted in Hazelhurst 1979: 285). Menzies wrote that governments had to create 'a state of affairs which would encourage the enterprise, resourcefulness, and efficiency of individuals and ... lead to the greatest possible output of the needed goods and services' (1967: 289). The spirit he desired was 'the spirit of sturdy independence of the great middle class at all times; of the people who save, who are frugal, who take out insurance policies, who yearn for and maintain education, who stand on their own feet' (1943: 145).

Fostering spirit

Politics was very much about creating or encouraging the right spirit. Opportunities to display initiative and enterprise in economic and non-economic pursuits had to be made available to individuals. Support was also required for the development and increase in intellectual capacities on the part of individuals. Good politics also meant fostering the expression of all forms of spirit by making intellectual and cultural pursuits available to all individuals. The defeat of the Nazis was a victory for the ennobling and enlivening elements of society. It meant the preservation of 'our spiritual freedom, that our goods will be more justly shared, and that a better recognition of human values will have quickened our sense of human responsibility' (Menzies 1943: 29).

Nation-building

Nation-building was central to the process of community-building. That Australian society was stratified meant that the interests of these strata had to be harmonised so that a larger national community was produced. Sound political institutions were to function as focal points for the expression of and enhancement of a national spirit. If people merely clung to their particular interests they would not recognise political institutions as expressions of a national will. Menzies encouraged people to 'see the state as a grouping of you and me and millions like us, retaining our individuality but seeking strength in unity'. If this attitude was taken people would realise 'that to rob the State is to rob myself; that to betray the State is to betray myself; that to become grumbling or cunningly hostile to the State is to start a civil war in my own household' (1943: 143).

Menzies wanted political institutions to bring Australians to set aside, or overlook, their differences in the pursuit of national goals. He was not seeking to radically alter the processes that tended to produce social stratification, but to overlay a national interest that encouraged people to contribute to the achievement of national goals. For him, 'there can be no complete national organization of men and materials and financial resources unless there is ever present and ever active a vital moral element in the community which produces an utter willingness to share in sacrifice and effort' (1943: 161).

Sound thinking

Menzies believed that the most important task of government was to 'educate a new generation ... for an enlightened citizenship based upon honest thinking and human understanding' (1943: 157). This could only be produced if individuals were educated to think beyond their particular economic situation and interests. The role of politics was to encourage and enable individuals to develop to their 'fullest capacity for thought, for action, for sacrifice and for endurance … and no prejudice, stupidity, selfishness or vested interest must stand in the way' (1943: 187).

People had to avoid demands that simply reflected a preoccupation with the interests of the social stratum to which they belonged. They had to be encouraged not to focus exclusively on their rights but to acknowledge and seek to satisfy those obligations that reflected their membership of the community. 'It all comes back to the sense of responsibility—that quiet and lovely virtue which can convert seven millions of individual people into a good and faithful community' (1943: 145). In Menzies' view, 'the successful working of democracy depends upon an educated intelligence, self-discipline, a community conception, and a capacity for selection and judgement' (quoted in Joske 1978: 279).

Concerted effort devoted to developing a communal orientation was essential to the creation of social conditions under which the human spirit could be fully realised. That people were capable of being other-oriented and required society for their development meant they needed and were capable of creating a strong and united community. Sound political institutions and practices were essential for such a community, and the conditions for the promotion of individuality that went with it. Menzies looked for 'a true revival of liberal thought which will work for social justice and security, for national power and national progress, and for the full development of the individual citizen' (quoted in Hazelhurst 1979: 283).

Active, enterprising individuals remained the pillars of a sound society, but were not isolated and anti-social creatures. Menzies considered the most desirable society was not one 'in which everybody looks to his neighbour hoping for something from him, but that in which every one looks to his neighbour, willing and able to do something for him'. This had to be carefully played out, however, for willingness to assist others was not a desire to interfere in their lives. The best environment was produced when people were encouraged to be 'strong, self-reliant, intelligent, independent, sympathetic and generous' (1943: 186).

Conclusion

Creating a nation of individuals who were able to exercise their initiative without having to deny their connection was an essential element of the sort of politics Menzies desired. To create this form of politics meant overcoming the division created when the elements of society failed to acknowledge a collective interest and simply acted to pursue narrow class interests. Social strata could not be entirely removed, but good politics and leadership could mitigate their effect by creating opportunities for cooperation and recognition of a national, and an international, interest.

That this was possible was mainly a reflection of the fact that individuals were not simply motivated by narrow economic interests. They also partook of a spirit that allowed them to recognise higher ends to life and interests that transcended their particular social stratum. Without this sense of the possibilities inherent in human nature, the sort of politics that Menzies imagined possible could not be achieved. Certainly the politics of his time was not one in which this had been achieved, but recognition of the 'forgotten people' who symbolised the possibilities for initiative and for community was an important step towards a desirable political and social order. Inequality remained a feature of this order. Social strata continued to produce differing interests, but a sense of community and responsibility were equally powerful forces.

Menzies rarely discussed social strata in terms of inequality. Unlike Higgins, he did not consider workers to be in a significantly disadvantaged position. Indeed, he believed that they had achieved a level of social influence and political power that was not fully in accord with their social and political significance. His project was close to Wentworth's, in that he championed the interests of a social stratum that lay towards the middle of the social hierarchy. His goal was to defend and promote their interests as these were given insufficient regard in Australian society and politics.

That the members of this stratum were not organised meant they were unlikely to be dealt with through formal political processes. No new political or judicial institution could be created in which their interests could be recognised. Their attitudes were closest to those that Menzies thought most desirable for Australia, which meant that change in the orientation of political institutions was required. To allow their interests to be taken into account would promote a sound and improving society.

Menzies' forgotten people were excluded because their interests could not find an avenue through which they might be recognised. There is some parallel between Menzies' attempt to find a place in Australian politics for the forgotten people and Dowse's attempts to gain recognition of women's interests. The crucial difference, however, was that the economic, social, and political systems were organised in such a way that women's interests could not be taken into account and could not be served. Women were not forgotten—they could not be remembered. Menzies' forgotten people simply needed to be provided with representation from political institutions that served a collective interest. Once this was done their individuality, enterprise, and full sense of spirit could be used to overcome the domination of Australian society and politics by the rich and by organised labour.

---

1   In 'Menzies and Hewson' (Cook 1994) I characterised Menzies as a conservative liberal (as against Hewson as an economic liberal) in order to highlight his sense of community, tradition, and morality, which can be identified in the 'organic' approach to society typical of conservative political philosophy.

8

SARA DOWSE
(1938–)

Women, blacks, migrants, kids, old people, the unemployed. We're the ones who need a public sector. Not the bastards who take it for their own, then disavow it. (Dowse 1983c: 265)

Sara Dowse was born in the USA in November 1938 and came to Australia in 1958. She received a Bachelor of Arts from the University of Sydney. In 1973 she was press secretary for the Federal Minister for Labour. Between 1974 and 1977 she was head of the Office of Women's Affairs (renamed Women's Affairs Office and then Commonwealth Office of the Status of Women) in the Department of Prime Minister and Cabinet. She resigned from this position after the 1977 federal election. Between 1997 and 1995 she held a number of lectureships and tutorships, for the most part in tertiary institutions in the Canberra region. In 1983 she published her first novel, *West Block*, which deals with one woman's experience as a senior member of the Australian Public Service. She followed this with *Silver City* (1984), *Schemetime* (1990), *Sapphires* (1994), and *Digging* (1996). She has published widely in various magazines and newspapers in Australia.

The focus of preceding discussions of responses to social stratification by Australian liberals has rested largely upon those differences in social position that derive primarily from the operation of economic forces. Sara Dowse's understanding of social stratification was more complex as it involved the interaction of a variety of factors. She acknowledged that economic factors were important, but she considered other factors, such as sex/gender, ethnicity, and race, to be just as important. Social stratification, in her view, was a result of the combined effect of these factors; society was systematically divided in more ways than are indicated by the notion of economic class.

While all of the factors contributing to social stratification were important for Dowse, this chapter is focused on sex/gender and is an examination of her understanding of the situation of women in the social stratification processes of Australian society. She was active in attempts to address the marginalising of women's interests in Australian society and politics. This was, in essence, a political project. Addressing systematically produced inequality in such a way as to recognise and further women's interests required change in the orientation and practices of political institutions. Her project involved both asserting women's rights and attempting to bring political institutions to recognise and respond to these rights.

The main effect of social stratification on women, in Dowse's view, was to limit the life opportunities available to them and to undermine their ability to express their individuality. Women, in short, were denied social justice. For liberals, social justice is deeply entwined with rights to equality of opportunity and fairness of treatment. Only under these conditions could women, like any other individuals, realise their full potential. Like the central character in her first novel, Dowse believed, 'if she believed in anything, that given a chance, people would flourish and develop their potential' (1983c: 234). She pursued ways in which women's rights could be recognised and protected and equality of opportunity afforded them. Her project required the reorientation and reshaping of Australian political institutions, one of which, essential to achieving justice for women, was the bureaucracy. It was here that Dowse made her most significant contributions to the pursuit of justice for women.

This analysis of Dowse's response to social stratification and its effects on women is presented in three sections. The first deals with Dowse's view on the effect of the social environment on women. The second presents aspects of her approach to pursuing social justice for women and the defence of women's rights. The final section is an examination of her views on the role of governments and the bureaucracy in achieving social change that would provide equal opportunity for women.

Women and the Social Environment

While liberals take people to be fundamentally individual, the extent and nature of that individuality can change from liberal to liberal. All liberals treat society as the context within which individuality is manifested. A significant number believe that the nature of this context can either facilitate or preclude some people's expression of individuality. Some societies may prevent people from manifesting individuality, thereby making individuality unavailable to some of their members.

Structural impediments

The expression of individuality requires a set of personal and social resources that enable people to act and to take advantage of opportunities present in their social environment. Those who are denied these resources are faced with structural impediments that limit, if they do not prevent, their expression of individuality. Thus while all liberals see people as individuals, those who believe that structural impediments may preclude the expression of individuality do not accept that all people share identical life opportunities. Some people exist in environments within which they have greater opportunities to manifest and develop their individual characters. Some liberals believe that inequality that exists among individuals is in part a reflection of different levels of opportunity and is not simply a function of individual difference.

Women, in Dowse's view, were often rendered incapable of manifesting or expressing their individuality. Indeed, some were so affected by the constraints in their social environment that they did not acknowledge their individuality or their value as individuals. These women were socialised to accept lesser roles in society and to surrender their initiative to others to whom they felt inferior.

Invalidating women's experiences

Devaluing, if not denying, women's experiences was an important way in which women were brought to question their worth and the validity of their perceptions. The effect of this devaluation is to induce a sense of inadequacy or even an incapacity to participate in society. For someone to believe that his or her experiences are somehow wrong or invalid produces significant psychological and social impediments to participation. Dowse's exposure to the women's movement gave her a profound and personal sense of the ways in which women's experiences and lives were devalued.

While studying at university, Dowse read D. H. Lawrence's *Sons and Lovers*. She

> identified very strongly with Mrs Morrell. She, too, was a middle-class woman who'd married a working-class man. It came as a great shock to me when I went to my lecture that she in fact was seen as the villain of the piece ... I think what the women's movement did for me was to

> validate all those immediate perceptions that I had had to reject. And
> there were all kinds of women in the movement who had read Mrs
> Morrell as a heroine of sorts, too. I mean, she wasn't the monster she
> was perceived to be by those people who were interpreting Lawrence
> to us. And I think it was just that shift of focus that allowed me, and
> so many other women, in fact, to say, well, this has been our experi-
> ence, and it's just as true as anything else. And I thought that was an
> enormously powerful emotional and intellectual experience, to find
> oneself validated in that way. (quoted in Ellison 1986: 93)[1]

This quotation describes a disjunction between Dowse's experience of
Lawrence's book and that presented by her, predominantly male,
university teachers. It also registers the effort it took to recognise that
her interpretation was not by nature inferior. It provides a microcosm
of the position of women whose exposure to the women's movement
offered a perspective from which they could see that their senses of
inferiority and worthlessness were trained responses and not reflections
of some natural inequality.

That opportunities to participate more fully in society have been
created is a reflection of changes to the way people think about women.
Most importantly, for Dowse, it indicates the extent to which the way
women think about themselves has changed. In a speech to the ACT
branch of the Women's Electoral Lobby, she discussed changes in
thinking over the preceding decades.

> Many women are politicians now, women read the news, drive buses,
> run businesses, are on the stock exchange. Terms like 'sexual harassment'
> and 'affirmative action' are part of the thinking person's parlance, and so
> the list goes. The unthinkable 20 years ago—that a woman could
> become Prime Minister of this country—is not so unthinkable now.
> Indeed for a woman to get 'to the top' in any field is not so much
> unthinkable as admired. (Dowse 1989b: 1)

That people, and particularly women, thought of women as inferior
and incapable of undertaking certain roles was part of a psychological
process that produced social inequality. Its effect was to constrain the
possibilities available to women by influencing the way men and
women thought about women.

The limits on women's participation

That both men and women thought of women as inferior was not, in
Dowse's view, the only factor explaining their inability to become fully
active and effective members of society. Women were also prevented

from participating fully in society because of the operation of social institutions that were predisposed to marginalise them and to diminish the recognition and valuing of their capacities and rights as individuals. One manifestation of this was that female workers did not receive the same treatment as male workers. In enterprise bargaining, for example, 'only large, powerful male-dominated unions … are in a good position to bargain. The presence of women or low-income workers generally at the bargaining table is not guaranteed, and the high concentration of women in low-paying occupations and industries seriously weakens their negotiating power' (Dowse 1992a: 15).

The problems women faced were not merely a result of underrepresentation and low status in industrial and political systems, though these certainly played a part in creating injustices. Women and their interests were also excluded as a result of the processes or mechanisms that were part of the normal operation of the systems themselves: the very *form* of these institutions precluded women's participation. Women's inequality could therefore not be redressed simply by attempts to adjust the *outcomes* of political and industrial institutions, but the institutions themselves had to be opened to women's participation. Thus 'campaigns against discrimination attack the cause and not the symptoms of women's powerlessness—principally, our lack of equal opportunity in employment and the barriers to economic and political power' (1983b: 218).

Women's inequality, however, was so subtle and pervasive that in Dowse's view it would not be displaced easily. She wrote that 'to talk of "post-feminism" can be laughably premature. In Europe as in Australia great structural inequalities still exist, even among the Scandinavians, where enlightened policies have been in place for several decades' (1992b: 20). That women's inequality was linked to economic processes made it an intractable problem. According to Dowse 'the problem of inequality of outcomes is one of the toughest and most enduring that women have to face. The experience of Scandinavia has shown that even the most advanced gender programs are hampered to a considerable degree by the operation of economics' (1992b: 20).

Inequality and participation

Changing institutional forms and practices to provide equal opportunities for women to participate and have their interests acknowledged constituted only one part of Dowse's project. A cultural change was required that resulted in women being seen and seeing themselves differently. The social environment had resulted in women failing to see themselves as capable of full participation in the social, political, and economic spheres. For them to express themselves as individuals, women had to undertake a personal transformation. One of the dangers that faced women was that expressing individuality could be taken to imply being selfish. True autonomy, for Dowse, involved a higher moral sensibility and not a descent into anti-social attitudes and behaviour.

Personal transformation

A central element of women overcoming inequality and expressing their individuality involved a re-evaluation of their sense of self. Dowse described the battles feminists fought as 'really existential ones of the highest order' (quoted in Ellison 1986: 99). The re-evaluation that she and others sought involved women imagining a new realm of possibilities for their lives. When Dowse first started to engage in women's movements 'it was visionary for us women to imagine a life of our own, economic independence, safe and cheap contraception and abortion, equal employment and educational opportunity ... The movement was about releasing women from their bondage, physical and psychological; it was about ... liberation. The goal, as I remember it, was autonomy' (1989b: 2).

The main point, in this context, was that the struggle to increase women's life opportunities began with women believing in themselves. Dowse had personal experience of the positive effects of an opening up of horizons. Her experience in the Public Service gave her 'a lot more confidence than I'd ever had that I could actually do something I wanted to do ... I suffered the classic inferiority complex, feeling that I could never do anything ... The next thing I knew, I was in the second division of the Australian Public Service and that did a lot for my confidence' (quoted in Ellison 1986: 95). Her experience led Dowse to stress 'the value of the experience of paid work and economic independence' (1989a: 8). While she rejected exploitation, she believed that 'even the most poorly paid jobs can have substantial psychological benefits ... Along with the badly needed pay cheque, work provides women with a social environment and a sense of worth' (1989a: 8).

Selfishness

While Dowse supported self-expression and individual autonomy, she rejected selfishness and the mere pursuit of individual material interests. She expressed disappointment that many women were approaching their increased opportunities in the same narrow and selfish way that men did. Women were being given greater choice, but they were not choosing to be any better than men were. Like most Australian liberals, Dowse rejected narrow egoism and an exclusive focus on material rewards. She believed that many women were ignoring the forms of individual expression that were consistent with recognition of membership of a community and were allowing their individuality to be channelled into competition and the struggle to acquire material possessions.

Dowse's belief in the possibility of social progress was not dampened. It was certainly tested, however, when many women took autonomy to be synonymous with selfishness. She argued that women were 'being very subtly subverted all the time. Our "freedom" is in danger of becoming the freedom to join the rat race, to exploit others or be exploited, to get "ahead" at all costs'. She was dismayed 'that feminism can be perverted into a kind of subsidiary to capitalism where some women can get fabulously wealthy and others can barely survive and what's worse are made to feel that they're failures because of it' (1989b: 2–3). For her, autonomy was not about individuals pursuing their personal interests independent of and isolated from others. Autonomy was not selfishness.

Creating conditions in which true autonomy was possible meant bringing people to recognise the social character of rights. Dowse believed that people could not consider their rights in isolation from others in their community and in every other community in the world. She was convinced that, more than ever before, people had begun to think with others in mind. 'Unlike previous generations, our consciousness is permeated by a sense of a global species. Our cultural artefacts are saturated with the scenes, settings, characters, language and history of other human societies' (1984: 143–4).

Thinking as if one were isolated from others was not autonomy. Human beings were not autonomous when they disregarded everyone else; they simply became less human. If women who sought to create a situation in which women gained true autonomy were defeated, this was a reflection of 'the lack of human qualities in the society that defeated us. It's not necessarily a statement about the weakness in women … sure, it would be easy, it's easy for anybody to "succeed", really, if you just jettison all your scruples, jettison all your humanity, your sensitivity, all the things that make it worthwhile being human. (Ellison 1986, p. 100) The struggle for women was not simply one of attaining greater freedom of choice and action. It was also a matter of achieving autonomy for women and men which allowed, if it did not require, people to act toward each other in a non-exploitative manner and not be punished or marginalised for doing so.

Dowse believed that the social environment in which they lived had a number of deleterious effects on women. Women, in her view, faced a variety of structural impediments that precluded their full participation in society. This undermined, if it did not prevent, their capacity to express themselves as individuals. A subtle and less direct, but no less effective, means of excluding women was by invalidating their experiences. The effect of this was to produce a sense among men and many women that women were not equipped to act effectively in most political, economic, and social roles. That women were excluded from full participation explains something of the failure of political, economic, and social institutions to reflect their interests. Their exclusion was only part of the explanation for this failure, however. For these institutions were underpinned by principles and practices that inhibited, if not precluded, any recognition of women's interests. Redressing the failure to provide for participation from women required changing women's senses of themselves. Women had to begin to see themselves as full members of society. Only then could they demand the opportunities for participation that were normally only available to men. These opportunities would allow women to express themselves and achieve true personal autonomy. Dowse was careful to maintain, however, that for women to attain full self-expression and autonomy did not imply that they should become selfish.

The Pursuit of Justice for Women

Before women could attain social justice, basic problems with Australian society had to be addressed. Women were not being treated justly even by the principles that were supposed to govern Australian society. They were denied equality of opportunity and their interests were neither recognised nor promoted by political institutions. In short, their rights were being neither acknowledged nor provided for. Promoting women's rights and achieving social justice required that governments legislate against discrimination. It also necessitated a general change in the way public policy was understood and administered. The most important element of this change was to see social justice in terms of the larger context within which any rights might be claimed. This section provides an indication of the various fronts on which the struggle for social justice had to be fought. Changes in the forms and practices of governments and bureaucracies through which social justice could be implemented are examined next.

Defending women's rights

Seeking social justice for women depended on having their rights recognised. Simply getting governments, bureaucracies, and the community generally to recognise women's rights was an important first step, though, as will be discussed below, getting them to do something about the problems women faced was more complex. Gaining acknowledgment that women were individuals who had those fundamental human rights normally associated with being a citizen in a liberal-democratic society was an important element of Dowse's political project.

Rights language has always been central to liberalism. A concern with promoting good character, such as is found in works by Pearson, Goldstein and Murdoch, reflected a desire to ensure that rights, especially citizenship rights, were being accorded to people who would use them well. Liberals' objection to social stratification can be understood as in part a result of their refusal to accept the legitimacy of a society in which only some people could lay claim to and fully capitalise on the rights that truly belonged to all human beings. Certainly one of Wentworth's main objections to government in New South Wales was that the normal rights of English people were being denied to all who were not exclusives. Higgins spent much of his life defending the rights of workers from attacks by those in superior economic positions. Menzies may have been hostile towards those who claimed rights without accepting responsibilities, but he was not hostile to the view that people had rights. Rights language represents both a set of claims about the nature of people (i.e. that they have fundamental characteristics that must be respected by others and by governments and their agencies) and a set of claims about the responsibilities of government.

One advantage that women had in Australia, as compared with women in the USA, was that a culture existed in which individuals looked to governments to obtain and further their rights. Australian men were already using rights claims to make demands for assistance from governments. They expected, and often got, government support for the rights that enabled them to pursue their interests. Those involved in the women's movement 'came into the political arena with the same expectation, that "the state means collective power at the service of individualistic rights". In this, we feminists were similar to primary producers and returned service personnel and all the other groups that lobbied for, expected and got government support, apparently without strings attached' (Dowse 1989c: 8).

The most important point that had to be made about rights was that they functioned as part of human relationships. That rights were individual did not mean that they were exercised against the community. The struggle was not simply one of claiming rights, but of gaining an acknowledgment that rights were about communities and not just about individuals. Dowse rejected simple egoistic models of human rights. For her, the definition and pursuit of rights was an expression of membership of society. Like autonomy, rights functioned within social relationships and were not mechanisms for denying connection, responsibility, or community membership. Rights were not about isolating oneself and had to be understood as more than abstract constructs that belonged to imaginary others.

This is illustrated in *West Block* when a male character, Jonathan, is faced with unwanted paternity. In Dowse's account of this part of the book, Jonathan is confronted by the contradiction between simple egoism and liberal rights theory.

> Jonathan's own theories were turned inside out by the woman wanting to go ahead and have the baby because she had, in his terms, every right to do so. It showed the poverty of that conception of life as a sort of free market, with everybody acting in a vacuum. Because what one person does obviously has a very large effect on what another person does. It wasn't that he was concerned about his individual happiness so much as that he learned that he couldn't find his individual happiness as long as he believed his pursuit was one he could undertake on his own. (quoted in Ellison 1986: 102)

For Dowse, rights function within a social matrix in which individuals pursue happiness as members of a community. Rights were not barriers erected in order to insulate people from each other. Instead they represented people's connection with others.

In this context, Dowse's views simply reflect the principle that all liberals accept: that individuals can develop fully only in society. To claim rights, then, is not to claim freedom *from* society but freedom *within* society. The main difference between liberals at this point is whether they see individuals as selfish or as self-centred. Selfishness implies a preoccupation with one's needs and interests and a lack of concern, if not inability to engage with, the needs and interests of others. Self-centredness simply reflects the fact that each individual is at the centre of his or her own life. It does not require that people ignore the needs and interests of others. Indeed it may, as it did with Jonathan, require them to understand that the quality of their lives reflects the quality of others' lives. That individuals are at the centre of their worlds does not mean, then, that they cannot recognise the importance of others to their well-being. Those liberals who assume human selfishness often understand rights claims as means to create barriers between individuals; those who, like

Dowse, assume self-centredness, but not selfishness, believe that individuals who fully appreciate their interests do not use rights as barriers but as means to realise themselves fully alongside others.

One of the real tests of the recognition of rights in a community comes in times of economic downturn. It is at this point that rights, especially for groups with limited power, may cease to hold. For Dowse, rights reflected, in part, the attitudes of members of the community to other members. If rights were a function of community attitudes then times of stress indicated the extent to which rights really existed—even when formal recognition of those rights in legislation was present. Any piece of legislation that sought to protect rights had to be evaluated in terms of whether it would survive economic downturn. Thus 'a crucial factor is whether the concept of positive discrimination … is sufficiently understood in the community and sanctioned in law to uphold the rights of vulnerable and subordinate groups during economic recession' (1992c: 4).

Rights claims were central to Dowse's response to the failure to provide social justice for women in Australian society. They were used both to create an awareness of the situation of women and to push that awareness into acceptance of a general failure to acknowledge and defend women's rights. Dowse's account of one of the first squats set up by women in Australia illustrates central features of her project. Elsie in Glebe, Sydney, was set up, in her view, 'to make several political statements: that there were homeless women; that women were often homeless because they were victims of domestic violence; that the state had a responsibility to protect such victims; that women had a right to demand such protection; but that women would take it into their own hands to help each other' (1984: 148). The language of rights was a vehicle for bringing women's claims into the political arena and for giving those claims moral force. Making demands on the basis of rights allowed otherwise hidden dimensions of the treatment of women in society, such as the amount and extent of domestic violence, to be brought into the open; it allowed women to call for these abuses of rights to stop.

Social justice and legislation

An important step in pursuing social justice for women lay in having their rights recognised in legislation. This was a complex problem in the Australian federation. Much of the legislation required had to come from state governments, which had not been quick to legislate against sex discrimination. A first step for the federal government was to 'legislate against discrimination on the grounds of sex and marital status in its own territories … and in its government operations' (quoted in Knuckey 1978: 9). Obviously this was only a small step, but social justice could not be achieved until governments, including federal governments, provided formal, that is, legislative, recognition of women's rights.

Social justice and public policy apparatuses

Legislation alone, however, could not provide social justice for women. A general public policy environment had to be created. According to Dowse, 'as well as equality of opportunity for women we need a stronger women's policy apparatus to ensure the development and implementation of more equitable policies for women' (1984: 159). Achieving a truly just society for women required that fundamental aspects of social organisation had to be addressed in terms of the way in which opportunities for women were limited and fairness of treatment was denied them.

Work

An important element of the denial of social justice for women was a failure to provide assistance to them to enter or re-enter the workforce. Governments often treated women's employment as simply a function of general levels of employment. More work would be available to women, from this perspective, when more work was available generally. Women could not rely on general economic forces, however, as economic forces did not have an identical effect on all people. For 'marginal workers (of whom women form the substantial part) are usually the last to benefit from any economic upturn, and therefore special measures for assistance may be required … for women seeking to enter or re-enter the workforce' (Dowse 1983d: 7).

Child care

Recognising women's right to work demonstrates the complexity of any real attempt to create conditions under which they were treated justly. Women who were mothers had no real right to work when they lacked high-quality and affordable child care. There was simply no basis to claim that all women had the right to work when child care was not available. Dowse argued that feminists were returning to the issue of child care in the late 1980s because they came to recognise its centrality to the struggle for justice for women. 'It is only now that the women's movement, armed with more sophisticated analyses of the sexual division of labour and the maintenance of patriarchy by women's predominant role in child-rearing, is turning once again to the child care issue' (1984: 209).

For Dowse, 'the question of children remains the central issue for women' (1984: 218). It was central because child care had a direct effect on opportunities available to women and because the struggle to achieve it revealed the extent to which society was organised around a denial of social justice to women. According to Dowse, 'even the limited objective of providing cheap, good quality community care for our children would make a significant change to women's lives. Such a goal is a necessary condition of women's liberation' (1984: 218).

Dowse's pursuit of social justice for women relied heavily on having women's rights acknowledged and supported among all sections of society. The pursuit of social justice also required a re-evaluation of the nature of rights. They were not to be understood simply in terms of the isolation of the individual, in which rights were claimed against others and against governments. Rights were part of the membership of the community. More importantly, the rights women most needed if they were to experience social justice required government action, not inaction. They required legislation and public policy apparatuses that could support them.

Government, Bureaucracy and Change

Like many Australian liberals, Dowse saw an immediate connection between making meaningful rights claims and having those claims supported by government, particularly the Commonwealth government. 'For over two decades community groups have depended on Commonwealth intervention for the initiation, expansion and equitable distribution of services. It is extremely doubtful, for example, whether child care would ever have developed to the stage it has if the states or local government had been left to develop programs themselves. Nor would we have seen the establishment of women's refuges and associated services on anything like the scale currently operating' (Dowse 1991: 15).

Parliaments may have been crucial sites for making rights claims, but bureaucracies were essential to putting them into effect. Dowse saw bureaucracies as an important instrument for addressing the structural inequalities and defending the rights of the socially and economically disadvantaged.

An immediate problem, in this context, was that government in general and the bureaucracy in particular continued to be dominated by men and their interests. They therefore had dual aspects: on one hand, they were among the few resources available for women to pursue their rights; on the other, they were mechanisms through with women had been denied basic human rights. This section deals with Dowse's views on the changes that had to be introduced to governments and bureaucracies to enable them to respond adequately to women's interests.

The public sphere

One of the main problems for women in Australia was that they found themselves in an economic system that had a limited capacity to respond to rights claims. Thus 'because of the difficulties women encounter in a laissez-faire, private-sector environment, we have often had cause to fall back on the pitiful resources of government assistance' (Dowse 1984: 143). The private sector provided only limited opportunities for individuals to develop, so the public sphere became a vehicle for pursuing social justice.

This was more than a coincidence. Since women's needs were unlikely to be met through the operation of a free market, the public sector was 'better suited than the private sector to helping individuals in satisfying their needs and achieving their aspirations' (1984: 143). Women and their children required 'decent parks, playgrounds, public transport, sewerage. They need low-cost, quality child-care facilities, education and health services. They need services to help them in their daily lives and in broadening their horizons, and few of these services can or should be provided on a profit basis' (1984: 145).

That government might be better suited to supporting an environment conducive to women's interests and rights did not mean that it regularly satisfied those interests or supported those rights. Legislative interventions were often inadequate. Even when specific legislative provisions might have been adequate to the task at hand, the resources necessary to support them were rarely provided. Dowse acknowledged that 'the combined impact of state and federal anti-discrimination legislation has contributed to the improved status of women in Australian society, and many individual cases of discrimination have been redressed'. But, she added, 'the machinery for dealing with complaints is under-resourced' (1992c: 3).

The fact that men dominated all elements of the political system meant that women's interests were often overlooked or constructed in terms of a narrow set of interests. An important example of this was Higgins' attempt to use the resources of government to address the inequalities that existed between employers and workers through conciliation and arbitration. His attempt, particularly as expressed in his calculation of a basic or family wage, worked against the interests of Australian women (see Chapter 6, note 4). In Dowse's view, 'Australia's system of conciliation and arbitration, once unique for its own protection of the basic rights of workers, nonetheless played an important role in extending and entrenching a deep and abiding sexism in Australian society' (1992a: 15).

Government

Women's reliance on the public sphere for achieving justice in society meant that they had a deep interest in the particular character of governing institutions. Their interests were rarely served by governments oriented to individuals as possessors of a narrow range of economic, or material, interests. Not all forms of government were the same, and some would be more able to reflect the interests of women. Well-constituted public institutions were vital to promoting women's rights and interests. 'If women are conscious of this, we can work towards a democratisation of the public sector, indeed find ourselves a pivotal part of this process. If not we will only find ourselves subsumed into the existing order, forever dependent upon a beleaguered, and therefore increasingly authoritarian entity' (Dowse 1984: 158).

Bureaucracy

The centrality of the public sector to the promotion of women's rights made it the focal point for many women seeking social justice.[2] The bureaucracy was also part of the problem, in part because it was highly segmented and organised hierarchically, which prevented it from responding adequately to women's interests because of their interrelated and multidimensional nature; in part because it contained few women in senior positions, which made it unable to interact effectively with women and women's groups. These characteristics produced a bureaucracy that largely excluded women's interests on the grounds that they were either illegitimate or incapable of being served.

Yet bureaucracy remained one of the few significant agencies through which women could have their interests registered and served. To do this properly, however, it had to be reorganised. Having been set up by men within a private enterprise system meant that the bureaucracy was suited to serving economic interests and to managing people as economic units. Other interests might be served, but they were always secondary to economic interests and would be abandoned during economic downturns.

Femocrats

It was essential to get into senior positions in the bureaucracy women who were sensitive to women's needs and who could design and implement appropriate policies. This would give that organisation the capacity to deal with all people fairly and consistently. When Dowse joined the Australian Public Service, it 'was a wholly masculine world'. Women had junior or supporting roles in this world. 'Women were sparse above the lower administrative ranks. They were poorly represented in middle management and virtually absent from the executive division. I was the only woman in the department on the top rung of middle management, one of a handful throughout the service' (1990: 29).

Dowse's approach reflected a strategy adopted by many Australian feminists, who believed that gaining senior positions in the bureaucracy would allow them to promote women's interests. Unlike their male counterparts, these bureaucrats were more likely to take women's interests seriously. They would seek to create appropriate policy processes and would attempt to provide the resources necessary for women to pursue full and satisfying lives. Femocrats, as these feminist bureaucrats are sometimes called, were vital, for they could 'work to make other policy-makers aware of the consequences of their policies on women, and to seek to change those policies accordingly. Without feminist bureaucrats we would not have quite so many refuges, child care centres, working women's centres, health centres as we have today' (1983a: 8).[3]

Changing bureaucratic culture

Gaining recognition and support for women's rights, however, required more than simply having women in the bureaucracy. A change in its intellectual climate was also necessary. Only if this happened would the bureaucracy be able to deal with women's interests in something like the same way it dealt with men's interests. Dowse cautioned women not to stop at getting women into senior positions. 'If we allow ourselves to be trapped into thinking that affirmative action is the sole strategy all we will end up with is a more efficient meritocracy. As well as equality of opportunity for women we need a stronger women's policy apparatus to ensure the development and implementation of more equitable policies for women' (1984: 159).

Women's interests could not be served effectively in the existing policy-making environment because those interests cut across the responsibilities of almost all Public Service departments. A group that coordinated and oversaw the various departments was required to deal effectively with women's interests. This group was likely to meet, and when created did meet, with considerable resistance from a bureaucracy used to working in vertical hierarchies (see next section). Those such as Dowse who sought to promote the interests of women through the Public Service 'had to deal with the fact that the function cut across conventional department jurisdictions. This would make the development and implementation of policy difficult and was bound to produce conflict' (Dowse 1981: 9).

Maintaining a multifaceted approach to supporting women's rights required resisting the process within the bureaucracy to focus on 'single' issues. Dowse illustrated the pressure on women within the Public Service to limit their objectives in *West Block*. A senior male bureaucrat offers the following advice to a female bureaucrat: '"Seriously now. We've had enough of your fingers poking in every pie. Causes no end of trouble. I can't allow it, do you hear? It's no way to run a department. So be a reasonable girl. Pick out one, two, maybe three things to concentrate on." He stopped for breath. "Discrimination legislation, for instance"' (Dowse 1983c: 251). While this advice may have been well-intentioned, to follow it would amount to narrowing and limiting her objectives and substituting this for serving the complete range of women's interests.

An important indicator of a change in the federal bureaucracy was having a women's policy coordinating group close to the centre of the policy-making process. Thus whether or not the Office of Women's Affairs (OWA) was in the Prime Minster's Department was crucial, for its location determined its ability to have an effective input into the policy-making process to ensure that women's interests were not overlooked or deliberately excluded. If the OWA worked properly from within the Prime Minister's Department it could 'encourage line departments to adopt initiatives which benefit women … [and] work to ensure that departmental practices do not disadvantage women' (Dowse 1988: 9). Having the backing of the Prime Minister's Department was essential to ensuring that everyone in the bureaucracy was aware that they had to change the way they acted and thought. Changing the bureaucracy 'was an education process as much as anything else, and it helped a lot to be able to chair this network of women's units from the Prime Minster's department' (quoted in Knuckey 1978: 9).

Dowse argued that an essential element of the downgrading of the bureaucracy's capacity to deal with women's interests occurred as a result of the transfer of the OWA out of the Department of Prime Minister and Cabinet to the Department of Home Affairs in 1977. She thought this move 'represents more than just the downgrading of a function. The establishment of a network of women's units was all but completed when it was damaged at the core'. Moving the OWA, then, represented 'a dampening down of the innovative impulse in administration' (1981: 20).

The culture of the federal and state bureaucracies was generally unsympathetic to women and their interests. This explained some of the resistance from some departments within the Australian Public Service to the creation of the OWA. These 'other departments resisted for no other reason than the basic threat a women's unit posed to the continuation of sexist policies and practices' (Dowse 1981: 11).

Changing bureaucratic structures

The hierarchical organisation of the bureaucracy meant, in Dowse's view, that it could not deal effectively with women and their interests. Change that brought about equal treatment for women would not simply result from having a policy-coordinating group. A change in the very form of the bureaucracy was required. Hierarchy was an important part of the masculine world of the federal Public Service. This made it a bearer of patriarchal norms and recreated the relationship of domination that was at the heart of discrimination against women. The task for women in the bureaucracy, in Dowse's opinion, was 'to try to develop this apparatus along more anti-authoritarian lines … Ironically, it is the refuges, and other feminist organisations, wh[ich] have much to teach the bureaucrats' (1984: 159).

Ultimately, in Dowse's view, 'feminism is a philosophy of co-operation: it opposes hierarchies and exploitation. In the bureaucratic environment, feminism is a force for change' (1983a: 8). Promoting women's interests required a different kind of bureaucratic style. Many feminists, including Dowse, worked within the bureaucracy to change it. They believed that discrimination was 'systemic, integral to the structures of social, economic and political institutions, and that radical change in these institutions was required if any significant social change was to be effected' (1981: 10). Dowse rejected the 'charge frequently levelled … that women can't change the system by working in it. To me that's like saying we can't breathe the air until it's no longer polluted' (1983a: 8).

Responding to the construction of women's interests as non-economic
An important element of the campaign to enable the bureaucracy to deal effectively with women's rights and interests was to overcome a tendency to construe these rights and interests as non-economic or social. This was a problem because it maintained a false distinction between economic and social interests. As a result of 'this ideological separation of the social and the economic, much of the mounting political pressure for women has been siphoned into a narrow range of "social policy" issues' (Dowse 1983b: 202). Women's rights and interests could not be dealt with without changes in the economic structure. If the distinction between economic and social interests was false—'a convenient fiction', as Dowse put it (1983b: 217)—then women's interests were economic as much as social.

Women had to force recognition of the interplay between economic and non-economic interests. They had to challenge 'the assumption that economic and social policies comprise two distinct spheres' (1983b: 201). Central to this project was 'to push forward with an alternative analysis of the total social structure, in which social, political and economic factors are demonstrably interlocked' (1983b: 217).

Another problem with the separation of economic and social interests was that it normalised expenditure on economic matters as essential and hid the cost of government support for private enterprise. In Dowse's view, the public sector had been mistakenly understood to be primarily involved in providing social welfare, with the result that people were not made conscious of 'the vast public resources placed at the disposal of the sphere of "private" production. Most of the activity, personnel and resources of the commonwealth bureaucracy are concerned with assisting the productive sphere. State governments are chiefly occupied with social services and social control, but even here vast public sector resources are channelled into support of the private sector' (1983b: 202).

Bureaucracy and change

Despite its limitations, and because there were few alternative avenues, Dowse saw the bureaucracy as central to the project of creating a just society in which women were accorded equal and fair treatment. 'The bureaucracy reflects the society it serves, it is overwhelmingly patriarchal and racist. It is competitive and hierarchical. For a feminist it is alien territory. Yet, for all its faults, the bureaucracy is one institution predicated on the belief in the worth of public endeavour' (1983a: 8).

Dowse's focus on the bureaucracy as a vehicle for change did not mean that she thought it was the only institution through which social justice for women could be pursued. Governments and bureaucracies might not be the only option, 'but the state is here, bureaucracy is ubiquitous; they cannot be discounted' (1984: 159). She believed that too many critics of Australian society and government dismissed the bureaucracy as a vehicle for change and consequently failed to acknowledge the efforts of those who were trying to use it to improve society for themselves and for other women (1984: 143).

Unfortunately the intellectual climate had changed. By the 1980s economic rationalism had become the prevailing philosophy of government, and those liberals who took a narrower view of human interests and government had recast the policy climate. In this new climate, 'bureaucratic reform has boiled down to reducing the role of the public sector and adopting the operational modes of the private one ... The pursuit of social justice has been tolerated, but only within parameters set by the economic rationalists' (Dowse 1990: 29). This environment was in fact inimical to the promotion of social justice for women. One of the few institutions that could assist women in claiming their rights was shifting its focus from social justice issues and moving back to being an institution that served only a limited subset of economic interests (that is, men's economic interests).

> The bureaucracy remained an important site for advancing and supporting women's claims to basic human rights. It was one of the few agencies within which the multiple and complex project of pursuing rights for women could be approached in something like a holistic way. This was so despite the fact that the bureaucracy was in itself a site of struggle and not simply a vehicle that was capable of supporting

change in its existing state. Despite these internal pressures and other problems with its culture, the bureaucracy was open to the sorts of interventions that could produce social justice.

Conclusion

By its importation of English liberal political institutions and philosophies, the cultural colonisation of Australia meant that asserting women's rights was a meaningful and legitimate way to respond to discrimination against women in Australia. The use of the fundamentally liberal notion of essential human rights to challenge this discrimination was also facilitated by the fact that few liberal thinkers had specified that women were not individuals and consequently could not claim rights. Women such as Dowse could criticise political and social institutions on the ground that women did not have access to rights such as were understood within liberal political thought to be basic to human beings. Certainly men could and did resent the fact that women were claiming and being given rights which liberal political thought indicated they deserved. It could not, however, be dismissed as immaterial that women were denied opportunities to express their individuality. Liberal principles do not allow for such restrictions on opportunity (even if they do not always require action to correct them).

Social stratification operated in this context to produce and reproduce a virtual underclass of women. A failure to recognise their rights and to ensure that they were treated equally with men reduced them to individuals of lower status, which affected the way they were viewed by men and the way they understood themselves as women. Women were not forgotten in the same way that Menzies' forgotten people were. If women could be thought of as forgotten, it was a very active and pernicious form of forgetting. Women were not united by a shared economic position, so they did not constitute a class in the way that the working class figured in Higgins' political project. Women's experience of social stratification may be likened to the emancipists' experiences in that it was an active form of exclusion, but it was also somewhat different. It relied in part on women having a limited sense of their own capacities so that, unlike the emancipists, they were more likely to accept as justified their exclusion from important aspects of social, political, and economic life.

The form of social stratification that women experienced operated in very different ways from the forms discussed by the other liberals whose works are dealt with in Part II. Discrimination was based on sex and required the overt and covert withholding of certain rights; it was therefore a highly pervasive and sometimes very subtle form of exclusion and structured inequality. That it had such a powerful effect on women's psyche was also part of the way it was able to endure and to be transmitted from generation to generation. The basic problem with social stratification remained, however, because it represented the denial of fundamental rights to a group of people who could not experience social justice in Australian society.

---

[1] 'Women's liberation. It came to Canberra and, as they wrote on the book jackets, changed her life. Not the daily routine of it, but the way she looked at things. She stopped dreaming of her husband's return. She thought about him, and the misery he'd caused her, but differently. He was a creature, like herself, of certain social forces' (Dowse 1983c: 238–9).

[2] The bureaucracy, however, was something of a double-edged sword. In Dowse's view, 'the bureaucratisation of women's affairs, if inevitable, had the equally inevitable effect of diluting Australian feminism, even though, ironically enough, this was symptomatic of its widening influence' (1981: 19).

[3] This is not to suggest that Dowse was unaware of the problems of co-option. 'Depending on your point of view a femocrat was a woman who'd been coopted into a cushy government job or one who had entered the government arena to fight for equality and the redistribution of resources for women' (1990: 29).

ECONOMICS: GOVERNMENTS AND MARKETS

According to Charles Lindblom (1977: i), 'the greatest distinction between one government and another is in the degree to which market replaces government or government replaces market'. Questions about economic organisation have always been important in any society, and liberals have always had this issue at the centre of their philosophical and political agendas. While Part III is constructed around a choice between government regulation and free markets, as Lindblom suggests, this issue is really one of the degree of government regulation and control. Completely unregulated or unsupported markets have never existed and are unlikely to be supported by any liberal.

The question then is the extent to which governments should intervene to control and direct market outcomes. The classical economists, and Adam Smith in particular, spent a lot of energy on constructing a defence of markets from government intervention. Early English liberals tended to accept this *laissez-faire*, or minimal government intervention, approach. Markets were to be left free according to this theory, with governments providing the necessary support for markets and overseeing them to ensure that people were protected from unscrupulous behaviour. Such behaviour was a problem because it might lead people to doubt market mechanisms and lose motivation. Many of the liberals who came later questioned the *laissez-faire* philosophy and supported various forms of government intervention into the economy.

An explanation of the centrality of this issue to liberal political theory is that it represents a return to issues of maximising individual freedom and providing incentives for individual exertion and participation in the economy. All liberals believe that, if they are working well, markets can provide people with freedom of choice with respect to goods, services, and careers. Markets are considered to provide a stimulus to individuals to act and to maximise their abilities, or at least some of their abilities. They are thought to produce continuous improvement in the productive capacities within a community. The supply–demand nexus that is at the heart of markets works to reward efficiency and creativity in the use of resources. This nexus is also thought to result in the closest match between what people want and what is made available to them.

A Need for Government Intervention

No liberals believe that markets can work perfectly without some form of government regulation and support. They all acknowledge that government has at least some role to play in the economy. They agree about some of the reasons for government intervention and disagree about others. Most liberals accept that governments have to provide some of the infrastructure required for markets to work. Most believe that governments must protect markets from the disturbing effects of unscrupulous behaviour. Some argue that governments must protect society from the effects of economic downturns. Others believe that government has a responsibility to support those who are unemployed. Most liberals believe that governments must protect those individuals who, through no fault of their own, are less able to compete effectively in the marketplace. Some believe that governments have a responsibility to provide opportunities for people to pursue activities that are not stimulated by market forces. All of these grounds for government intervention provide a justification for direct interference in markets by way of taxation, legislation, supervision, or a redistribution of resources.

This interference has to be handled carefully, since markets can be undermined though excessive intervention. Intervention can often reduce the rewards for full and efficient action in a market environment. It certainly interferes with the system of incentives and disincentives that markets create. This means that arriving at the right mix of market operation and government regulation is a difficult and contentious issue among liberals.

Infrastructure

The first reason that government intervention in markets is justified is to provide the infrastructure necessary for markets to operate. Individuals or companies do not provide the entire infrastructure because it is often 'uneconomic' for them to do so. Liberals have different views about what infrastructure governments may justifiably provide. Government provision of armed forces, roads, railway lines, schools, and lighthouses is often justified on this ground; provision of universities and research facilities is sometimes justified on the same ground.

Dishonesty

Yet another reason that governments may justifiably interfere in markets is to prevent dishonest or other types of action that reduce the operation of market forces. Theft is a simple example. Thieves are not stimulated to engage in market-focused behaviour. Those stolen from are no longer able to satisfy their needs to the extent that they might have done, because they no longer have what they earned in the market. A more complex example is collusion by suppliers of goods and services that can lead to price-fixing and other anti-market behaviour. Other actions, which have the effect of driving competitors out of business, are also a problem because they reduce the level of competition within markets. Only government action can prevent these more subtle, but possibly more significant, forms of undermining market processes.

Economic downturn

Another ground on which liberals justify government intervention in markets is to mitigate the effects of economic downturns (otherwise known as recessions, depressions, slowdowns, meltdowns, and market corrections). These periods produce great distress for many people. They may even lead some people to question the wisdom of using markets to produce and distribute goods and services. A number of liberals, relying on the work of the English economist John Maynard Keynes, argued that governments had to intervene in markets to reduce the extent to which economics slumped, to promote savings, and to ensure that investment was directed to increasing the efficiency or productivity produced by market forces.

Unemployment

Unemployment is not, in itself, a problem for liberals. Some may even celebrate the stimulus it provides to individual initiative. It is a problem for other liberals because of the distress it causes individuals and families or because it can provide a stimulus to theft and other anti-social or anti-market behaviour. Unemployment can also contribute to economic downturns through the dampening effect it has on demand. Thus some liberals may justify government intervention in markets on moral or economic grounds to support the unemployed. Governments are also justified in granting pensions, or other forms of assistance, to those who suffer from problems which make them largely unable to seek and retain a job.

Artificially unequal competition

Some liberals believe that government must intervene in markets to ensure that competition is fair. Those liberals who accept the existence of systemic or structural inequality, that is, social stratification, believe that some people are artificially made less competitive than others and that some have advantages that are not natural advantages (this may be a reflection of the effects of social stratification). They do not accept, therefore, that market outcomes reflect people's true abilities, but believe that overcoming these problems requires government intervention. This intervention can overcome some of the artificially produced inequality: it can provide means by which those who have been disadvantaged can overcome their disadvantages. It may not make competition truly fair, but it may make it fairer.

Opportunities for unmarketable activities

Some liberals believe that markets provide a stimulus to undesirable, or less desirable, aspects of human beings. They consider markets to stimulate only certain capacities in people. They believe human nature contains potential that cannot be realised if markets are not supplemented by opportunities to pursue other activities, usually understood as higher or more uplifting activities. They look to governments to support activities that enrich society and encourage people to develop their full range of capacities. Government support for the arts and higher cultural activities is justified on this ground. Society as a whole is thought to benefit, even if only a limited number of people take advantage of the opportunities that governments provide. Such a society is enriched, made more varied, and is simply better for everyone if these activities are valued. Most liberals acknowledge that markets will not ensure that they are treated as valuable.

Taxation, legislation, supervision, redistribution

Each of the justifications for government action involves direct or indirect, and sometimes both, forms of government interference in markets. In part, this is simply a function of the taxation, imposition of duties, or charges that a government is required to levy in order to maintain itself and undertake any of the activities listed above. Taxation takes resources out of the hands of individuals and companies, which then affects the structures of individual and company motivation that are part of market systems. Some of the forms of government action required by liberals will necessitate the passage of legislation that will make certain behaviour, including that by actors in markets, illegal, or that will direct the behaviour of actors in markets. Oversight is also required to ensure compliance with legislation. Finally, some of the justifications of government intervention described above necessitate a degree of redistribution of economic resources, which must occur outside or against market forces.

Australia

All of these grounds for justifying government intervention in markets have been put forward by liberals in Australia. Some have been more important because of the particular environmental and social conditions in Australia. Geographical factors have been particularly important in shaping both Australian society and the level and form of government intervention in the economy. That Australia is a sparsely populated country located a considerable distance from like cultures has meant that markets for goods and services are limited. This has impeded economic development. That the resources necessary for economic development have not always been available in private hands has also meant that governments in Australia have had to be more involved in promoting economic development than governments in other countries.

Australia's origin as a penal colony has also contributed to an acceptance of government intervention in the economy and society among some liberals. Australia's origin as a convict settlement meant that it was a creation of government and that political authorities were understood to be responsible for the success of the colony and society. Government, in short, preceded the very existence of white society in Australia. Australians were quite used—some liberals might think overused—to government assistance and support in the creation of a healthy and prosperous society.

Protection versus free trade

In Australia, the choice between government and market regulation of the economy was often constructed around the choice between protection and free trade. 'Protection' meant using government to protect local industries from outside competitors. This usually implied a responsibility on the part of government to ensure that all members of the Australian community shared the benefits of protected markets. Free trade meant minimising, but not removing, barriers to external competition and, in most instances, resisting pressure to ensure some equity in the distribution of economic goods.

Deakin, Coombs, and Hewson

The three liberals whose works are dealt with in Part III are Alfred Deakin, Herbert Cole Coombs, and John Hewson. Each offers a somewhat different approach to the issue of the proper relationship between governments and markets. Deakin and Coombs have more in common with each other than they do with Hewson. Hewson might be said to have had more in common with the earlier, *laissez-faire*, liberals than he had with Deakin and Coombs.

Alfred Deakin's principles came to define the Australian liberal response, at least in government, to the choice between 'free' markets and government regulation. Deakin was a protectionist who supported government intervention in the economy to create and sustain a local economy that was insulated from competition from industry in other countries. He saw protected industries as the basis for a healthy and prosperous community. As a significant actor in the federation movement, Deakin was able to translate the principles he had developed for the colony of Victoria into a political practice at a federal level. This philosophy dominated Australian economic practice from federation until the 1980s.

H. C. Coombs' importance, for the purposes of this book, lies in his role in introducing Keynesian economic principles into Australian politics and, most importantly, into the Australian bureaucracy. Keynes' theories justified and even required significant government intervention into the economy. The main purposes of intervention were to reduce the effects of economic downturns and to control investment in order to achieve greater productivity and economic efficiency. While control over investment was rarely attempted in Australia, the Keynesian approach to managing the economy was practised in order to reduce the effects of economic downturns. Coombs was significant in introducing and shaping the Australian use of Keynes' ideas, particularly in the period immediately after the Second World War. He was also influenced by the problems of environmental degradation and the depletion of natural resources in Australia. He believed that markets were not providing incentives that would induce individuals and companies to conserve natural resources and that governments had to intervene to promote conservation, either directly or through shifting market incentives.

John Hewson's approach to these issues represents a significant shift in the practice of Australian liberalism that became prominent in the 1980s. As leader of the Liberal Party of Australia, Hewson was a principal spokesperson for those who adopted a free-market approach to economic organisation. One of the most prominent advocates of what is now known as 'economic rationalism', he rejected government as a legitimate means of economic regulation and advocated minimal government. Although he failed to lead his party to victory in the Australian election of 1993, his ideas represent the modern practices of Australian liberalism, at least in the context of economic policy and practice.

Deakin and Coombs were clearly less confident about the efficacy of markets for achieving economic and political goals. Both thought that markets would not deliver the outcomes that Australians required. Hewson, on the other hand, had far greater faith in markets. He also looked to non-political agencies, sometimes called voluntary associations, to provide many of the services and opportunities that Deakin and Coombs sought from government. Hewson was convinced that market processes could not tolerate a significant level of government intervention. Deakin and Coombs thought they could. Thus whereas Deakin and Coombs sought to extend government intervention in the economy, Hewson sought to reduce it.

9

ALFRED DEAKIN
(1856–1919)

A Colonial Liberal is one who favours State interference with liberty
and industry at the pleasure and in the interest of the majority, while
those who stand for the free play of individual choice and energy are
classed as Conservatives. (Deakin 1968: 12)

Alfred Deakin was born in Fitzroy, Melbourne, on 3 August, 1856.
He received a law degree from the University of Melbourne, practised
as a barrister, and worked as a journalist at the Melbourne *Age* newspaper. He entered the Victorian parliament in 1879 and quickly
became one of the leaders of the various liberal parties that formed
and re-formed during this period. Between 1883 and 1886 he was
Minister for Public Works. In 1885 he was president of the Royal
Commission on Irrigation and Water Supply, and from 1886 to 1890
was Chief Secretary and Minister of Water Supply. He was a leading
figure in the Victorian movement supporting the federation of the
Australian colonies. He won a seat in the first federal parliament as
Member for Ballarat. Between 1901 and 1903 Deakin was federal
Attorney-General. He was Prime Minister of Australia between 1903
and 1904, 1905 and 1908, and 1909 and 1910.

Alfred Deakin articulated essential elements of the economic and political philosophy that was to dominate Australian politics until the mid-
1970s. This philosophy justified the systematic use of government
intervention in the economy to achieve specific social objectives. To
understand Deakin's liberalism requires developing both a sense of his
economic and social objectives and an understanding of the policies he
thought necessary to achieve those objectives. These two aspects of his

thought are examined in separate sections. The first gives an overview of Deakin's economic and social objectives, which broadly were to create an autonomous Australian economy that provided the basis for a healthy society. The second section takes up the specific policies Deakin adopted, which included tariffs, government support for and ownership of industry, and industrial legislation to protect workers.

These aspects of Deakin's principles and policies provide a general overview for his political practice. Careful note must be taken, however, of the fact that Deakin was negotiating a difficult political environment. Federation required bringing together colonies that had been developing along different economic lines and had different productive bases, and in which different social conditions prevailed.[1] His involvement in the creation of the institutions of Australian government meant that he abandoned aspects of his economic and social objectives when he felt that their pursuit threatened federation.

Economic and Social Objectives

Deakin's economic and social objectives can be understood in terms of interlocking ambitions. His initial objective was to increase the productive occupation of the Australian continent. Increased productive occupation provided the foundation for his second objective: to create locally based industries that were tailored to meet local demand. This, in turn, would allow for the realisation of his ultimate objective, which was to create an integrated and self-sufficient Australian economy. Achieving this required both productive occupation and local industry. It also required the reduction, if not eradication, of antagonisms that had developed within and between the states/colonies.

Deakin's economic objectives were bound up with social objectives. He sought the 'utilization of [Australia's] unoccupied areas, a reorganization of our methods and a redistribution of its energies' in order 'to enable a civilised life to be led from shore to shore in all callings and in all our climates' (1906: 25–6). Productivity, in his view, was not simply a technical and mechanical matter; it was also an intellectual and spiritual phenomenon. Deakin believed that 'those who are responsible for the nation's destinies realise … that these depend on the numbers, health, efficiency and culture of the people of Australia. We may be in machinery and material possessions the wealthiest nation in the world, yet the weakest in manhood and womanhood if our masses are stunted or morally and mentally starved' (1910a: 12).

Increased productive occupation

An increase in the productive occupation of the Australian continent could only be achieved, in Deakin's view, under the right conditions. Above all, it required an increase in the population and especially an increase in those who could assist in the exploitation of the natural resources to be found in Australia. 'Australia requires to be peopled', Deakin wrote, 'and peopled soon, by those who will better their own circumstances and add to the national wealth by the development of our agricultural and mineral resources' (1906: 25). Australia was rich in these natural resources. 'The misfortune is that we have nothing like an adequate population to develop them as they deserve' (1968: 197).

An increased population would be able to support local industries. The creation of these industries, however, necessitated 'the adoption of a well-thought-out and scientific system for the development of national industries' (1906: 8). Deakin was not driven by a desire for simple self-sufficiency or some narrow nationalistic fervour. He thought it was only through the creation of a separate Australian economy that Australians could control the nature and future of their society. This meant that 'the Liberal ... in this country is associated with the development of our own industries by our own people' (1906: 9).

Deakin's desire to create economic independence required him to pursue the federation of the Australian colonies, since none of the colonies could hope to be self-sufficient. People in the colonies could achieve this goal only if they joined together. Economic interdependence was an essential step towards a fully unified federation. For 'the necessary beginning of national union is a binding together by commercial ties. When one part of the continent is capable of supplying the wants of another, the first duty of Australian citizenship is to ensure that the interchange of the products raised should take place within ourselves' (1906: 9).

Economic issues were central to debates about federation. Ensuring that sound economic principles were adopted was one of the primary tasks of early Australian governments. Deakin believed that the economic principles under which the federation was to operate had to be carefully laid down before any other aspects of his desired Australian society could be created: 'The first condition of the transaction of the business of this country is to lay down once and for all the conditions upon which Australian investments and Australian labor shall be employed in this country' (1906: 10).

Promoting local industries

Economic development, for Deakin, would provide the basis for a sound Australian society only if it led to diversification and greater technical sophistication in production among local industries. While in the first instance production might be largely in primary industry, other forms needed to develop. Only when these other industries existed could Australian society be thought of as encouraging the development of the skills and technical sophistication that would mark it as a modern society. In his view, 'the industries which skill, intelligence, and capital have built among us should be encouraged as a means, not only to the development of the country, but to the higher practical and technical education of its people. They should not all remain hewers of wood, drawers of water, shearers of wool, and growers of wheat' (1906: 11).

Economic and social objectives were inextricably linked for Deakin, and one could not be mentioned without the other. Thus his Liberal Party aimed 'to unlock the lands, develop national industries, and to safeguard the rights of those engaged in them' (1906: 5). Local industries had to develop 'because they are the means of livelihood to and advance the interests of scores of thousands of our fellow citizens' (1910a: 12).

Overcoming intra-state and interstate tensions

Creating an environment in which Australian industry and society would flourish required overcoming the antagonisms that existed between the colonies/states, between the various producer groups, and between workers and employers. Each of these often overlapping antagonisms prevented the cooperation that was required, so they impeded the creation of a healthy society. In the end, in Deakin's view, government had to create the economic and social order in which Australians would flourish. The first objective was to break down the domination of privileged groups whose defence of their privileges held all of society back. The second was to mobilise government to intervene in the economy to provide opportunities for those in less privileged positions.

Deakin's experiences in Victorian politics in the late 1880s and 1890s led him to the view that powerful forces inhibited economic and social development in that colony and in Australia generally. In Victorian politics, Deakin belonged to those who are known as radical liberals. Against the radical liberals, who sought change to benefit all members of society, stood 'the propertied classes, squatters and other capitalists, the land-owners opposed to free selection and desiring to pervert the provisions intended to encourage settlement so as to allow them to accumulate large areas of the public estate'. Those who supported these groups included 'the civil service except its poorest paid members, the professions and the tradespeople who thrived on their relationships with the well-to-do' (Deakin 1957: 11).

These divisions were not confined to Victoria and posed significant problems for anyone interested in fostering a national interest. Problems increased when intra-state divisions interacted with interstate rivalries. Deakin's assessment of the pre-federation situation indicates something of the problem at hand. The colonies, in Deakin's view, had 'waged fiscal war' and protected their 'frontiers with lines of hostile Customs Houses … Though men of the same stock, of the same type of thought, and living, broadly speaking, in similar surroundings, our differences, small at first, have been multiplied and increased until some marked divergences have become manifest and have been gradually intensified by various rivalries' (1968: 10).

Divisions among the colonies prevented the combination and cooperation required for a prosperous national economy and a flourishing society. Deakin lamented the fact that Australian 'agriculturalists are slow to unite even with their neighbours, while pastoralists find union impossible except for certain general purposes of self-protection' (1968: 9). Further complications were created when antagonisms between worker and employer were added.

Deakin's solutions to these problems were political. He looked to an active interventionist government to create an economic framework that undermined privilege and encouraged the recognition of a shared interest in the development of the Australian economy and society. For only government could contain both the power of the privileged and the revolutionary pressures created by the growing power of workers. Deakin had to negotiate a political environment within which hostile forces aimed to ensure that society was organised in a way that reflected their interests. As Clark (1981: 186) suggested, Deakin believed that 'a judicious use of state assistance to economic activity could create a society in which there was both material well-being for all and equality of opportunity without the evil of servility or the vice of mediocrity. The task of Australian liberalism was to steer that middle course between the conservatives and Labor'.

Behind Deakin's economic objective were a set of social objectives. To create a thriving society and civilisation in Australia meant achieving self-sufficiency. This required both overcoming the divisions within and between colonies and the development and increasing sophistication of local industries. 'We look to commerce, we look to industries and machinery', he wrote, 'because we see through them to our own people' (1910a: 12). These, in turn, required an increased population. These outcomes could only be achieved, in Deakin's view, if there existed governments at both federal and state levels that were willing and able to interfere in economic processes.

Political Implications

An active government was an essential element of Deakin's political agenda. Only governments would be able to promote a collective interest. Liberals such as Deakin rejected 'the conservative argument that State interference was both an infringement of individual liberty, and a sapping of that individual initiative essential to the full development of the personality' (Clark 1981: 123). In the end, Deakin's liberalism meant 'equality of rights and opportunity, some re-distribution of wealth by taxation, some legislation to curb the impact upon men and women of capitalist enterprise concerned with profit' (La Nauze 1965: 106–7).

Rejected *laissez-faire* approaches

In direct contrast to John Hewson, Deakin's principles led him to firmly reject *laissez-faire* or minimal government theories. He believed that liberals could reject these theories of the proper role of government because they were based on pre-democratic assumptions and principles. Once 'the powers of government and Parliament have passed into the hands of the people', he argued, liberals 'have asked themselves why they should refrain from using, in the interests of the whole community, the powers originally used in the interests of the classes. That is the distinctive development of liberalism of our own day' (1906: 6).

These ideas could not be carried too far, however. Deakin emphasised the need for governments to be careful not 'to destroy private enterprise—the energies which make modern life, that have built up our civilization … in favour of some mechanical government management of every human activity' (1905a: 5). He dismissed as a flight of fancy the socialist view that extensive government regulation of society or the economy was either possible or desirable. But he was always ready to use the power of government where he thought that it was necessary to serve some ultimate purpose. 'I shrink with no dogmatic or doctrinal horrors from the use of the machinery of legislation and administration', he wrote, 'but … recoil from using it further than is proved necessary' (1905a: 7). Deakin's mind was open, then, on the question of government intervention. He adopted a more careful approach than those whose minds were closed on this issue by their ideological prejudices, so he was always ready to support government intervention when he was persuaded that it was required.

Deakin's political program required four specific forms of government action. First, governments were responsible for fostering private enterprise through regulation, investment, and the provision of social and economic infrastructure. Second, governments might need to create or acquire industries, where this was necessary to protect the public interest. Third, governments had to create tariff barriers to imported goods to protect local industries. Finally, governments needed to take control of industrial relations. These actions do not exhaust Deakin's political program but, for the purposes of this study, they are its most important elements.

Fostering private enterprise

Deakin advocated three main roles for government in fostering private enterprise. The first was to support local industry through bounties to encourage particular industries, to provide irrigation to allow for an expansion of agriculture, to create specific technical and scientific agencies to help solve problems facing industry in Australia, and to ensure that education was available to all. A second role was to regulate economic interactions to ensure that the society was free from negligent, fraudulent or other practices that undermined the market. The third way of fostering private enterprise was to protect Australian industry from combinations of major producers seeking to control a particular industry.

Bounties for industry

Deakin believed that supporting local industries often required governments to provide bonuses or bounties in the early stages of an industry's development. For example, he sought to introduce an iron bounty to encourage the development of this industry. He saw the development of an iron-producing capability as vital to the future of the country 'because all of our industries are associated with our iron resources. We cannot lag behind industrially without finding ourselves in a most unsatisfactory, unbusinesslike and, what is more, a most defenceless condition' (1905a: 15). He supported a similar intervention to ensure the viability of the sugar industry, which 'has been enabled to support itself against the subsidised beet sugars of Europe only by means of indirect bounties or subventions' (1968: 46).

Irrigation for agriculture

Government support for private enterprise was also required, via the provision of water through irrigation schemes. Irrigation schemes would allow agriculture to develop in areas that received insufficient annual rainfall. This would encourage settlement of these areas and greater productivity in agricultural industries. 'We have the land, the climate, and the rainfall in the coastal belt. We have rivers capable of filling storage reservoirs which, if used for irrigation, would go far towards producing abundant harvests' (Deakin 1968: 124–5).

The system Deakin developed for Victoria under the Irrigation Act of 1886 involved cooperation between colonial and local government agencies. In this scheme, 'irrigation works were to be constructed by local Trusts with the aid of state loans, repayable from rates which the Trusts were empowered to levy. The government itself would construct some "national works" such as weirs to serve large areas' (La Nauze 1965: 86). The failure of this system did not diminish Deakin's sense of the need for government-sponsored irrigation, but it did make him more cautious about governments attempting such ambitious projects.

Technical and scientific support

Deakin was more confident when it came to providing technical and scientific support to help industries develop and adjust to Australian conditions. An important element in this support was an agricultural bureau. This bureau represented a government initiative to assist local industry. It also symbolised the way in which a federal government could serve interests spread throughout the states. He advocated 'the employment by the Commonwealth of a half-a-dozen experts, paid good salaries, masters of diseases that decimate stock or destroy orchards or crops, and of the pests that prey upon them ... Difficulties, facing the whole, or large parts, of this country, are great national questions which a great national bureau can deal with' (1910a: 15).

Education

Deakin also recognised the need for governments to ensure that education was available to all Australians. This reflected his desire to enlighten and generally raise the standard of Australian society. It was also important for economic development. He even supported government-provided education, and acknowledged that it was Carlyle's and Ruskin's influence that had brought him to this position (1957: 4–5).[2]

Regulation of economic interactions

Like all liberals, Deakin also defined a role for government in the regulation of economic interactions to ensure that markets operated free from fraud or other dishonest practices. Liberals have always accepted government regulation to ensure that markets functioned properly. Deakin believed that this was the responsibility of the federal government and would result in a significant increase in federal responsibilities and a diminution in those of state governments. The federal government, Deakin argued, needed to make uniform the provisions governing trademarks, copyright, secret commissions, and the adulteration and false advertising of goods (1968: 165). He acknowledged that the result would be to 'increase the control of the federal Parliament and Government over the trade, commerce, industry, and the legal obligation of its citizens incidental to these all over Australia' (1968: 165).

Protecting local industry

Just as Deakin sought to prevent a variety of unfair dealings within the Australian economy, he also sought to protect that economy from acts by foreign companies that would undermine local industries. He wanted to create 'a just commercial system under which our own people shall be protected against invasions either of trust or dumper' (1906: 26). He pursued legislation directed 'against those mammoth trusts which are coming into prominence in the Western world' (1906: 21).

> Take the case of the harvesters. They are the invention of Australian brains, the work is carried out by Australian workmen, and they are doing credit to Australia wherever they are employed. The proposal is made that we should protect these fruits of Australian industry against the deliberate attacks of great capitalists abroad, aimed not at fair competition in the open market, but used with all the destructive powers which would be possible if an hostile foe landed on these shores and endeavoured to wreck our factory. What I say is that an

attack of this kind ought to be resisted, fiscal issue or no fiscal issue. Our endeavour should be to protect an Australian industry against a great monopoly which we cannot control, because it exists outside Australia, whose object is to crush our local production in order to mulct our purchasers of agricultural machinery undisturbed. (Deakin 1905a: 14)

He argued that there was no point in fostering local industries 'if they are then to lie absolutely at the mercy of these great combinations of capital and ability which unscrupulously and with piratical tyranny work for the destruction of local industry' (1906: 21). Such destruction would lead to 'a helpless dependence of our people'. If foreign attacks on local industries were successful, Australians would 'be compelled to pay toll to the multi-millionaires' (1906: 21).

Protecting local industries did not require the complete destruction of these combinations. Instead, they could be 'allowed to exist under conditions equitable to the country, their employees, and the employers'. They had to be dealt with in such a way that they lost their destructive capability. The general principle was to 'allow those who have chosen to unite their businesses to conduct them under the control and supervision of the commonwealth, so long as their operations are such as to make for the general welfare of the community' (1910b: 49). Australian industry could not be sacrificed to outside powers because this would render Australians subservient to foreign interests.

Government ownership of industries

Deakin's desire to create an economic environment that sustained a progressive society led him to accept public ownership of industries where this was conducive to the general good. The failure of his program to provide irrigation in Victoria made him less certain that government ownership was always a solution. He did not rule out public ownership, however, even when he knew that it would be expensive and was unlikely to recover the funds that had been invested. That government ownership could be a problem was evident from 'the great debts which the municipalities of Great Britain have incurred, and the great indebtedness of the Australian States, for railways, water works, etc.' (1905a: 7). He argued that, despite occasional problems with indebtedness, governments in Australia had successfully administered 'railways … post office, telegraphs and other State enterprises' (Deakin 1905a: 8).

Deakin was not naively supportive of government intervention and ownership. He recognised 'that when you substitute for private enterprise public enterprise you get rid of one set of difficulties and raise another' (1905a: 8). Nor did he dismiss, or otherwise diminish, the positive effects of free markets. He argued that despite 'all its faults, the system of private enterprise … brings an amount of intelligence and character to direct and to scrutinise even the smallest parts of business workings, which governments have never yet succeeded in securing in their own administration' (1905a: 8). He simply contended that the free market could cause problems and that it needed to be used carefully and regulated where necessary.

Deakin was even disposed, 'if no other means be available, to favour the nationalisation by the Commonwealth of those industries which become weapons of abuse and oppression' (1905a: 8.) Nationalisation was necessary 'when no other device can be found to protect the public against pillage by the unscrupulous' (1905a: 8), but 'regulation comes first because it costs least' (1905a: 8–9). Nationalisation was very much a last resort. That it was an option at all marks Deakin's liberalism as going well beyond the minimalism of some liberals' conceptions of the proper role of government.

Tariffs

A central element in Deakin's political program was the creation of tariff barriers designed both to protect local industry and to ensure that the conditions under which Australians worked were conducive to their well-being and improvement. He had not always been a protectionist. He was encouraged to reconsider his views when he worked at the *Age* under its editor, the protectionist David Syme. 'In journalism', Deakin recalled, 'my Spencerian laissez-faire, including Free trade and individualism in excelsis, crumbled away almost at once' (quoted in Gabay 1992: 17).

His change of mind on the issue of tariff protection caused him no particular problem, once he was satisfied that well-conceived government interference would benefit local industries. The principal residue of his original commitment to free trade was his view that 'the undue or unnecessary increase of duties tended toward monopoly and was to be resisted on that score' (1957: 6). He supported only that level of duties which would allow local industries to compete with their overseas counterparts. He also wanted to restrict tariffs to 'those classes of products from which our country, climate and circumstances offered natural advantages and promised a permanent output of sufficient extent to render state action profitable' (1957: 6).

Deakin's approach reflected his general social objectives and not some hostility to markets. He supported tariff protection because he believed that it was a means 'to promote regular employment, to furnish security for the investment of capital in new as well as existing industries, to render stable the conditions of labour and to prevent the standard of living of the employees in these industries from being depressed to the level of foreign standards' (quoted in Pons 1994: 130).

Deakin's support for tariffs was also fuelled by his sense that the revenue raised by import duties would allow the federal government to become fully independent of the states. This would enable it to initiate and fulfil significant legislative programs. His struggle to introduce a federal tariff on imported goods was part of his struggle to achieve a sustainable and meaningful Australian federation, and the imposition of a federal tariff was a significant milestone in the development of this. When tariffs were finally introduced, supporters of a meaningful federation could begin to relax. Those with a full understanding of what a failure to bring in a federal tariff would mean 'felt a more profound relief as they became assured that the Commonwealth was out of the toils at last, and fast escaping beyond the reach of its enemies' (quoted in La Nauze 1965: 20).

That Deakin's support for tariffs was partly a reflection of his desire to achieve a viable Commonwealth government should not obscure the fact that it reflected his general social objectives. Deakin believed tariffs were essential for the promotion of local industry: they would create an environment in which Australian initiative and enterprise would flourish. Protection was designed to stimulate initiative, however, and could not be allowed to produce lethargy or inefficiency. Protection would operate best in the early stages of development of an industry and in situations of unfair competition. Enterprises were not to be protected from ineptitude or inefficiency on the part of those who directed them, for 'the Australian manufacturer is not to be sheltered against competition from abroad if he is understood by reason of his own omission to obtain the latest machinery or processes or his inability to manage his business' (Deakin 1968: 161–2).

Protecting wages and conditions

Deakin's concern with promoting local industry was a direct reflection of his desire to protect Australian wages and working conditions.

Protecting workers would not be possible with free trade, 'which allows the importation here of the cheapest labour of the world for them to compete against' (1905a: 15). He argued that it was an essential element of liberal philosophy to protect workers 'against occasional dumping or continuous invasion by underpaid, overworked, or uncivilised labour elsewhere' (1905a: 10). Tariff protection was simply one manifestation of 'the obligation not only of maintaining within ourselves the necessary productive power to make this nation wealthy, but also of supervising the conditions under which work is performed' (1906: 10).

Conciliation and arbitration

Tariffs were only one means of providing protection for workers. This also required the creation of a system of conciliation and arbitration designed to protect local industry from disruption caused by tensions between employers and employees. Deakin wanted to introduce 'a judicious tariff and industrial laws, well considered and worked out in detail, so as to dovetail into each other' (1906: 12). He believed that liberals were required to do whatever could be done to pursue social justice. In his view, 'no measures ever submitted to any legislature offer greater prospects of the establishment of social justice and of the removal of inequalities than those which are based upon the principle of conciliation and arbitration' (quoted in La Nauze 1965: 299).[3]

Deakin's commitment to social justice was only one of the motivations behind his desire to introduce a national system of conciliation and arbitration. His experiences of industrial unrest in Victoria during the 1890s and in the early years of the Commonwealth made it clear to him that governments and courts had an important role in ensuring the maintenance of productivity. This meant resolving industrial disputes before they resulted in strikes and other disruptions to production. In his view, strikes and lockouts were 'modes of war which rend our industrial system to pieces, and … have cost civilized countries many millions sterling, and many thousands or tens of thousands of lives' (1904: 4).

Deakin's faith in human rationality and his belief that political institutions could represent a collective good sense led him to think of the system of conciliation and arbitration as the intercession of the higher authority of reason. They represented, in his view, 'a noble effort to lift out of the field of strife and of mutual hatred the keen issues which have severed employers and employed, and to raise them to a higher level in the light of day and by impartial judgement' (1904: 4).

The White Australia Policy

A commentary on Deakin's liberalism could be left at this point. His intention to support government intervention in the economy, government ownership of particular industries or services, tariff barriers, and industrial legislation paint the picture of a liberal employing various means for creating a healthy, productive and just society. Any full consideration of Deakin's economic theories, however, must address his commitment to what came to be known as the White Australia policy.

This policy represented not only a commitment to a particular social framework, but also represented a commitment to a particular set of economic conditions and a particular form of trade policy. It was also a commitment to the maintenance of a white Australia. The question of whether or not Deakin was a racist will not be canvassed here, as this does not bear upon the issues at hand.[4] Certainly, racism does not preclude anyone from being a liberal and should not be taken to disqualify Deakin from being thought of as a liberal. His defence of the White Australia policy was a direct reflection of his conception of the most desirable economic framework under which Australian society could function. For Deakin,

> a white Australia does not by any means mean just the preservation of the complexion of the people of this country. It means the multiplying of homes, so that we may be able to defend every part of our continent; it means the maintenance of conditions of life fit for white men and white women; it means equal laws and opportunities for all; it means protection against underpaid labour of other lands, it means the payment of fair wages. A white Australia means a civilisation whose foundations are built upon healthy lives, lived in honest toil, under circumstances which imply no degradation; a white Australia means protection. (Deakin in Crowley 1973: 51)

As this quotation indicates, many of the features of Deakin's economic and political objectives discussed above were repeated in the context of his defence of the White Australia policy. A productive and progressive society meant, in Deakin's use, a healthy society for white Australians.

Deakin's desire to foster a healthy and productive society is manifested in a variety of ways in his political program. The first manifestation was his rejection of *laissez-faire* approaches, as he considered them inadequate to the task. Government, in his view, had to participate actively in the development of industries, which meant providing direct supports such as bounties and irrigation programs; it also meant less direct assistance through technical and scientific support and through education. Government regulation of the economy was also necessary, especially in light of the operation of overseas manufacturers, which acted singly and in combination to drive out local industries. Unlike some other liberals, Deakin even accepted that supporting local industries might require that they be owned and operated by governments. A combination of tariff protection and various means of protecting workers' wages and conditions, particularly through conciliation and arbitration, was also necessary because it would allow all Australians to share in the benefits of economic development. The level of cooperation and commitment to shared principles that Deakin sought could not be achieved, in his view, in a community in which some people could not commit themselves to the values shared by Caucasians.

Conclusion

Deakin believed that government had a central role in defining and pursuing a particular form of society. Market forces were insufficient for or ill-suited to meeting his economic and social objectives. They were an important element of his ideal economy and society but had to be directed, managed, and controlled by governments. Local industries would be supported through government incentives, investments, and publicly provided infrastructure. Public ownership was acceptable, and in some cases required, when this was conducive to the national interest. Tariff protection was also necessary. A system of tariffs would allow local industries to develop and provided a basis on which workers' wages and conditions could be improved. For only a strong domestic economy could support a society that provided opportunities for all Australians to lead satisfying lives.

Deakin's approach to the relationship between governments and markets was to dominate Australian society and politics for the first seventy years after federation. His approach was developed, adapted, and even extended by those liberals who followed, including H. C. Coombs. Certainly, liberals like Frederick Eggleston argued against such an approach, and liberals in New South Wales, such as George

Reid, supported free trade with some enthusiasm. Those liberals who disagreed with Deakinite liberalism did not become chief spokespeople for liberalism in Australia until the 1970s and 1980s. It was at this stage that liberals who returned to classical free trade, or *laissez-faire*, approaches became dominant. One of their better-known spokespeople was John Hewson.

---

1 'The narrow prejudices, the petty jealousies, and miserable envies of our days of division have to be gradually crushed out under the play of the Federal forces that were created by union, but at present they exist and require to be allowed for' (Deakin 1968: 98).

2 Thomas Carylyle (1795–1881) and his follower John Ruskin (1819–1900) rejected *laissez-faire* approaches because they believed that they caused the immiseration of workers and the degradation of society more generally. Ruskin in particular rejected unrestrained competition and sought to create a more cooperative and, in his view, higher form of civilisation (see McDonald 1962: 447–9).

3 Deakin had pursued legislation to regulate the conditions under which people worked when he was a minister in Victorian governments. He had been given personal responsibility for introducing the Factories and Shops Act of 1885. He considered this Act to be 'the first social legislation of its kind in the Australian colonies'. It 'provided for the registration and inspection of factories, the enforcement of sanitary regulations, limitation of hours of work of women and young persons, and compensation for injuries' (La Nauze 1965: 83).

4 'People try themselves by their own standards, and, naturally, return a verdict which is favourable to themselves. But assertions of superiority are neither conveyed nor implied in this Bill, which simply recognises the incontestable fact that, despite the unity of humanity, its diversity is more operative in fact. The branches and families into which the human race is divided have followed different paths for ages. They have developed in different directions to such an extent that it is now found that any attempt to suddenly blend their blood, unite them in institutions which are foreign to them—or in politics or economic relations—lead to disruptions and disturbances of a serious kind. These blends are apparently of advantage to neither race directly—and certainly not to the advantage of any hybrid races which spring from them' (Deakin 1905b: 3). 'From such gross [racist] attitudes Deakin was free. He realized well enough that in Australian discussions there were elements of a "purely selfish desire to escape competition" and "a spice of the unreasoned hostility to strangers and foreigners for which no justification can be offered". His own justification of a White Australia avoided cruel general implications of "superiority". He was too well read, and too long acquainted with Eastern thought, to think in that way' (La Nauze 1965: 278).

10

HERBERT COLE
COOMBS
(1906–1997)

A person's life, even the most private parts of it, is lived within a context which to an important degree sets limits to, or imposes a character on, the way in which that life is lived … While that context was largely determined for one, it responds to human decision and effort. I had myself therefore been aware of the opportunity and had felt some obligation to help build a context which offered the greatest freedom and opportunity for myself and others to work out our personal lives. (Coombs 1970: 7)

Herbert Cole 'Nugget' Coombs was born on 24 February 1906, in Kalamunda, Western Australia. He studied economics at the University of Western Australia and gained a scholarship to the London School of Economics, where he was awarded a doctorate. Coombs was an advisor to seven prime ministers from both sides of politics (Curtin, Chifley, Menzies, Holt, Gorton, McMahon and Whitlam). Coombs was Director of Rationing during the Second World War. After the war he was Director-General of Reconstruction, until he became the governor of the Reserve Bank from 1949 to 1968. In 1968 he was elected chancellor of the Australian National University. In 1974 he headed the Royal Commission into Australian Government Administration. Later he became chairperson of the Australian Council for Aboriginal Affairs, the Aboriginal Treaty Committee, the Australian Council for the Arts, and the Elizabethan Theatre Trust.

H. C. Coombs' role in the introduction of Keynesian economic theory and practice to public policy in Australia makes him an important figure for any understanding of liberalism in Australia. Coombs' views on the appropriate forms and levels of state intervention into markets underwent some changes over time, but at no stage did he retreat from the view that significant government intervention into markets was required to create a prosperous, healthy, and sustainable society. Markets were necessary to provide choice for people and to stimulate individual initiative, but governments also had an important role to play in modifying and controlling their effects. Both markets and governments had important functions in creating an economic and social environment within which people were given the greatest degree of freedom and opportunities for self-expression.

Coombs expressed his commitment to liberal principles in a variety of ways and in a number of contexts. While all are relevant for an understanding of his liberalism, only two figure in this chapter. The first is his application of Keynesian economic principles to the project of development in Australia after the war. The second is his promotion of ecological sustainability. Coombs was not as well placed to implement principles associated with economic sustainability as he was to apply Keynesian economics. His application of basic economic principles to issues of ecological management is nevertheless important to an understanding of his contribution to liberalism in Australia.

This chapter is presented in two sections. The first deals with Coombs' views on the nature of growth and how it might be achieved in Australia; it is in this context that his articulation of Keynesian economic principles figures. The second deals with what he understood as the management of scarcity in Australia. This led him to return to older economic principles, especially those articulated by Thomas Malthus. These sections do not represent markedly divergent approaches to the relationship between governments and markets. Coombs remained convinced that markets were necessary, but were only one element of sound society and could only function effectively when governments actively managed them.

Governments, Markets, and Growth in Australia

In his role as Director-General for Post-War Reconstruction, Coombs had to deal with the promotion of growth in Australia. The first issue I discuss is Coombs' broad understanding of 'growth', which included both economic and cultural dimensions. After that I consider his ideas on the relationship between governments and markets best suited to achieving growth in Australia. While markets were essential for achieving growth, the Keynesian principles he applied placed final responsibility for it in the hands of governments.

Growth

For Coombs, growth included but was not exhausted by economic growth. He did not dissociate economic growth from other forms of growth. Economic growth was strongly affected by other forms and provided a basis on which they became possible. Growth referred to an increase both of material goods and of the environment conducive to human well-being. The economy was a key to achieving this environment, but only governments could assure that economic growth occurred and that it facilitated social growth. Coombs argued 'that the economic system could … satisfy only part of human needs and that the "real business of life" is in its human relationships and … the quality of these will depend in part on the physical and social environment in which they are conducted' (1981: 26). Coombs accepted the importance of economic growth, but he questioned 'the prevailing obsession with economic growth which is distorting the values which we attach to different components in human welfare and over-valuing market goods as against the rest' (1970: 55).

Society was not simply an association of economic actors, to be understood and judged according to the degree to which basic economic needs were met. Economic systems had to be judged in terms of the way they provided 'the members of the relevant social groups with access to a livelihood; to the material, social, intellectual and (to a degree) spiritual means to a healthy, secure and stimulating life'. Certainly the quantity of goods and services delivered by an economic system was important to this, 'but the end products of the system are qualitative—the health, security and the lifestyle of the members of society' (Coombs 1990: 2). In his view, society was to be judged according to the general environment it created for individuals. 'The components of the good life are a combination of goods and services available in a total environment, physical, social and cultural' (1990: 56).

Coombs believed that, within their societies, individuals required identity, security, and stimulus:

> A healthy and balanced personality accepted within the general society of which he is part, confident that his 'belonging' and his 'differences' will be acknowledged and respected, can, in his continuing exploration of his universe, come to see himself as belonging to a great

variety of groups. His family, his schoolfellows, his workmates, his church, his sporting associates, his fellow club members, persons of common political or cultural interests, all provide contexts within which he can find various kinds of identification and security from which he can venture forth to issue and to encounter an infinity of challenges. (1978: 123–4)

He argued that in Australia, however, overly rapid change, the loss of traditional social structures and uncertainty among individuals as to their social roles had combined with 'persistent pressure to the consumption of goods' to degrade society. This degradation reflected the fact that, in Coombs' view, Australians had 'so sacrificed identity and security to the demands of stimulus that we no longer have any sense of who or what we are or any consciousness of personal or community purpose' (1990: 58).

Coombs was always an economist. He did not reject or belittle the economic dimensions of growth, particularly in less industrialised nations, but he thought that in a more industrialised nation an obsession with economic growth had inhibited growth in those other dimensions of human being that were equally if not more important for the determination of quality of life. He carried this dual or multi-faceted understanding of growth throughout his career.

Governments, markets and growth

No matter what understanding of growth is adopted, the question that faced an Australian liberal engaged in public life concerned the relationship between governments and markets in achieving growth. Like most liberals, Coombs was committed to markets as essential for maximising individual freedom and for producing various forms of social coordination. He did not believe that markets were necessarily stable, however, nor did he think that they produced the best outcomes for a society. He argued that markets required consistent and systematic intervention from government in order to produce both economic stability and socially desirable outcomes.

Markets and growth

Coombs was committed to markets as essential to economic organisation and growth. Obvious advantages, in his view, attached to market mechanisms. A market-based system made 'it possible for men and women to choose work in which they are competent or which pleases them … and it leaves to individual choice the final real content of the reward itself. Diversity of occupational opportunity and the power to choose between experiences open to consumers are sources of real stimulus and satisfaction' (1990: 120). The fact that they relied on individual choice was one of the main advantages of markets. This availability of choice was an important part of providing quality of life for people.

Markets were also important, in Coombs' view, because they provided incentives to innovation and adaptation. Government interference in markets might be necessary, but it had to be done in terms of basic economic principles. Coombs did not dismiss import restrictions out of hand because he believed they had played a positive role in the early stages of development in Australia (1971: 167–8). In the end, however, 'the lack of competition from imported goods results in rises in the prices of home produced goods; whilst the incidental protection afforded to inefficient industries raises costs' (1971: 132–3).

Governments and growth

While Coombs accepted that markets were central institutions for the achievement and maintenance of growth, he did not consider them perfect vehicles. He believed they could not maintain themselves without various forms of government intervention. He argued that 'the self-regulatory character of this system is, as we well know, imperfect. It appears to need continuous or occasional intervention of a supervisory character to keep it working effectively at an adequate level' (Coombs 1971: 12–13).

Keynes

Keynes' economic theories gave Coombs the theoretical base for pursuing government intervention in markets. Coombs described the appearance of Keynes' *General Theory of Employment, Interest and Money* as 'the most seminal intellectual event of our time'. He became

> convinced that in the Keynesian analysis lay the key to comprehension of the economic system. This conviction was strengthened by the almost simultaneous development of National Income Estimates … It was this combination of the Keynesian model of the economic system with the National Income assessments … which made it possible to give quantitative expression to the components of the relationships on which that model was based, and which made it so useful to economic policy. (Coombs 1981: 3)[1]

Coombs' support for Keynesian economic theory ran counter to economic orthodoxy at the time. This meant that the first step in implementing Keynesian economic approaches was to convince economists, politicians, and bureaucrats that the theory was viable and that governments had a much greater role to play in economies than had hitherto been accepted. Acceptance of Keynesian theories came 'only gradually and in the face of impassioned resistance from traditional centres of wisdom and authority within the economic and political system' (Coombs 1970: 20–1).

Coombs was not simply an economist advocating and defending Keynesian ideas. He was also a bureaucrat who practised them. The members of the Department of Post-War Reconstruction that Coombs created and presided over believed 'in the power of government intervention to contribute positively to the sum of human welfare, to civilise the content and distribution of the product of the economic system without impairing its essential freedom or its efficiency'. Members of the group also 'had faith in the intellectual model of the economic system and our capacity to manage it; we believed that it could in practice deliver benefits to both producer and consumer ... We were conscious that there was in the community generally a conviction that a better world could be built' (Coombs 1981: 27).

Coombs argued that a general commitment to achieving growth was an important factor in the positive reception of Keynes' economic theories. 'The wastes and bitterness of the depression years were still fresh in the minds of many and the Keynesian revolution in economic thought offered hope of making full employment a reality' (1971: 151). While it may not have been essential to or required by Keynesian economic theory, 'growth quickly became the more dominant element in the credo of the advocate of progressive or active economic policies'. This, in Coombs' view, was because growth 'was a more dynamic objective and expressed more adequately the demand for a better world which wartime experience made vocal' (1971: 151).

Coombs was a keen participant in debates about the role of government, particularly its role in achieving full employment. For him 'the most important debate was centred around the central core of the strategy for full employment—the control of investment' (1981: 51). Government control of investment was not the only idea that economists, politicians, and the public had to accept. They also had to 'accept action through interest rates and by other means to restrain any tendency towards too rapid growth of the flow of funds through the capital market' (1971: 55).

Planning

Implementing Keynesian economic principles relied heavily on governments developing and implementing economic plans. Economic planning required the production of a detailed model of the economy that 'could serve to demonstrate how growth depends on the co-ordination of the elements of private decision-making and public policy. It could indicate the implications and possible inconsistencies of unco-ordinated sectional planning, perhaps allowing us to forecast points of pressure within the economy as a whole'. The resources that were invested in producing this model would be justified, in Coombs' view, if it became 'a framework for more informed decision-making in the public and private sectors' (1971: 150).

Coombs was careful to point out, however, that 'planning does not offer a means of escape from the problems of decision-making and the hardships of economic life'. Stability and growth were still to be understood as a result of 'the skill and initiative of management in the public and private sectors and this can best be encouraged by sound and forward-looking economic institutions and by a highly educated and adaptable industrial and commercial community' (1971: 150).

Savings

Coombs believed that growth in Australia was retarded by a lack of adequate investment in equipment, research, and development—a function of the inadequacy of savings in Australia. It was here that government had an important role; it was 'dangerous to leave the adequacy of saving to finance development to chance or the uncertain influence of interest rates' (1971: 126).

He offered two suggestions as to how government might promote savings. The first was a compulsory superannuation scheme. 'A second possibility … is that the government should accept responsibility for determining the proportion of our gross national product which should be devoted to development, public and private, and to modify its tax system to ensure adequate savings to provide the necessary resources' (1971: 126). Governments had a crucial role to play in controlling investment and fostering savings. They were the only institutions capable of ensuring not simply a functioning economy but an economy that produced equity and a desirable social environment.

Non-economic growth

Coombs' view that growth was not registered simply in increasing GDP, or any other simple economic measure, required an extended role for government in society and the economy. Governments had a crucial role not only in regulating markets but in ensuring that the outcomes produced through market forces contributed to a healthy and just social environment. This was particularly true, Coombs argued, when a high level of material affluence existed. In his view,

> as incomes and standards of living rise, more of the goods which can add appreciably to the quality of life are characteristically provided collectively and it is increasingly necessary to take collective action to conserve and improve our physical environment. A well-planned town or city, with uncluttered roadways and an effective transport system, which is rich in parks and gardens, has fine buildings, libraries, art galleries, theatres and the like, with easy access to areas of unspoilt rural and natural environments, is the foundation of a good life for the citizen and it becomes increasingly difficult to preserve and more expensive to create. *And only public authorities can do a great many of these things.* (1971: 162, emphasis added)

Education

Achieving a sound economic and social environment in a democracy was not simply the responsibility of those engaged in markets and governments. A high degree of understanding within the community of the issues and the policy options available was also necessary. Coombs came to this view because of his experiences in implementing Keynesian principles in Australia. That democratically elected governments were now central to economic policy formation meant that 'the broad requirements of policy suggested by theory must be thrashed around and mulled over in communication and controversy between academics, scientists, politicians and the community generally until they become … part of the ethos of the community' (1970: 51).

An appropriate education system was central to producing a community able to adapt to and support sound economic policy. This system would also produce a variety of experts able to provide sound analysis and advice and, in many instances, direction and leadership. He considered the Australian National University as an important part of this system. He, and others like him, looked on it 'as a place where research directed at problems arising immediately from the social, economic and cultural context would bring us the knowledge with which to build wisely. We saw it as the power-house of social reconstruction' (1970: 11).

A sound educational system would also contribute directly to the development of a better and more productive community. Coombs sought 'an effective educational policy which makes available to the work force an appropriate range of skills and knowledge and equips them to recognise and seize the opportunities which economic growth can offer' (1971: 157). He supported government expenditure to promote research and education on the ground that they were 'the sources of the growth of knowledge and of skills from which increasing productivity derive. They also form a contribution to the quality of life itself' (1971: 126). Of course, governments were responsible for supporting such a system and ensuring it achieved those ends.

An expanded conception of growth coupled with the adoption of Keynesian economic theory meant that Coombs understood economic growth somewhat differently from many economists of his time. This gave him a different conception of the institutions responsible for economic growth and consequently a different sense of their relationships and responsibilities. Markets remained important because they promoted diversity, maximised choice, and generally provided appropriate systems of incentive and disincentive. But they required government intervention if they were to remain stable and produce socially desirable outcomes. Governments were responsible for the planning that would ensure long-term prosperity and development. They also bore primary responsibility for producing an education system that would facilitate growth. A sound education system was necessary to ensure that members of the Australian community were able to follow and respond appropriately to debates on economic policy informed by experts also produced by that system. High levels of education were also essential for a productive community that was also able to enjoy the enriching experiences offered within a healthy social environment.

Governments, Markets, and Managing Scarcity in Australia

His involvement in the pursuit of growth in postwar Australia provides only one perspective for an understanding of Coombs' sense of the proper relationship between governments and markets. Keynes was a powerful influence on Coombs' economic and political theories and had a profound impact on earlier periods of his public life. He did not forget his exposure to Malthus's economic theories, however. If Coombs' earlier public life was dominated by growth, his later public life reflected his response to environmental degradation and resource depletion.

For an economist like Coombs, dealing with environmental degradation and resource depletion meant a return to the problem of managing scarcity. 'The optimum use of scarce resources has always been the basic concern of the discipline. It was also an economist, Malthus, who first (almost 200 years ago) drew attention to the potential conflict of rising populations with limited resources' (Coombs 1990: 40). Coombs' apparent shift from achieving growth to dealing with scarcity did not mean abandoning economics: 'The achievement by market and non-market forces of a use of scarce resources which is more efficient in terms of human satisfaction is a purpose to which both economist and ecologist are professionally committed' (1990: 126). He did not reject growth as a social objective in his later work; he simply had to situate it in the context of the need to manage scarcity.

To understand Coombs' views on the proper relationship between markets and governments in the face of scarcity requires a consideration of three aspects of his thought. The first is the form of scarcity that Coombs thought Australians faced and consequently the environment they were to try to preserve. The second is his return to classical economic thinkers such as Thomas Malthus for principles that would allow for the management of scarcity. The third is his views on the way in which markets must be regulated and directed by governments in the management of scarcity. If markets required government intervention for stability and to ensure that they produced socially desirable outcomes, then governments had an even greater role to play when to these responsibilities was added that of ensuring that scarce resources were properly managed.

Scarcity

Coombs believed Australians who lived in the 1990s were living in 'an era of economic change dominated by increasing scarcities of natural resources' (1990: 104). Dealing with scarcity in Australia, in his view, required significant changes in economic and social policy. Major shifts in the dominant attitudes within the Australian community were also required if scarcity was to be managed effectively. The first shift that had to occur, in Coombs' view, was for all sections of society to accept the reality of scarcity. For 'until the community generally and the decision-makers of industry and commerce, as well as governments and their agencies, accept the facts of increasing scarcity, there is little prospect of reaching a consensus about environmental and resource policy' (1990: 103).

A necessary attitudinal change was for Australians to develop a new understanding of and approach to growth. Australians could continue to pursue growth, but they would 'do so at the expense of other values. Growth is indeed a jealous god' (Coombs 1970: 36). Those who could not lose their obsession with economic growth had to cease approaching it in terms of exploitation. Coombs looked for an understanding of growth in terms of efficiency. The most important change that was required was that growth no longer be understood as a product of population increase and further exploitation of natural resources. It had to come 'only from more effective use of known resources and from the development of new goods and services employing little or no scarce materials ... It derives from more effective use of capital, from increasing knowledge, from improved organisation and from imaginative entrepreneurship' (1990: 53–4).

Like Malthus, Coombs took population expansion to be the key to the problem of scarcity. Thus 'growth in human population causes more severe ecological imbalance than any other factor, since it presses us on to technological change at an exponentially increasing rate, in forms the ecological consequences of which we cannot hope to foresee'. Unlike Malthus, Coombs could not accept disease and warfare as legitimate constraints on population, but he argued that 'unless we find others as effective the prospects of ecological balance are remote indeed' (1978: 28).

A new (old) economics

A change in the basic approaches to economic theory and practice in Australia was fundamental to a transition to an economic system oriented to managing scarcity and based on a different conception of growth. At a theoretical level, the change required reassessing the indicators used to measure economic performance. At a practical level, it required developing an economic system that produced positive responses to ecologically sound choices.

Measures of economic performance

Coombs was highly critical of standard economic measures such as GDP, which provided measures of economic activity but not of the medium- to long-term economic consequences. Australians had adopted, in his view, 'an accounting system which records the running down of capital as a contribution to income' (1990: 102). Under such a system, outputs from extractive industries and other industries with environmentally damaging effects were treated as contributing to national wealth. The problem was that these activities 'progressively reduce the national wealth and its capacity to sustain the citizens of the future' (1990: 9). The result, Coombs argued, was that both governments and markets were responding to misleading signals. His solution was to develop new measures that, among other things, made clear the degree to which the proceeds of the sale of resources were used 'to create other capital assets, or how far their distribution represents a net reduction in the nation's capital assets' (1990: 9).

Standard cost-benefit analyses were inadequate, in Coombs' view, because they were limited to what could be readily calculated in monetary terms. Such analyses could not 'take account of the destruction of a wild life habitat or the direct enjoyment of aesthetic pleasures lost except where these are capable of being identified with and measured by revenue derived from tourist traffic' (1990: 92).

Coombs looked to newer techniques within economics that registered qualitative changes to the environment. These could facilitate the adoption of a new approach to economic decision-making based on new economic models. They would provide the basis for more rational economic decision-making. Coombs thought that 'the exploration of such theoretical models for resource management, particularly those involving environmental factors … will perhaps provide better guides to action than a simple cost-benefit analysis which … provides the basis for most such decisions in the public arena' (1990: 94–5).

Registering 'quality' of life

Problems with economics were not limited to deficiencies in economic measures used to shape public policy. Inadequacies could be found, in Coombs' view, at the very heart of market mechanisms. Markets could not register or respond to choices that reflected an appreciation of 'qualitative' improvement in life. They were only able to deal with choices about the possession and consumption of goods and services. As it became harder to find an untarnished natural environment, Coombs argued, 'the need to choose between direct experience of it and the goods it could be used to produce has become more urgent. At the margin there is a trade-off relationship between them but the market does not provide an effective mechanism by which preference for direct experience can influence the negotiation of the trade-off' (1990: 119).

Governments, markets and scarcity in Australia

Coombs' approach to tackling the problems associated with increasing scarcity does not represent a significant departure from his attitudes towards creating growth in Australian society. Market mechanisms remained significant because they responded to individuals' choices. Coombs thought that the price mechanism could also be used to promote the efficient use of scarce resources. Markets needed to be carefully and continuously managed, in his opinion, if they were to play a part in managing scarcity, for 'the market response to scarcities is likely to produce results incompatible with the best social aspirations of our society' (1990: 37).

Coombs believed that markets could not and should not be relied on for two reasons. First, they had already been influenced by decisions by previous Australian governments that amounted to giving away control over natural resources to the private sector. Second, to create an environment in which Australians were able to control the use of natural resources required interventions to reverse overseas ownership of these resources. One of the most important reasons for government control over natural resources was that they were collective property. This meant, Coombs argued, that their use ought to be controlled by representatives of the community, in other words by governments. In the end, for him, a community in which scarcity was properly managed was one in which 'resources industries are owned by their own citizens; they are able to finance the development of their own enterprises from their domestic savings; the technology employed in their enterprises is owned by their own members; and they are not "anxious" sellers on international markets' (1990: 10–11).

Using markets: the price mechanism

Coombs believed that the price mechanism was an essential means of dealing with scarcity. It meant leaving people to decide for themselves, within a given price framework, about their consumption patterns. In the face of resource depletion and pollution, then, 'the logical behaviour from an economist's point of view would be to increase the prices of the resources concerned or the offending process until their use was brought effectively under control' (1990: 44).

The price mechanism was not functioning adequately in Australia, Coombs contended, because the economic system was failing to protect the community from increasing scarcity. Creating an ecologically sound economic system was a matter of 'adapting the pattern of prices so that long-term equilibrium is achieved between the demand for and supply of scarce resources. But it is obvious that the present institutional pattern of our economic system is not going to produce such an adaptation' (1990: 45–6). He was particularly critical of the failure to use the price mechanism to control water use in one of the driest continents. Australians were extravagant in their use of water. Such extravagance 'could be restrained and more economical techniques stimulated if greater reliance were placed upon the price mechanism in its distribution' (1990: 84).

The price mechanism had to be continually monitored and modified to avoid an excessive burden for the use of natural resources being placed on those with limited wealth. He recommended the use of differential prices such that resource use to satisfy basic needs was relatively inexpensive, while price disincentives functioned to deter use in excess of that required for the satisfaction of basic needs. 'For water, electricity, petrol and other important components in the cost of living using exhaustible resources, it would be possible to provide a basic per capita quota at a price designed to limit the burden of scarcity on needs and to impose sharply graduated price increases for supplies above that level' (1990: 162).

Market mechanisms were not enough, however, because they failed to distinguish between people in different socio-economic positions. Indeed, the unequal ownership of scarce resources meant that an increasing advantage accrued to those who owned these resources. Scarcity, Coombs believed, would result in 'increasing affluence among proprietors of these resources but entrepreneurs in other industries will face mounting difficulties and there will be downward pressure on wage rates and low incomes. These effects are the inevitable result of relying solely on market prices to ration scarce resources' (1990: 104–5).

Taxation

Ensuring that the price mechanism was functioning effectively was only one of the roles that government had to take on to conserve natural resources. An even more important role was that of creating a taxation system designed to foster conservation and other ecologically desirable outcomes. Coombs saw this as a crucial role for government.

He proposed a number of measures that would be part of this taxation system. He argued that payroll tax should be abandoned in favour of a tax on non-renewable energy sources. He advocated 'a special capital asset replacement royalty or resources tax on the export of exhaustible resources' (1990: 14). He believed that a tax of this sort ought to be applied to 'enterprises engaged in agriculture, pastoralism, forestry, fishing, or other resource uses capable of depleting the productivity of the land or seas concerned' (1990: 15). The proceeds of this tax were not to be included in general revenue, but 'allocated to a special fund for investment in sustainable enterprises' (1990: 14).

> These measures to reduce the pressure of consumption on scarce resources should be supplemented by direct taxation at expenditure rather than at income. I do not mean indirect or value added taxes which are usually designed to shift the burden of taxation more on to lower and middle incomes. I mean a graduated percentage tax which falls on funds coming to the taxpayer from both income and the sale of assets, but allowing substantial rebates for the saving and investment of those funds in financial assets. (1990: 162–3)

Maintaining a sound economic, social, and natural environment was not simply a matter of impeding the operation of industries that relied on the use of exhaustible resources, produced pollution, or resulted in land degradation. In these instances, Coombs argued, 'it would be necessary to rely on complex regulations involving supervision and the imposition of penalties, or alternatively on excise taxes on the commodities produced by the offending processes, or preferably on the polluting effluents themselves' (1990: 48–9).

Public ownership

To those who argued that the use of resources should not be controlled by government, including by a taxation regime designed to promote conservation, Coombs replied that natural resources were collective assets. 'In Australian society all natural resources—land, forests, water and minerals—have belonged originally, at least since 1788, to the Crown; that is, to the community generally' (1990: 34–5).

One of the problems facing attempts to manage scarcity was that Australian governments had already ceded ownership of these resources to private enterprise, usually at minimal prices. Where governments could not regain ownership of these resources, Coombs argued that they had to charge for the use of these resources at appropriate rates.

'J. S. Mill pointed out that ownership of scarce resources constitutes a monopoly which cannot be prevented from existing. He also added … that the monopoly and, therefore, the rent derived from it can be held as a trust of the community' (1990: 33). Coombs believed that such a trust could be used 'to offset, to some extent at least, the adverse effects of scarcity on the distribution of wealth and income without impairing the effectiveness of the economic system' (1990: 33).

The alternative to this was the free market. The operation of the free market, in Coombs' view, would be disastrous for Australian society. Private ownership of scarce resources would result in a monopoly over these resources being held by some members of the community and would result in increasing disparities in income in Australia. Governments had to ensure that the community was protected from this eventuality. It was necessary to

> reassert, and where necessary re-establish, the public ownership of the natural resources of the continent, its minerals, forests, seas, soils, vegetation and wildlife; vest title in these resources in an authority independent of corporate and political control; empower that authority to grant licences for the use of these resources only on terms which will ensure their conservation, regeneration and sustainable development, and which will provide a rent determined by tender in a competitive market, so as to return to the authority a major proportion of any monopoly rent the resources extract from the consumer; empower the authority to carry out or support research programs designed to develop the potential of these resources on a sustainable basis. (1990: 16–17)

Conditions of scarcity could not be properly dealt with by an unregulated market in which the taxation system provided little by way of incentives to conservation and investment in sustainable industries and technologies. The only alternative was a system that involved significant government ownership, control over, and regulation of the use of scarce and exhaustible resources. Only in this way could a healthy economy and society emerge.

Coombs' proposals were and are somewhat radical. Nonetheless he thought them practical and evolutionary, rather than revolutionary. He argued that there was 'nothing inherently impracticable in these proposals. They would preserve an economic system based upon private (largely corporate) ownership of economic enterprises motivated by profit and the accumulation of personal and corporate wealth'. This new economic environment 'need not destroy the attractions of wealth nor require a monastic or Buddhist lifestyle among the community generally. They could be implemented without expropriation, revolution or even major constitutional reform' (1990: 19).

> The role of economists, in Coombs' view, was to protect the economy and to contribute to the effective management of scarcity. Their primary responsibility, in this context, was to ensure that increasing scarcity did not result in social dislocation and the checks on population that Malthus took to be the only ways to escape the effects of increasing scarcity. A changed conception of proper economic practice required abandoning the understanding of growth as a consequence of increasing exploitation of scarce resources. Australian society needed a new form of accounting that registered the use of scarce resources as the depletion of collective goods rather than as an increase in productivity. Managing scarcity required the use of the price mechanism to reflect the true present and future costs involved in the use of scarce resources. Most of all, however, managing scarcity required a government able to intervene in economic activity in such a way as to promote sound choices rather than enforce them.

Conclusion

While the objectives of fostering growth in postwar Australia and of dealing with scarcity produced different emphases in his writings, Coombs' basic principles remained largely unchanged. He was always convinced that governments had an important role to play in promoting economic and social outcomes. At no stage, however, did he reject markets as vital instruments for providing freedom and individual motivation. The primary goal was to produce a society in which prosperity was understood to involve more than simple increases in the production and possession of material goods. His notion of an ideal society involved a more rounded lifestyle:

> For my part I would like to live in a society where taxes fell only on the surplus above the national wage level; where education and health services were unambiguously free; where every citizen had the right and opportunity freely or cheaply to enjoy access to an unspoilt natural environment, to ample, convenient and diverse playing fields,

to the creative works in the arts of all ages, to the opportunity fully to develop natural talents—a society which would offer to its citizens a widely ranging choice of activities and enjoyment. (1970: 55)

To achieve this required the use of market forces that were controlled, directed, and otherwise shaped by governments.

While some differences in their positions resulted from the fact that Coombs addressed the problem of managing scarcity and Deakin did not, basic symmetry may be asserted with respect to their views on the proper relationship between governments and markets. Coombs' background in economics and the influence of Keynesian economic theories provided a very different background from which he made his recommendations, but both Deakin and Coombs outlined a significant role for government in determining economic and social outcomes.

Some of the differences between the approaches Coombs and Hewson took to basic economic issues related to the general orientation of the different economic theories on which they relied. Coombs relied on theories designed to address deflationary pressures, Hewson on theories designed to address inflationary pressures. This represents a more superficial difference than the real division between the approaches that Coombs and Hewson took to the relationship between governments and markets. Coombs, and for that matter Deakin, was positively disposed towards governments and sceptical about markets and their effects. Hewson, on the other hand, was positively disposed to markets and sceptical, if not hostile, to governments.

---

[1]   Coombs' initial enthusiasm for Keynesian theory was slightly diminished by subsequent experience. 'Unfortunately the very means employed to banish the evils of unemployment and depression have themselves had "side effects" … of profoundly disturbing character. Broadly the strategy to sustain total expenditure at an adequately high level has been to build a growth factor into the economy. Such growth requires private and public investment spending high enough to guarantee the required total. The risk of excessive expenditure has been contained by variable degrees of restraint through fiscal and monetary policies. Several unhappy sets of consequences flow from this strategy despite its general effectiveness for the immediate purposes for which it was designed. Firstly, it means that, since there will always be a slight and variable tendency to excess of expenditure, there will be a persistent upward trend in prices subsidising those profiting from production and commerce at the expense of wage earners, pensioners and others on fixed incomes … Secondly, the growth factor has been a function of increasing population (in Australia stimulated by migration), more complex technology and increasing use of natural (and in many cases inexhaustible) resources' (Coombs 1970: 21).

11

JOHN HEWSON
(1946–)

As a political philosophy, liberalism means, in its classical definition, the greatest possible freedom of the individual consistent with the equal freedom of all other individuals. In the abstract, everyone is in favour of greater freedom. But in reality, many are appalled by new freedoms which cut across old vested interests. (Hewson 1990a: 4)

John Robert Hewson was born in Sydney on 28 October 1946. He received a Bachelor of Economics, with honours, from the University of Sydney. He gained a doctorate from Johns Hopkins University, Baltimore, and worked for the International Monetary Fund in Washington as an economist in 1973 and 1974. He was an economics advisor to two federal treasurers, John Howard and Phillip Lynch, between 1975 and 1986. He was Professor of Economics and head of the School of Economics at the University of New South Wales between 1978 and 1987. From 1985 to 1987 he was executive director of the Macquarie Bank. In 1987 he was elected to federal parliament for the Liberal Party of Australia (in the seat named for William Wentworth). Between 1990 and 1994 he was leader of the parliamentary Liberal Party and, as a result, Leader of the Opposition.

John Hewson's ideas are representative of a fundamental shift in the form of liberalism articulated by key actors in Australian society in the 1980s and 1990s. Hewson's approach to the relationship between governments and markets became the dominant approach in public discourse in this period. This change in the conception of the proper relationship between governments and markets was central to an ideological shift within the Liberal Party of Australia which was, as Kelly

(1992: 35) has suggested, 'a revolt … against the Deakin-inspired Australian Settlement of the early post-Federation period which, in the post-war context, was embodied in the Menzies-McEwen-Fraser heritage'. In this reconceptualisation of the proper relationship between governments and markets, markets were systematically preferred to governments in any context in which a choice between the two was available. The idea that governments had an obligation to intervene in the economy to control and otherwise affect the consequences of market forces had little place in the new consensus.

This characterisation of Hewson's conception of the proper relationship between governments and markets is discussed in three sections. In the first, general principles of the relationship between governments and markets are outlined. The second deals with Hewson's assessment of the economic and social problems that developed as a consequence of the improper relationship between governments and markets that existed in Australia. This discussion sets the scene for the third section, which is an examination of Hewson's strategies for correcting the relationship between governments and markets in Australia in the 1990s and beyond. In short, Hewson advocated a greatly reduced role for governments in controlling decision-making and other aspects of individual and corporate behaviour. The result was a significantly increased role for markets, especially international markets.

Markets and Governments

Fundamental to Hewson's approach was his positive attitude to markets and his negative view of governments. His belief that national markets were of decreasing importance relative to international markets magnified his sense of the limited possibilities for government action. Indeed, he looked to international market forces to provide the impetus required to change Australian economic policy and practice. International market forces would also require, if they did not force, a change in popular attitudes to work and the economy.

Little scope was available to governments, in Hewson's view, to resist the imperatives of the international economy. Politicians and bureaucrats could either accept that the international economic order required freer markets and smaller government, or allow the country for which they were responsible to suffer economic and social decline. This decline in the capacity of those in government to control domestic economic outcomes was not something to be lamented, however, as

Hewson preferred markets to governments in all contexts. Free markets were, in his view, the principal means through which a better society was created: 'I do not believe that smaller government and freer markets will produce a perfect world—just that anything else will be even less perfect' (Hewson 1990a: 7).

The following material deals with Hewson's belief in markets, his negative attitude to government, and his sense that an international economy was developing which required changed practices on the part of those in government, businesspeople, and workers. It gives a sense of the fundamental principles that conditioned Hewson's assessment of the malaise into which the Australian economy and society had fallen and provides a basis for an explanation of the policies, attitudes, and practices he saw as necessary to overcome this malaise.

The virtues of markets

Hewson's liberalism was characterised by an absolute commitment to markets as the only viable means for providing a sound system of incentives and disincentives to individuals, corporations, and governments. Markets were superior because they were more efficient, more flexible, and more responsive to people's wants, and because they stimulated initiative and discipline. This is not to say that Hewson had no sense of market failure, but that he was convinced that markets were so superior to any other form of economic organisation that failure was not the problem others might have taken it to be.[1]

Promoting morality

The superiority of markets was not simply in their economic consequences, in Hewson's view, as they also provided the basis for a superior society. 'Moral community and economic freedom ... are closely related to each other. Properly functioning markets are based on voluntary co-operation and de-centralised decision-making, they ... create the only conditions in which a moral community can emerge and be sustained.' Thus while 'economic freedom does not guarantee morality ... it fosters it and ... requires it' (Liberal Party of Australia 1991: 27).[2]

Efficiency

The primary advantage of markets, in Hewson's view, was that they resulted in efficiency. 'I believe that the market is the best—indeed, the only—means of ensuring and testing economic efficiency' (1990: 6). While he rarely spelt out what he meant by efficiency, it probably reflected the standard construction of efficiency within economics. Efficiency, as economists use it, takes two main forms: technical and allocative. Technical efficiency 'exists when a firm, an industry, or an economy is attaining maximum output by means of the best use of available resources'. Allocative efficiency 'exists when the organisation not only has achieved technical efficiency but also is satisfying consumer preferences by producing the combination of goods and services consumers want with their current earnings' (Shim and Siegel 1995: 119–20). Both of these forms of efficiency seem implied in Hewson's use of the term.

Choice

One of the most important aspects of allocative efficiency is that it satisfies consumer demand. Markets were the most desirable forms of economic organisation because they offered the greatest possibility of satisfying consumers. Markets were superior to all other forms of economic organisation, in Hewson's view, because they continually offered choice. 'Liberals believe in market and market competition because markets are the way that millions of individuals make the choices that best suit them. Politics offers people one choice every three years. Markets offer people almost limitless choice as often as they like it' (Hewson 1992b: 12).

Choices about goods or services were not the only ones markets made available to individuals. Markets also provided choices on the sorts of work that people did and allowed them to change or improve their life situations. 'A freer and more competitive market system creates a more equal, fairer society—a society where people can work hard and improve the standard of living for themselves and for their family' (Hewson 1992b: 12).

Discipline

Increased choice, in Hewson's opinion, was only one of the positive effects of markets. They also enforced discipline on individuals and the corporate sector by rewarding sound decisions and punishing mistakes. Hewson drew a parallel between newly deregulated financial markets and the Australian Golf Club course. Like the golf course, these markets 'now have a real capacity to punish a bad shot. And it's no good standing back and saying that the course, or those markets, are irrational. Certainly, you might think so. You might even lose control of your mouth for a time, as they cursorily deal with your best shots. But you live with the discipline they provide' (1985a: 109).

The discipline of markets also operated, and was extremely valuable, at the government level. That is, market discipline would bring governments to adopt what, in Hewson's view, were sound decisions. 'The decision to float the Australian dollar was wise', he argued, 'not least for the sort of discipline it will ultimately impose on this and any other government. It does presuppose the adoption and maintenance of a stable and realistic stance and mix of macro economic policies' (1986f: 82).

The vices of governments

If Hewson could say little against markets, he could say almost nothing for governments. Whereas once he had had some faith in government, this had long since ceased to be the case. In the 1960s he told an interviewer: 'we were all going to go out and get into government and fix all the world's problems. It wasn't until the 1970s that we started to realise that a lot of the world's problems were in fact being created by government' (quoted in Abjorensen 1993: 52).[3] Governments did not work, in Hewson's view, because they inhibited initiative and were unable to generate and implement policies required by the prevailing economic and social circumstances. These were not the only problems with governments, but they give some indication of Hewson's predisposition against governments. Hewson argued that 'Liberals start with the assumption that people know best. We have a disposition in favour of people and against government' (1992b: 12).

Inhibiting initiative

One of the main problems with governments, in Hewson's view, was that they tended to frustrate individual initiative and generally interfere with people's capacity to pursue their goals. 'The problem with modern government is that it is still too busy giving people what they think they want, rather than what they really need. And in doing so, it can easily destroy the self respect and self-confidence that people need most' (1990a: 14). Government involvement made people less able to look after their interests by impeding free choice and leading people to become overly dependent on governments. Governments should not seek to resolve problems in people's lives, 'first, because experience demonstrates that the bigger government gets, the more problems it creates; and second, because people with all their problems solved for them could hardly lead satisfied and fulfilled lives' (1990a: 8). Smaller government was preferable, in Hewson's view, because 'people are best left to shape their own destiny' (1990: 6).[4]

Individuals were not the only ones who suffered when government intervention in society and the economy exceeded a minimal level. Business also suffered when governments interfered with market forces. Government intervention in the mining industry provided 'a classic illustration of how government can impede human progress. From our earliest colonial governors we had examples of their attempts to discourage the search for gold because it would create social instability. Pre-war governments prevented the export of iron ore because it could jeopardise the steel industry. All-too-current governments smother vital projects in red, green and black tape' (Hewson 1992d: 41).

A further problem with government intervention into the economy and society was that extensive taxation was required to fund those interventions. According to Hewson, the taxation system necessary to support government intervention reduced incentives for business to expand and to create employment. If businesses were going to employ more people, Hewson argued, governments had to eliminate the 'mountain of taxes … used … to fund programs. That batch of hidden taxes needs to be abolished if business is to get on and do the job … of giving Australians the opportunities of employment that they really want' (1991c: 3572).

Failure to make sound decisions

Governments, in Hewson's view, were also a problem because of their inability to produce policies appropriate to the economic circumstances that prevail in a community. Modern governments were unable to serve the interests of the people, partly because they were captives of special interests and partly because they were afraid to adopt initiatives in case these proved unpopular. Governments were more likely to service vocal or influential minorities and were unable to adjust policy quickly to suit changing circumstances. They tended to ignore longer-term social benefits in the face of shorter-term political costs. Politicians had one eye on special interests and the other on the opinion polls. The result was that they failed to pay attention to the needs of the community more generally and everyone suffered.

The desire to maintain electoral popularity had an important effect on the capacity of governments to pursue effective economic and social policies. Governments changed economic policy because of popular opinion and not, according to Hewson, because of sound economic principles. They adopted policies that were 'subject to day-to-day or week-to-week or month-to-month manipulation for short-term political gain' (1991a: 5).

While Hewson believed that good economics was good politics, he believed that governments tended to ignore this basic principle. He told what he took to be the salutary tale of a former prime minister, Malcolm Fraser, who became 'the main stumbling block to rational economic policy'. Fraser, in Hewson's view, provided a lesson that his successors ought to heed. He 'became so concerned about the electoral consequences of his decisions that he stopped taking decisions and ensured the electoral consequence he most feared' (1986b: 101).

Unfortunately, the problem with governments was more than a preoccupation with electoral outcomes, to the detriment of sound economic policy. Governments went awry because they developed too close an association with specific interests in the community. These relationships precluded a concern with the general interest and impeded the government's capacity to respond to other interest groups. Hewson argued that the main reason for

> much of the expansion and distortion of government has been the desire of private or special interests—businesses, producers, trade unions, professions, and bureaucracies—to entrench in law, in regulation and in government practice a privileged position for themselves. In persuading government to guarantee a trade monopoly or market share, in imposing restrictions on trade, in making membership of unions compulsory, in gaining a special status within the tax system, in locking in to government grants available to a limited few, the economic freedom of many others has been restricted. As a result, incentives have been undermined, competition has been weakened, and inefficiency in the use of our national resources entrenched. Big government has given power to the few, and the corporate State where decisions are made by big unions, big business and big bureaucracy has been the inevitable outcome of a century's restriction on freedom. (Hewson 1992b: 12)[5]

Hewson's experience as a policy adviser gave him a particular perspective on the contribution of the bureaucracy to the failure of governments. His account of the factors that lay behind government failure in the area of economic policy reflects his sense of government as a battleground of insiders seeking to further their own causes. For him, 'the official and other advisers ... are usually running their own selfish games strategies, probably in the context of a host of other issues, all designed to get the government to take their view' (1986c: 73).

Governing in an international economy

Hewson's preference for markets over government must also be understood in light of his belief that an international economy was developing which was, for the most part, beyond the control of national governments. His work on eurocurrency markets led him to conclude that the international economy was largely ungovernable. In this context, good government involved responding to international market forces or imperatives. Governments could do nothing to resist them, in Hewson's view, and those in government had to understand that they were no longer fully in control of their national economy.

Eurocurrency markets

Hewson's understanding of the development of the international economy was deeply influenced by his work on the so-called eurocurrency markets, which he studied for his doctoral dissertation and at the International Monetary Fund. Eurocurrency markets 'are a group of international money markets where financial intermediaries (largely commercial banks) borrow and lend currencies outside (or "offshore") to the country of issue of those currencies' (Hewson 1976: 32). Eurocurrency markets were an important marker of the end of governmental control over international trade and commerce. This was not simply a function of the collapse of the Bretton Woods agreement[6] but reflected the development of technologies and philosophies that resulted in the full development of an international economy.

The international economy

Eurocurrency markets represented one part of a much broader phenomenon. They indicated the existence of transnational economic relationships and phenomena that had not previously existed. To understand eurocurrency markets fully, Hewson argued, they should 'be viewed in the broader context of the general process of internationalisation of economic and financial activities that has taken place in the last two decades or so. The development of the Eurocurrency markets is, therefore, just one aspect of a more fundamental development—the growing interdependence of the world economy' (1976: 40).[7]

The development of a more fully integrated world economy was not simply an economic phenomenon; it was a political phenomenon, and its significance needed to be understood by national policy-makers. The most important thing national policy-makers had to understand about the international economy was that they had a limited capacity to determine, or even exert significant control over, national economic outcomes. Hewson and Sakakibara examined the question of whether governments, singly or in combination, could control eurocurrency markets. They concluded that any attempts by national governments to exert control over this type of market 'in the highly integrated and interdependent world economy ... are likely to be futile. For unless the authorities imposing the controls are prepared to control all transactions (trade and capital) the direct impact of particular controls is likely to be offset by variations in other items of the balance of payments' (Hewson and Sakakibara 1975a: 399).

A clear example of the process, and a sign of things to come, occurred in October and November 1985 when pressure from overseas investors forced a change of government policy and Reserve Bank practice. This was a salutary lesson, in Hewson's view, on 'the fragility of business and market confidence'. According to Hewson, the weakness of the Australian dollar had led many Japanese investors to consider withdrawing from the Australian bond market. This would have resulted in $1 to $1.5 billion being withdrawn from that market. 'Recognition of the damage of such a portfolio shift was an important factor, if not the most important factor, contributing to the decisive tightening of monetary policy and the noticeably more active intervention in support of the $A by the Reserve Bank since that time' (1985b: 97).

That a government had its monetary policy determined by financial markets could not be treated, Hewson argued, as an isolated phenomenon. This was the way governments had to learn to conduct themselves. 'The international monetary system is evolving; understandings about appropriate policies and policy co-ordination (both domestic and exchange-market) are being forged' (1983: 29). As Wallace (1993: 99) put it, eurocurrency markets 'pointed to the future, to a world where international financial markets would make government policy fit in with them rather than vice versa'.

The most important lesson was that national governments had to accept the policy 'discipline' of this newly developing international economy, especially international financial markets. The existence of this international economy was a function of the collapse of Bretton Woods, and no similar agreement was likely. Some form of control might be initiated as a result of cooperation among national governments. The reality, however, was that national governments were relatively powerless and had to understand their role as one of responding to, and adjusting policy in the face of, the international economic order.

To understand Hewson's conception of the proper role of governments requires understanding his belief in markets, his lack of faith in governments, and his view that governments were losing control of the domestic economy as the international economy developed. Markets were desirable, in Hewson's view, because they promoted initiative and efficiency. Governments were to be treated with caution, if not outright antipathy. They acted as the antithesis of markets: stifling initiative, undermining economic efficiency, constantly being enmeshed in deals designed to promote the interests of the few at the expense of the many. No matter what one thought of national governments, however, an international economy was developing that was largely beyond their control, and this would call the policy tune.

The Australian Malaise

These general problems with governments manifested themselves in particular ways in Australia. In Hewson's view, Australia's current economic and financial difficulties were a result of 'recent short term "cyclical" pressures and a number of long term structural problems and trends … Many are, in large measure, the direct result of the inadequacies of the policy responses of a succession of post war governments' (1987: 31). Hewson believed that federal and state governments had failed to capitalise on Australia's significant advantages relative to other countries. The result of these failures was that Australians were faced with economic decline, when they could easily be relatively prosperous. In Hewson's assessment, Australia was bedevilled by a general lack of competitiveness that resulted from tariff and other forms of protection, the over-provision of welfare, and problems with its labour market.

Australia was seriously under-performing economically and socially. Instead of increasing prosperity, Australians in the 1980s and 1990s were faced with a lower standard of living that was unlikely to rise in the middle to long term. This might not be a problem if it reflected Australia's potential, but it did not. In the end, the lack of performance in what could otherwise be a prosperous country was, for Hewson, simply embarrassing. In his view, Australia 'should be back up towards the top of the heap in terms of standards of living … We used to be a major trading nation, we have slipped off the pace there. A lot of that has come for a lot of reasons, a lot of bad policy' (quoted in Abjorensen 1993: 197).

Lack of competitiveness

The main problem with the Australian economy was that Australian industry was losing the capacity to compete with overseas rivals. The three main causes of this were tariff protection, welfare and, by far the most important, problems with the labour market. Clearly these factors operated together and interacted, but each made its own contribution to the problem. Government had a direct role in tariff protection and welfare, and played an important part in supporting a deficient labour market.

Tariff protection

Hewson argued that the system of tariff protection favoured those companies that did not compete overseas and penalised those that did; Australia had built up a system in which tariffs penalised the efficient and internationally competitive. He believed that those businesses that were not seeking to service overseas markets were holding back those that were. His approximation was that 20 per cent of Australian companies were seeking to be internationally competitive, while 80 per cent were not. Outward-looking companies, in his view, were struggling 'as the comfortable 80 per cent increasingly constrains them. So all the waterfront inefficiencies, all the domestic transportation inefficiencies, the cost disadvantages of the telecommunications system, the role of government—it's all right for the 80 per cent. But it is constraining the other 20 per cent that has to go offshore' (quoted in Duffy 1990: 14). The problem with protection was clear in an increasingly internationalised environment: it created a comfort zone in which inward-looking, self-serving attitudes and policies inhibited innovation, efficiency, and engagement with the international economy.

Welfare

The counterpart to protection, for Hewson, was welfare. Whereas protection operated to encourage business people to look to government and not to rely on their own abilities, so welfare encouraged individuals to do the same. The economic malaise in which Australians found themselves was exacerbated, in his opinion, by the culture of dependence created by an excessive welfare system. He argued that Australians were being encouraged to believe that governments had the responsibility and capacity to 'take care' of them without their having to do very much for themselves. They were developing what Hewson and a number of other commentators described as a welfare mentality.

Hewson believed that Australia had 'an unbelievably large social welfare system' (1985c: 93). The problem with such a system was that people no longer sought to look after themselves but relied on government to meet their needs. The result, he argued, was an attitudinal shift that undermined feelings of self-worth. Labor governments 'go about building a social security and welfare structure that in time locks people into a situation in which they cannot have a job or do not want to have a job. They change people's attitudes, they change their livelihood' (1991e: 2080). The result was 'a welfare system which makes it easier to put out your hand than to help yourself or to lift your game' (1990c: 1484).

The problem with social security, for Hewson, lay in the word 'security'. Security created an environment within which ambition was stunted and risks avoided. This resulted in a situation in which many, if not most, people failed to achieve their potential. 'The people who built this country had big dreams and if many of them failed', Hewson argued, 'we are much the better for their efforts … If they had wanted security they would never have left London or Melbourne. If our distant past shows that hardships can build a nation, more recent experience shows that comfort risks producing a society of under-achievers' (quoted in Abjorensen 1993: 198). Social security was central to the creation of a society of under-achievers and in particular to creating an environment in which a powerful work ethic did not operate.

Labour market deficiencies

The third, and for Hewson most important, reason for the lack of international competitiveness in Australian industry was the industrial relations system. The main problem, he argued, was that wages reflected neither productivity nor a firm's capacity to pay. The award system meant that wage increases were not linked to agreements on the part of workers to increase productivity (which meant they were not linked to decreases in the cost of producing goods or providing services). This made Australian products and services less competitive in the international environment. Hewson argued that Australia 'cannot have full [wage] indexation when none of our trading partners have anything like it. We also need a system where we can have significantly different wage adjustments in different industries—specifically in industries that are declining. We should probably see significant cuts in nominal wages' (1986a: 114).

The main stumbling block to labour market adjustment was the craft union structure, 'which is … economically inefficient, primarily because it fails to explicitly recognise differences in economic performance between different industries and ultimately between different firms in the same industries' (Hewson 1986d: 93). At the very peak of this structure was the Australian Council of Trade Unions (ACTU), which was responsible for many of the problems with Australia's economic performance. Hewson argued that 'the key issue at the present time concerns our need to increase our rate of production, to increase our productivity, to increase our exports—to trade our way out of our economic difficulties. Yet in every key area in which a decision needs to be taken the ACTU effectively blocks that decision' (1989a: 764).

The essence of the problem, said Hewson, was that industrial relations had gone 'out of the hands of management and into those of the ACTU and industrial bureaucrats. This substantial inability to manage their workforce is a key explanation of our firms' low labour productivity, the resultant reluctance to invest in manufacturing and the flight of some important business off-shore' (Liberal Party of Australia 1991: 20). If managers could be freed from the power of unions and the ACTU, they could make decisions based on sound economic principles. They would not be placed in a situation in which they could not control wages and conditions.

Hewson looked on the relationship between governments and markets that had developed in Australia as a failure. The system had promoted an inward-looking approach to economic issues that had resulted in a fundamental lack of competitiveness in Australia. This inward orientation had been promoted by protection and was expressed by a welfare mentality in which people thought they did not have to strive for themselves and their families. One of the major causes of this lack of competitiveness was that trade unions were able to pursue agendas that were in their interests but inimical to the national interest. Australians were, in Hewson's view, 'left with a society where there is very little incentive left to work, little incentive left to look after yourself, increasing restriction on competition, increasing centralisation of Government and increasing reliance by Government on things like compulsion rather than choice' (1991b: 33).

Reconstituting the Relationship between Governments and Markets

Turning Australia around, in Hewson's opinion, required a complete reconstitution of the relationship between governments and markets. The first step was to make government smaller. Then a new economic climate had to be created. This was to be based on an attitudinal shift in almost all sections of the Australian community, but particularly among politicians, bureaucrats, business leaders, and workers. People, whether they were inside or outside government, had to change their expectations of governments, and governments had to make themselves less of a burden on business and society.

The reforms Hewson advocated were major and involved change in most aspects of the economy and society in Australia. His reform agenda meant 'no tinkering at the edges, no little marginal changes, no playing bits and pieces here, but an overall reform agenda with the specific objective of rebuilding the economy from the bottom up, brick by brick' (1991d: 379). No other option was available but the pursuit of fundamental economic reform, for 'Australia has no choice but to face up to its very vulnerable situation and to commit itself to a reform agenda that will restore a competitive economy and rising standards of living' (1993: 11).

Creating a productive climate
Attitudinal shift

If governments had any role to play in Hewson's reform agenda, it was to lead businesspeople, consumers, employers, and employees to adopt a new mindset. Governments had to encourage these people to free themselves of attitudes that had resulted in Australia's inability to compete in the world markets. They had 'to make fundamental changes in Australia. We have to break the mould, change attitudes, change values and change policies' (1991c: 3583). They had to create an environment in which people were more independent and looked less and less to government in all aspects of their lives. Hewson wanted 'an alternative society in which the individual plays a much greater part, where individuals are left very much to themselves, beyond those who need genuine assistance from government' (1991e: 2080).

The changes Hewson advocated would have two main effects: they would increase individual initiative and produce a competitive attitude, and they would encourage business to look to the international arena as its avenue for growth. Hewson saw this project as one of 'rebuilding a sense of individual effort, independence, competition in private enterprise, in simple terms rebuilding a bit of a business ethic in this country' (1991b: 34).

Business leaders

A central element of Hewson's project was to bring business leaders to change their attitudes and practices. They were no longer to seek tariff protection and other barriers to competition from goods produced overseas that insulated them from the realities of market discipline. Australians 'just can't afford to keep the subsidies going. We just can't afford to promote inefficiency instead of efficiency—we just can't settle for anything less than best international practice' (quoted in Abjorensen 1993: 194).

They also needed to make sacrifices to demonstrate their commitment to change. One of the policies Hewson promoted during the 1993 federal election campaign was a 10 per cent pay cut for government ministers. He argued that 'if business leaders and others in positions of influence in Australia were to respond similarly, we would go a very long way to building a fairer Australia and … developing a more genuine sense of partnership that is fundamental to making the sorts of changes we need to make' (1992a: 8).

Business leaders also needed to change their attitudes. This included engaging with workers and interacting with them in a more cooperative manner. Hewson could not understand employers' concerns about dealing with their workers directly, rather than via systems of conciliation and arbitration. He believed that most of them 'would find the benefits of getting closer to their workforce in the process of reaching an enterprise agreement preferable to the financial chaos that they have had to endure with third-party wage settlements that are totally inapplicable to their own circumstances' (1992c: 52).

Hewson supported the idea of involving workers in certain management decisions. He thought this would encourage them to see their company's situation from their employers' perspective. He argued that 'there's nothing better than a deal between the employee and his employer which looks at the circumstances of the company or the plant and works out an appropriate way of paying people [and] under what conditions should they work' (quoted in Sykes 1992: 38). He wanted a greater sense of partnership between workers and employers. He wanted to get them 'to sit down together at the workplace to negotiate the terms and conditions—a common shared sense of direction for their company, just as we all have to have a common shared sense of the direction of the nation' (1991c: 3582).

Changing workers' attitudes

Business leaders were not the only ones who had to change the way they approached industrial relations. Workers also had to change. Indeed, Hewson tended to make this point more frequently than the one about business leaders. He believed that the unions had encouraged poor attitudes among workers. The insulation from competition given by protection had resulted in an overly powerful union movement. In Hewson's view, 'one of the main reasons for the consolidation of union power over the decades has been that they have been able to operate behind high tariff walls and have not had to face the reality of competition' (quoted in Abjorensen: 195).

Hewson argued that a national system of arbitration and conciliation was a mistake. He thought that workers had to organise at the enterprise level. Enterprise unions were 'the only way that we will get internationally competitive wage outcomes which tie wages to performance and genuinely protect the interests of workers' (1990c: 1488). Enterprise-based negotiations, in his opinion, made it 'easier to achieve rewards more readily matched to performance, and employees and employers can look after each other's benefits' (1990b: 304).

Reducing the burden of government

Changing attitudes among major economic actors was only part of the recipe that Hewson advocated. Central to his strategy was making government smaller by reducing its role in society. The first thing that was required of politicians, bureaucrats, and voters was to regain a sense of the limited capacities of governments. The true role for government was not to undermine choice and responsibility but to facilitate them. A significant reduction in the level of regulation was required. So too were lower tax rates, and a change in the form of taxation from indirect taxes to a consumption tax. The result of these reforms would be that business was left free to grow, produce jobs, and create greater material wealth in society. Welfare was to be retained only for the genuinely needy.

Reducing the role of governments

Hewson's main complaint about governments in Australia was that they did too much. This meant that they cost too much and provided services better provided through markets. In Hewson's view, governments had 'to trim itself back … to step out of some functions and cut quite a lot of its own expenditure. It will have to be prepared to face the reality of contracting out a lot of services which it knows it can't provide as efficiently as the private sector can'. That governments were inefficient managers of the enterprises they owned meant that 'privatisation is the fundamental part of what has got to be done in reducing the role and influence of Government' (1991b: 34).

Hewson looked to a new environment 'in which individuals have an elevated position, one in which they are left to make choices for themselves, one in which the role of government is significantly reduced, one in which the reliance on centralised control is gradually broken down' (1991e: 2080). However, 'privatisation of government activities should not be seen as a substitute for restraint on government expenditure which should be seen as a desirable end in itself' (1986e: 83).

Hewson believed that economic improvement would play a significant part in creating an environment in which the less well off were supported. 'By improving economic management you do a lot to improve your capacity to look after the disadvantaged, the needy and so on' (quoted in Burrell 1989: 12). Hewson believed that governments tended to do too much in the area of social security, mainly because of a failure to distinguish between genuine cases, in which support was needed, and those cases in which people received funding they did not deserve. He thought that social security payments could be better targeted: 'we probably pay out too much money to people who really shouldn't have the benefits to that extent and the genuinely needy don't get enough' (quoted in Burrell 1989: 13).

Reducing regulation

One of the most important things that government was to do less of was regulation and other forms of interference in the conduct of business in Australia. Without this regulation, Hewson argued, individual initiative would be encouraged, and market forces could function properly. Finance sector deregulation was a start.

> But why stop there? The financial sector is not the only one that has been burdened, distorted and noticeably inefficient as a result of regulation and excessive or ill-conceived government intervention. What about the labour market? It is probably the most excessively regulated, excessively legislated and noticeably inefficient 'market' of all. And what about our goods or trading markets that, in general, labor [*sic*] … under excessive regulations, tariffs and other non-tariff barriers,

not to mention the vast array of legislation, incentives, subsidies, concessions and implicit or explicit taxes and other forms of government involvement and regulation that disadvantages some industries' markets more than others. (1984: 116)

Changing the taxation system

The taxation system also had to change, Hewson argued, so that government ceased to rely on a combination of indirect taxes and income tax and relied instead on a retail or consumption tax. He advocated the 'full introduction of a retail turnover tax … or a VAT to raise a very big sum, with a substantial corresponding … reduction in personal income taxes' (1984: 85). One of the effects of such a change was 'that individuals will be given money back in their pockets and they can then decide how much tax they pay by what they buy' (1990c: 1486).

The main reason that he supported this change in the taxation system was that he believed it would make Australian business more competitive in world markets. In order to make it competitive, it was necessary to 'develop an alternative tax system which cuts business costs, which abolishes certain key taxes and charges on the business community, which … lowers a lot of the infrastructure costs and other disadvantages on our business community in Australia' (1992e: 3709). He saw a broad-based goods and services tax as 'a fundamental element of becoming internationally competitive as a business community'. Introducing such a tax would allow for the abolition of a variety of indirect taxes which increased production costs. 'That is why we will not only introduce a broad-based goods and services tax … but also go ahead and abolish other major cost imposts on business, like payroll tax, petrol excise, sales tax' (1992e: 3709).

Central to Hewson's formula for economic recovery was reducing the role of government. This involved a reduction in government regulation, a reduction in the activities in which government was engaged, and a change to the taxation system. One effect of these reductions would be to increase the scope for individual initiative. Another, and probably more important effect, would be to make Australian businesses more competitive in international markets. This would be particularly realised as a result of a shift in the taxation system away from income and indirect taxation to a goods and services tax.

Conclusion

When this change in the role of government was combined with a change in attitudes in Australia, particularly among business people and workers, the results, in Hewson's view, would be spectacular. Australians would throw off their welfare dependency, cease to rely on protection, and participate in a more competitive economic environment. They would change their expectations of government. Those in government would see themselves as facilitators and not controllers of economic processes. The main thing Australians had to realise was that governments were ineffective and markets effective.

The changes that Hewson advocated clearly reflected his general economic principles: that markets were a superior form of economic and social coordination, that governments were generally inefficient and corrupt, and that Australia had to face the reality of an international economy in which it was a competitor. It was not an effective competitor, Hewson believed, because the social, industrial and business climates that had developed were inward-looking and not viable in the new situation. If Australia was to have a healthy society it required a fundamentally changed economic environment, and basic to achieving this was a substantial reduction in the role of government and an increased reliance on markets.

Hewson's views on the proper relationship between governments and markets can be seen as a direct refutation of the principles that Deakin and Coombs supported. Deakin had had a central role in the systems of protection and conciliation and arbitration that Hewson sought to dismantle. Coombs had participated in the creation of an active interventionist government that took up a leading role in the economy and community. Hewson sought to reverse this to make markets central and governments peripheral. In rejecting much about Australian society and economic policies, Hewson rejected many of the principles that Deakin and Coombs had advocated and applied.

---

[1] 'But even where markets underprovide social services, and therefore governments have an important role to play, there is still a need for market processes and discipline in the implementation of that role for government. Moreover, the initial response to market failure should always be to see what can be done to correct or improve the operation of the market—government intervention should always be a last resort' (Hewson 1992b: 12).

[2] While *Fightback!* was a policy document to which many people contributed, I agree with Abjorensen's view that the '*Fightback!* package ... represents ... the culmina-

tion and distillation of more than twenty years work of a model Hewson has had in his head which has been constantly reworked, redefined and tested' (Abjorensen 1993: 20).

3   According to Abjorensen (1993: 63), Hewson's experiences at the IMF shaped his thinking about governments. 'Case studies on which he worked, such as that of runaway inflation in Brazil, convinced him that government intervention was the cause, not the remedy, of a whole range of economic ills.'

4   'Free markets work because individual people, co-operating peacefully and voluntarily through markets, can achieve much that politicians and bureaucrats cannot achieve using compulsion and direction' (Liberal Party of Australia 1991: 26).

5   Hewson seemed to assume that governments would always be captured and corrupted by 'special interests' of 'the few'. Other Australian liberals, such as Higgins, Deakin, and Coombs, did not assume this. They might have responded, then, that Hewson was unfairly treating a particular problem with some Australian governments as a general problem with all governments, or at least all Australian governments.

6   'The United Nations Monetary and Financial Conference at Bretton Woods, New Hampshire, 1–22 July 1944, established the International Monetary Fund (IMF) and the International Bank for Reconstruction and Development (the World Bank) as a cornerstone of a system of international cooperation for orderly balance of payments adjustments and post-war reconstruction' (Cate 1997: 51).

7   Hewson went further and argued that the expansion of 'Eurocurrency markets, as well as the activities of other non-financial multi-national corporations, has served as a vehicle for the transition of the world economy from the essentially controlled regime of the 1950s to the essentially free regime of international transactions today' (1976: 40–1).

Conclusion

This is not a conclusion

Readers who may be looking for some summation of the nature and state of liberalism in Australia will be disappointed. This is not a conclusion in the sense that it summarises an argument that I have been developing throughout this book. I have reached no conclusions about liberalism in Australia. The first reason that I will not attempt this here is that I have not designed the book in such a way that it would provide a basis for such a conclusion. I have attempted to provide separate discussions of ten thinkers whom I have designated as liberals. The book is not constructed in a chronological order and the various parts are not intended to dovetail into a framework from which pronouncements on the nature and status of liberalism in Australia may be delivered.

The need for more work

A number of other reasons have also led to this refusal of the position of authority with respect to liberalism in Australia. The first is that more work needs to be done to provide anyone with a perspective from which they can draw conclusions of the type that might be sought. So little sustained and careful work has been done, in terms of actually documenting political thought in Australia, that no one ought to be acknowledged as in a position of being able to make pronouncements of a conclusive sort.

That so little work has been done in making the ideas produced by liberals in Australia available to Australians led me to believe that the more important step was to make those ideas more readily available for study and reflection. My decision to rely heavily on quotations from the thinkers' works was also a reflection of this desire to make their ideas more accessible than they have hitherto been. A desire to simply present the ideas of another can never be completely satisfied, but using this as a primary motivation made it necessary to consciously resist any attempt to provide some over-arching argument that made sense of liberalism in Australia.

More than one story

Another reason that no story of liberalism in Australia has been presented here is a reflection of my sense of the very real dangers associated with providing over-arching accounts that purport to summarise an intellectual position in a country (even when it is a summary of one with a history as short as that of liberalism in Australia). I must admit to a deep scepticism about any project that requires providing an account of social phenomena that deals with millions of people and spans several generations, each of which was affected by different domestic and world events.

Certainly, this can be an interesting and entertaining project. It is an activity, though, that seems better suited to more informal occasions, such as cafes, restaurants, and hotels. Perhaps it might be formalised into discussions among expert panels or provide the subject matter for radio programs, television documentaries, or newspaper columns. All of these venues provide important and valuable contexts within which generalisations, and even over-generalisations, are necessary for conversation. Generalisations have to be handled carefully, in my view, and are simply inappropriate in some contexts.

Why a conclusion?

All of this might lead some readers to wonder why I have included a chapter in this book entitled 'Conclusion'. Lee Cameron Macdonald (1968: 606) has summed up the main reason in his *Western Political Theory*. 'Why conclude at all then? One concludes out of a decent respect for all that has not been said and all that might have been said. One concludes, in other words, in order not to leave a false impression of conclusiveness.' In this spirit, I have devoted the remaining section of this book to a discussion of what was said in order to distinguish this from what has not been said.

Liberalism in Australia

Given the points made above, I have chosen to present liberalism in Australia through largely discrete studies of the works of ten individuals. These thinkers shared certain presumptions and orientations, but they present significantly divergent views on certain issues. Some of the positions they shared result from the fact that their views were underpinned by certain ideas brought to Australia in the process of colonisation. Some of the similarities in their positions result from particular characteristics of the Australian physical and social environment. Neither derivation nor situation is necessarily singular, however, and difference might be argued to result from particular elements of the liberal intellectual heritage interacting with different aspects of the Australian situation. Liberal thought contains a variety of assumptions and positions, not all of which may be adopted by a particular liberal thinker. Australia may be understood as a set of situations that reflect differences in physical location, socio-economic position, and historical circumstance. Thus liberalism in Australia may be understood as the intersection of a limited set of derived ideas with a particular set of situations.

Liberalism and particular thinkers

Rather than constructing liberalism as some tradition of thought that emerges in the works of particular writers, it has been treated as a means of collecting the thought of specific individuals. Individual authors provide the foreground; liberalism provides a background that makes sense of some of what appears, but not as a single source from which thinkers consciously drew. Liberalism was approached, therefore, as something akin to an organising principle that provided a means for examining particular works. To read works as expressions of liberal ideas is not intended to imply that there exists some form of thought, in this case one called liberalism, that inhabits the mind of particular thinkers at particular times.

Who share certain positions

The set of thinkers whose works have provided the subject matter for this book have been chosen because of certain shared positions. Each sought to extend and promote the opportunities available to individuals. They all saw individual freedom as one of the most important aspects of people's lives. Each saw society as a means of securing and promoting the interests of individuals; individual interests, under most conditions, were not to be sacrificed to a collective interest unless individuals agreed to this. All of them believed that markets had some role to play in society.

Almost all the liberals whose works are examined in this book had reservations about markets, which brought them to accept and propose various forms of government intervention. Most of them would have argued that economic pursuits reflected only a limited range of human possibilities and that governments were responsible for promoting these other possibilities. Goldstein and Dowse had a very strong sense of the ways in which market forces had unequal effects on women. Dowse was particularly conscious of the ways in which commitments to supporting markets diverted significant resources to the private sector, leaving the public sector relatively impoverished.

All but one of the liberals examined in this book supported democratic movements and giving voting rights to all adults of sound mind. Their belief in the importance of individuals meant they were predisposed to favour political institutions through which individuals could articulate and defend their interests. Most of them—Menzies stands out particularly here—shared reservations about the state of mind of many voters. Of these thinkers, some were convinced of the educational effects of involvement in democratic processes and consequently supported popular suffrage. Most believed that some opinions were better formed than others. Their faith in human beings led them to the view that these opinions would prevail if they were effectively articulated in public debates.

Even when they were democrats, many of the liberals dealt with in this book believed in the existence and importance to society of cultural elites. Their sense of natural inequality provides one explanation for this. Those who accepted the existence of systemically produced inequality had a further explanation. Liberals who acknowledged such inequality often argued that government had a significant role in giving individuals the means by which they might overcome an impoverished background.

Who do not share other positions

Liberalism is such an open and variable category that people designated as liberals can occupy different positions in debates on social and political issues. Many of the ten liberals disagree on significant issues. While they all accept that individuals are important, they often disagree about the extent to which they are self-forming. That is, they disagree about the extent to which the environment of individuals shapes their being, their life chances, and their sense of life possibilities. Another point of difference is their attitudes to governments. All liberals are careful not to overuse governments, but some are positively hostile to them.

John Hewson showed the greatest degree of hostility to governments. Goldstein and Dowse were also suspicious of governments, but for different reasons. They saw governments in terms of the maintenance of male domination of society and so were equivocal towards them; governments were a means to further their political projects, but they remained full of men. Deakin, Coombs, Menzies, Higgins, and Pearson were generally positive towards governments. Governments could go terribly wrong, but there was no essential hostility towards them.

Goldstein and Dowse also differed from the other liberals in their view of the effects of the social environment on individuals. They had a strong sense of the effects of environment. Coombs, Murdoch, and Higgins saw the social environment as significant, but to a lesser degree. Wentworth, Menzies, and Hewson believed that social environment was not particularly important; individuals were able to resist environmental effects and determine their futures free of those effects.

The only thinker of the ten liberals who was openly hostile to granting democratic rights to all adults was Wentworth. He was not convinced that the majority of people in his time were worthy of being given such rights. He did not think they would vote in a way that reflected the general interests of the colony, and he demanded that people demonstrate their worth before being given democratic rights. He lived at a time when these rights had not been granted, so this position was more readily available to him.

Derivation meets situation

One explanation of the consistency in views to be found across these Australian liberals is that, consciously or unconsciously, they all accepted premises fundamental to liberal political thought, and were therefore likely to agree on a range of issues. Points of disagreement may be taken to reflect differences in their interpretation of those fundamental principles. Alternatively, they may be seen as products of differences in their historical, social, or personal situations. Wentworth's divergent views on democracy, for example, may be attributed to the operation of liberal ideas in a very different social context.

That Hewson stands out in his general antipathy to governments may reflect the fact that the views of the other liberals reflected a community that had come to accept as normal the fact that government had a major role in shaping the economy and society. Hewson's economics differed from Coombs' as a function of both their intellectual influences and the times in which they wrote. Hewson may be thought of as more influenced by ideas produced by American liberals, and Coombs by those of British liberals. Hewson might be understood to be reacting to economic problems caused by inflationary pressures, Coombs to those caused by deflationary pressures.

Just as the nexus of derivation and situation might explain differences, so too might it explain similarities. That Higgins and Menzies were lawyers might explain something of their similar views about the role of government and, in particular, legal institutions in the creation of a healthy society. That Goldstein and Dowse were women might explain something of their similar views on the effects of environment on human being. That all the other thinkers were men might be understood to explain something of their tendency to seek reform in the public sphere and to neglect the private sphere in their political thinking.

Some final points

Before I leave this book, some general points need to be reiterated. First, I have not provided some totalising or holistic account of the life of a doctrine in Australia. Rather I have sought to represent liberal thought as it has been expressed by people I have chosen to designate as liberals. The chapters were intended to be capable of standing alone as distinct studies of Australian thinkers. While they were grouped according to certain themes, this was by way of providing something other than a straight chronological presentation. This was not done out of a hostility to chronological approaches, but simply because the idea of looking to an alternative organisation was suggested to me and I was interested in pursuing that alternative.

Nothing in the organisation of this book is intended to be taken as definitive. This is not a definitive account. Nor is it a definitive list of thinkers (but simply one chosen after careful consideration of an extensive list of candidates for treatment). That the studies have been arranged thematically is not intended to imply that thinkers whose works have been studied in one part might not have been chosen for inclusion in another.

In the end, it came down to making a start on examining works by Australians as political thinking or political theory. This was an endeavour that seems largely absent in Australian scholarship. Historians had made some contribution, but political theorists had done little in the form I attempted here. If some readers take this to be a starting-point, and believe that the endeavour requires someone else's efforts, then their acting upon this view would be the happiest outcome of all.

REFERENCES

Abbreviations
ANU Australian National University
APAIS Australian Public Affairs Information Service
CPD *Commonwealth Parliamentary Debates*

Abjorensen, N. (1993), *John Hewson: A Biography*, Lothian Books, Melbourne.

Bacchi, Carol (1980), 'Evolution, Eugenics and Women: The Impact of Scientific Theories on Attitudes towards Women, 1870–1920' in E. Windschuttle, *Women, Class and History: Feminist Perspectives on Australia 1788–1978*, Fontana, London.

Barnard, Majorie (1978), *A History of Australia*, Angus & Robertson, Sydney.

Bomford, Janette M. (1993), *That Dangerous and Persuasive Woman: Vida Goldstein*, Melbourne University Press, Melbourne.

Brett, Judith (1992), *Robert Menzies' Forgotten People*, Macmillan, Sydney.

Burrell, Steven (1989), 'The Hewson Economic View', *Australian Financial Review* 29 May, pp. 12–13.

Callaghan, P. S. (1983), 'Idealism and Arbitration in H. B. Higgins' New Province for Law and Order', *Journal of Australian Studies*, 13, November: 56–66.

Cass, Bettina (1995), 'Gender in Australia's Restructuring Labour Market and Welfare State', in Anne Edwards and Susan Msagarey (eds), *Women in a Restructuring Australia: Work and Welfare*, Allen & Unwin, Sydney.

Castles, A. C. (1982), *An Australian Legal History*, The Law Book Company, Sydney.

Cate, Thomas (1997), *An Encyclopaedia of Keynesian Economics*, Edward Elgar, Cheltenham.

Central Committee of Women's Political Association (1912), *The Life and Work of Miss Vida Goldstein*, Australian Authors' Agency, Melbourne.

Chisholm, Alec H. (ed.) (1963), *The Australian Encyclopaedia*, vol. 3, The Grolier Society of Australia, Sydney.

Clark, C. Manning (1955), *Select Documents in Australian History 1851–1900*, Angus & Robertson, Sydney.

—— (1981), *A History of Australia*, vol. 5, Melbourne University Press, Melbourne.

—— (1987), *A History of Australia*, vol. 4, Melbourne University Press, Melbourne.

Clarke, F. G. (1992), *Australia: A Concise Political and Social History*, Harcourt, Brace, Jovanovich, Sydney.

Cook, Ian (1994), 'Menzies and Hewson', in Geoff Stokes (ed.), *Studies in Australian Political Ideas*, University of New South Wales Press, Sydney, pp. 168–95.

Coombs, H. C. (1970), *The Fragile Pattern: Institutions and Man*, Australian Broadcasting Commission, Sydney.

—— (1971), *Other People's Money: Economic Essays*, ANU Press, Canberra.

—— (1978), *Kulinma: Listening to Aboriginal Australians*, ANU Press, Canberra.

—— (1981), *Trial Balance*, Macmillan, Melbourne.

—— (1990), *The Return of Scarcity: Strategies for an Economic Future*, Cambridge University Press, Cambridge.

Crisp, Finn (1990), 'Federation Prophets Without Honour', in J. Hart (ed.), *Federation Fathers,* Melbourne University Press, Melbourne.

Crowley, Francis K. (1973), *Modern Australia in Documents*, vol. 1, Wren, Melbourne.

Deakin, Alfred (1904), 'Speech by the Hon. Alfred Deakin on Moving the Second Reading of the Conciliation and Arbitration Bill', *Parliamentary Debates*, 22–3.

—— (1905a), 'The presessional speech of Mr. Alfred Deakin, MP to his constituents, at the Alfred Hall, Ballarat', 24–6 March 1905.

—— (1905b), Speech by the Honourable Alfred Deakin (MP) on the Immigration Restriction Amendment Bill and Contract Immigrants Bill, *Parliamentary Debates*, 10–11 March 1905.

—— (1906), *The Liberal Party and its Liberal Programme: Speech of the Prime Minster (Alfred Deakin) at Adelaide, March 29^h*, Vardon & Prichard, Adelaide.

—— (1910a), *Prime Minister at Ballarat*, Berry, Anderson, Ballarat.

—— (1910b), 'Speeches on the Constitutional Alteration (Legislative Powers) Bill and Constitutional Alteration (Monopolies) Bill', *Parliamentary Debates*, 19/26/27/28–10 and 2–11.

—— (1957), *The Crisis in Victorian Politics, 1879–1888: A Personal Retrospect*, (eds) J. A. La Nauze, and R. M. Crawford, Melbourne University Press, Melbourne.

—— (1968), *Federated Australia: Selections From Letters to the Morning Post 1900–1910*, Melbourne University Press, Melbourne.

Deer, Lewis, and John Barr (date unknown), *Australia's First Patriot: The Story of William C. Wentworth*, Angus & Robertson, Sydney.

Dowse, Sara (1981), 'The Transfer of the Office of Women's Affairs', in S. Encel, P. Wilenski, B. Schaffer (eds), *Decisions: Case Studies in Australian Public Policy*, Longman Cheshire, Melbourne.

—— (1983a), 'The Plight of the Femocrat', *National Times*, 22–8 April: 8.

—— (1983b), 'The Women's Movement's Fandango with the State: The Movement's Role in Public Policy Since 1972', in C. Baldock and B. Cass (eds), *Women, Social Welfare and the State in Australia*, Allen & Unwin, Sydney.

—— (1983c), *West Block: The Hidden World of Canberra's Mandarins*, Penguin, Victoria.

—— (1983d), 'Women Suffer at the Summit', *National Times*, 15–21April: 7.

—— (1984), 'The Bureaucrat as Usurer', in D. Broom, *Unfinished Business: Social Justice for Women in Australia,* Allen & Unwin, Sydney.

—— (1988), 'Good Luck, Helen', *Australian Society* 7(11): 8–9.

—— (1989a), 'A Great Swell in the Tide', *Australian Society* 8(10): 8–9.

—— (1989b), 'Address to the WEL-ACT Dinner', 5 June.

—— (1989c), 'Keep At It—Often and Loud', *Australian Society* 8(2): 8–9.

—— (1990), 'Dilemmas in the Femocracy', *Australian Society* 9(6): 29–30.

—— (1991), 'Confessions of a Centralist', *Australian Society* 10(9): 15.

—— (1992a), 'Equal Pay: The Rising Stakes', *Modern Times*, June: 15.

—— (1992b), 'From Europe and Back', *Modern Times*, May: 18–20.

—— (1992c), 'The Sex Equality Counter-Offensive', *Modern Times*, March: 3–4.

Duffy, M. (1990), 'Can Hewson Make It', *Independent Monthly*, August: 13–15.

Ellison, J. (1986), 'Sara Dowse: An Interview', in *Rooms of Their Own*, Penguin, Victoria, pp. 92–109.

Encel, Sol, Norman Mackenzie, Margaret Tesbutt (1974), *Women and Society: An Australian Study*, Cheshire, Melbourne.

Evans, Ray (1985), 'Justice Higgins: Architect and Builder of an Australian Folly', in J. Hyde and J. Nurick (eds), *Wages Wasteland: A Radical Examination of the Australian Wage Fixing System*, Hale & Iremonger, Sydney.

Fifer, D. E. (1984), 'Man of Two Worlds', *Journal of the Royal Australian Historical Society* 70(3): 147–70.

Gabay, Al (1992), *The Mystic Life of Alfred Deakin*, Cambridge University Press, Cambridge.

Goldstein, Vida (1901a), 'What is to be Done?', *Woman's Sphere* 1(5): 37–8.

—— (1901b), 'Women and the Sceptre', *Woman's Sphere* 1(6): 45–6.

—— (1903a), 'Senate Election Manifesto', *Woman's Sphere* 10 October: 360.

—— (1903b), 'Should Women Enter Parliament?', *Review of Reviews*, 20 August: 135–6.

—— (1904a), 'The Australian Woman in Politics', *Review of Reviews*, 20 January: 47–50.

—— (1904b), 'The Political Woman in Australia', *The Nineteenth Century*, July: 105–12.

—— (1905), 'The Need of the Hour', *Woman's Sphere* 5(53): 1–2.

—— (1907), 'Socialism of Today—An Australian View', *The Nineteenth Century*, September: 406–16.

—— (1916), 'Manifesto Australian Women's Peace Army: Conscription Vote No', *Woman Voter*, 5 October: 2.

—— (1918), 'Open Letter to Workers, Unarmed Australia', *Woman Voter*, 18 April.

—— (1930), 'Women Can Help Australia More', *Herald*, 11 January: 17.

—— (1948), 'The Struggle for Woman Suffrage', in I. McCorkindale (ed.), *Pioneer Pathways: Sixty Years of Citizenship*, Women's Christian Temperance Union of Australia, Melbourne.

Gowland, Pat (1980), 'The Women's Peace Army' in E. Windschuttle, *Women, Class and History: Feminist Perspectives on Australia 1788–1978*, Fontana, London.

Hartz, Louis (1964), *The Founding of New Societies: Studies in the History of the United States, Latin America, South Africa, Canada, and Australia*, Harbinger, New York.

Hazelhurst, Cameron (1979), *Menzies Observed*, Allen & Unwin, Sydney.

Hewson, John (1976), 'Myths and Mysteries in Eurocurrencies', *Economic Papers* 52, June: 31–45: 40–1.

—— (1983), 'Sir John More Holds a Wild Card on Wages', *Business Review Weekly*, 4–10 June: 29.

—— (1984), 'Deregulation Boundaries Should Be Widened', *Business Review Weekly*, 18–24 August: 116.

—— (1985a), 'Hawke's Hook Shot Skirts The Issue', *Business Review Weekly*, 26 April: 109–10.

—— (1985b), 'How Japanese Nearly Scuttled $A', *Business Review Weekly*, 29 November: 97.

—— (1985c), 'Time to Get Serious on Spending Restraints', *Business Review Weekly*, 14 June: 93–4.

—— (1986a), 'Hawke's Tough Line Is Too Soft', *Business Review Weekly* , 20 June: 114.

—— (1986b), 'Bob Hawke Wanders With Fraser Disease', *Business Review Weekly*, 5 September: 101.

—— (1986c), 'Keating and Co. Must Act Now', *Business Review Weekly*, 7 February: 73.

—— (1986d), 'Last Chance to Free Up Labor Market', *Business Review Weekly*, 4 April: 93–4.

—— (1986e), 'Seeing The Good In Privatisation', *Business Review Weekly*, 28 February: 83.

—— (1986f), 'Time For Johnston To Get Tough', *Business Review Weekly*, 1 August: 82–3.

—— (1987), *The University Of New South Wales Occasional Papers* no. 12: 31–8.

—— (1989a), 'Speech on Appropriation Bill (No. 1) 1989–1990', *CPD*, 31 August.

—— (1990a), 'Address by Dr. John Hewson, MP Leader Of The Opposition', the 1990 Sir Robert Menzies Lecture. Monash University, Melbourne, 27 November.

—— (1990b), 'Address in Reply', *CPD*, 10 May.

—— (1990c), 'Speech on Appropriation Bill (No. 1) 1990–1991', *CPD*, 23 August.

—— (1991a), 'Commonwealth–State Relations', *Australian Quarterly* 63 (1): 4–14.

—— (1991b), 'Extracts From: Address by Dr. John Hewson, MP, Leader of The Federal Opposition To The Annual General Meeting Of Business Council of Australia', *Business Council Bulletin*, November: 32–5.

—— (1991c), 'Motion of Censure Against the Prime Minister' *CPD*, 28 November.

—— (1991d), 'Speech on Appropriation Bill (No. 1) 1991–1992', *CPD*, 22 August.

—— (1991e), 'Speech on Social Security Legislation Amendment Bill (No. 3) 1991', *CPD*, 16 October.

—— (1992a), 'Fightback!—Fairness and Jobs Summary', *Business Council Bulletin Supplement*, December: 2–10.

—— (1992b), 'Free Market Fosters Fair Society', Alfred Deakin Lecture, *Australian Financial Review*, 16 October: 12.

—— (1992c), ' Hewson Answers The Critics', *Australian Business Monthly*, October: 52–3.

—— (1992d), 'Mining Exemplifies The Qualities Australian Industry Needs Now', *Mining Review*, Canberra, 16(3): 40–3.

—— (1992e), 'Speech on Matter of Public Importance: Taxation', *CPD*, 26 November.

—— (1993), 'Immigration Program Requires Urgent Reforms', *B.I.R. Bulletin* 8, February: 11–16.

—— (1994), 'The Unravelling of Mabo', *Australian Business Monthly*, March: 80–2.

Hewson, John, and Sakikibara Eisuke (1975a), 'A Qualitative Analysis of Euro-Currency Controls', *Journal of Finance* 30(2): 377–400.

—— (1975b), *The Eurocurrency Markets and Their Implications: A 'New' View of International Monetary Problems and Monetary Reform*, Lexington Books, Massachusetts.

Higgins, Henry B. (1896), *Another Isthmus in History*, Creswick, Melbourne.

—— (1902), 'Australian Ideals', *Austral Light*, 1 January: 9–19.

—— (1906), Harvester Judgment (*Ex parte H. V. McKay*), *Commonwealth Law Reports* 2: 2–18.

—— (1911), Report of Cases Decided and Awards Made Between The Federated Engine-Drivers and Firemen's Association of Australia and The Broken Hill Proprietary Company Ltd. *Commonwealth Arbitration Reports* 5: 14–17, 25–29.

—— (1915), 'Socrates, The State and War', paper delivered at the Classical Association of Victoria, November 16, Melbourne.

—— (1917), 'Toleration', address delivered at the Workers Educational Association of New South Wales, 21April.

—— (1919), 'On Seeing Both Sides', address delivered before the University Public Questions Society, 28July.

—— (1922), 'The Future of Industrial Tribunals', *New Outlook*, April 19: 8–9.

—— (1924), 'The (Australian) Commonwealth Court of Conciliation and Arbitration', address delivered at Oxford, 24 June.

—— (1968), *A New Province for Law and Order: Being a Review by its Late President for Fourteen Years of The Australian Court of Conciliation and Arbitration*, Dawsons, Sydney.

Jary, David, and Julia Jary (1995), *Collins Dictionary of Sociology*, 2nd edn, Harper Collins, Glasgow.

Joske, Sir Percy (1978), *Sir Robert Menzies 1894–1978: A New Informal Memoir*, Angus & Robertson, Sydney.

Kelly, Paul (1992), *The End of Certainty: The Story of the 80s*, Allen & Unwin, Sydney.

Knuckey, Marie (1978), 'Conversations with Marie Knuckey: Look! Centuries of Prejudice Against Us, Says Sara', *Sydney Morning Herald*, 5 January: 9.

La Nauze, John (1965), *Alfred Deakin: A Biography*, vols 1 & 2, Melbourne University Press, Melbourne.

La Nauze, John, and Elizabeth Nurser (eds) (1974), *Walter Murdoch and Alfred Deakin on Books and Men: Letters and Comments 1900–1918*, Melbourne University Press, Melbourne.

Landes Joan B. (ed.) (1998), *Feminism, the Public and the Private*, Oxford University Press, New York.

Lees, Kirsten (1995), *Votes for Women: The Australian Story*, Allen & Unwin, Sydney.

Liberal Party of Australia (1991), *Fightback! Fairness and Jobs*, Canberra.

Lindblom, Charles (1977), *Politics and Markets: The World's Political Economic Systems*, Basic Books, New York.

Macintyre, Stuart (1991), *A Colonial Liberalism: The Lost World of Three Victorian Visionaries*, Oxford University Press, Melbourne.

Mackenzie, Norman (1960), 'Vida Goldstein: The Australian Suffragette', *Australian Journal of Politics and History* 6: 190–204.

Marshall, Gordon (ed.) (1996), *The Concise Oxford Dictionary of Sociology*, Oxford University Press, Oxford.

McDonald, Lee Cameron (1968), *Western Political Theory: Part Three, Nineteenth and Twentieth Centuries*, Harcourt, Brace, Jovanovich, New York.

McNeill, Kate, Sue Jackson, Pat Morrigan (1986), 'A New Phase for Equal Pay': "Comparable Worth" Signals a New Approach to a Long Campaign', *Australian Society*, January: 22–6.

Melbourne, Alex (1972), *William Charles Wentworth*, Discovery Press, Sydney.

Menzies, Robert G. (1941), *To The People of Britain at War*, Longmans, Green & Co., London.

—— (1943), *The Forgotten People*, Angus & Robertson, Sydney.

—— (1961b), *The Changing Commonwealth*, Cambridge University Press, London.

—— (1964), 'The Universities—Some Queries', Inaugural Wallace Wurth Memorial Lecture, University of New South Wales Press, Sydney.

—— (1967), *Afternoon Light: Some Memories of Men and Events*, Melbourne, Cassell, Melbourne.

—— (1970), *The Measure of The Years*, Cassell, London.

—— (1961a), *The Challenge to Australian Education*, Australian College of Education, Melbourne.

Murdoch, Walter (1911), *The Struggle for Freedom*, Whitcombe & Tombs, Melbourne.

—— (1912), *The Australian Citizen: An Elementary Account of Civic Rights and Duties*, Whitcombe & Tombs, Melbourne.

—— (1935), *Some Fallacies*, issued by the Australian Broadcasting Commission.

—— (1932a), *Moreover*, Angus & Robertson, Sydney.

—— (1932b), *Saturday Mornings*, Angus & Robertson, Sydney.

—— (1934), *The Wild Planet*, Angus & Robertson, Sydney.

—— (1939), *The Spur of the Moment*, Angus & Robertson, Sydney.

—— (1941), *Steadfast*, Oxford University Press, Melbourne.

—— (1945), *Collected Essays*, Angus & Robertson, Sydney.

—— (1947), *72 Essays: A Selection*, Angus & Robertson, Sydney.

Nyland, Chris (1987), 'Scientific Management and the 44 Hour Week', *Labour History: A Journal of Labour and Social History* 53, November: 20–37.

Palmer, Nettie (1931), *Henry Bournes Higgins: A Memoir*, Harrap & Co., London.

Pearson, Charles H. (1867), 'On The Working of Australian Institutions', in G. C. Broderick et al. (eds), *Essays On Reform*, Macmillan, London.

—— (1875), 'The Higher Culture of Women', lecture delivered at St George's Hall, 11 February, 1875, Samuel Mullen, Melbourne.

—— (1877), *Political Opinions on Some Subjects of The Day*, Fergusson & Moore, Melbourne.

—— (1878), *Public Education: Royal Commission of Enquiry, Report on The State of Public Education in Victoria, and Suggestions as to the Best Means of Improving it*, John Ferres, Government Printer, Melbourne.

—— (1879), 'Democracy in Victoria', *Fortnightly Review* 31 (old series), May: 688–717.

—— (1880), 'The Liberal Programme', *Victorian Review* 1: 523–45.

—— (1893), *National Life and Character: A Forecast*, Macmillan & Co., London.

—— (1896), *Reviews and Critical Essays*, Methuen & Co., London.

Persse, Michael D. de B. Collins (1972), *W. C. Wentworth*, Oxford University Press, Melbourne.

Pons, Xavier (1994), *A Sheltered Land*, Allen & Unwin, Sydney.

Rawls, John (1973), *A Theory of Justice*, Oxford University Press, London.

Rickard, John (1984), *H. B. Higgins: The Rebel as Judge*, Allen & Unwin, Sydney.

Rowse, Tim (1978), *Australian Liberalism and National Character*, Kibble Books, Melbourne.

Sawer, Marian (1990), *Sisters in Suits: Women and Public Policy in Australia*, Allen & Unwin, Sydney.

Searle, Betty (1988), *Silk and Calico: Class, Gender and the Vote*, Hale & Iremonger, Sydney.

Seth, Ronald (1960), *Robert Gordon Menzies*, Cassell, London.

Shim, John, and J. G. Siegel (1995), *Dictionary of Economics*, J. Wiley & Sons, New York.

Stebbing, William (ed.) (1900), *Charles Henry Pearson*, Longmans, Green & Co., London.

Sykes, Trevor (1992), 'The True Believer and the Heretic', *Australian Business Monthly*, May: 26–38.

Tregenza, John (1968), *Professor of Democracy: The Life of Charles Henry Pearson 1830–1894, Oxford Don and Australian Radical*, Melbourne University Press, Melbourne.

Wallace, Christine (1993), *Hewson: A Portrait*, Macmillan, Sydney.

Wentworth, William Charles (date unknown), 'Mr. Wentworth's Reply to the Governor's Speech on the New Zealand Bill', held in the Mitchell Library, NSW.

—— (1855), 'Mr. Wentworth's Reply to Mr. Robert Lowe's Speech to Confer a Constitution on New South Wales, And To Grant a Civil List To Her Majesty', held in the Mitchell Library, NSW.

—— (1978), *Statistical, Historical and Political Description of the Colony of New South Wales and its Dependent Settlements in Van Dieman's Land*, Doubleday, Sydney.

Women's Political Association (1916), *Recommendations in Favour of Voluntary Methods of Dealing with Venereal Diseases*, Fraser & Jenkinson, Melbourne.

RESEARCH NOTES

General Notes

Most of the thinkers dealt with here were chosen because their works were held in relatively accessible locations and because commentaries on their works were also available. This does not mean that all of their works are readily available, and the Mitchell Library (State Library of New South Wales), the La Trobe Library (State Library of Victoria), and the National Library of Australia hold many of their less accessible works. The National Library also holds collections of the private documents of many of the thinkers whose works were dealt with here. In this section I have included other works that I consulted but did not use and other notes on doing research on these thinkers. The APAIS (Commonwealth National Library, Canberra) is an excellent index of material, especially newspaper articles. It can be found in hardback or as a computer-delivered index. Menzies and Hewson were Members of Federal Parliament in recent years, and their speeches may be found in Hansard (*CPD*). Parliamentary speeches by others who were MPs may prove somewhat more difficult to acquire. Once again, the National, Mitchell, and La Trobe libraries would be good places to begin a search for these.

PEARSON

Most of the material by and on Pearson and which is relatively accessible is contained in this book (apart from books of maps he published early in his career).

Additional Material

Pearson, Charles H. (1869), 'On Some Historical Aspects of Family Life' in J. E. Butler (ed.), *Woman's Work and Woman's Culture: A Series of Essays*, Macmillan, London.
—— (1889), 'Religious Teaching in Schools', a speech by Charles H. Pearson, Samuel Mullen, Melbourne.

GOLDSTEIN

The best source for material by and on Goldstein is Janette Bomford's *That Dangerous and Persuasive Woman: Vida Goldstein* (1993). A considerable amount of material written by Goldstein is contained in the National Library of Australia, the La Trobe Library, and the Mitchell Library. Editions of *Women's Sphere* and *The Woman Voter* are also held in these libraries.

Additional Material

Amery, Kerryn (1986), 'Vida Goldstein: 1869–1949', in *Hidden Women: Locating Information on Significant Australian Women*, Melbourne College of Advanced Education, Victoria.

Bomford, Janette (1996), 'The Lady Politician: Vida Goldstein's First Senate Campaign', in *A Women's Constitution? Gender and History in the Australian Commonwealth*, Hale & Iremonger, Sydney.

Caine, Barbara (1993), 'Vida Goldstein and the English Militant Campaign', *Women's History Review* 2(3): 363–76.

Goldstein, Vida (1911), *Woman Suffrage in Australia*, Women's Press, London.

—— (1936), 'Notes by the Way', *Australian Women's World*, 1 July: 7, 37.

Mulraney, Jenni (1988), 'When Lovely Woman Stoops to Lobby', *Australian Feminist Studies* 7–8, Summer: 94–111.

Sawer, Marian (1987), 'Shades of Vida Goldstein', *Australian Society* 6(6): 41.

Theobald, Marjorie (1989), 'The PLC Mystique: Reflections on the Reform of Female Education in Nineteenth Century Australia', *Australian Historical Studies* 23(92): 241–59.

MURDOCH

Most of the material written by Murdoch, apart from his collections of Australian poetry, is referenced here. So too are most of the commentaries on his work.

Additional Material

Dale, Leigh (1993), 'Walter Murdoch: A Humble Protest?', *Australian Literary Studies* 16(2): 179–89.

Dutton, Geoffrey (1984), 'Pundits and Gurus: Walter Murdoch and Max Harris', in G. Dutton (ed.), *Snow on the Saltbush: The Australian Literary Experience*, Viking Press, Melbourne.

Hasluck, Sir Paul (1970), 'Sir Walter Murdoch', address delivered by His Excellency the Governor-General, The Right Honourable Sir Paul Hasluck, Aug. 9 1970, *University News* 1(6): 1–7.

La Nauze, John (1974), 'Walter Murdoch: A Centenary Tribute', address delivered by J. A. La Nauze for the Inaugural Murdoch Memorial Lecture, 17 September, Perth.

—— (1977), *Walter Murdoch: A Biographical Memoir*, Melbourne University Press, Melbourne.

Murdoch, Walter (1935), 'Three Popular Prophets', Australian Broadcasting Commission, Sydney.

Phillips, A. A. (1979), *Responses: Selected Writings*, Australia International Press, Melbourne.

Triebel, L. A. (1946), 'The Essential Murdoch', *Australian Quarterly* 18(3): 106–9.

WENTWORTH

The best source of material produced by Wentworth is the Mitchell Library.

Additional Material

Anon. (1903), 'Makers of Australian History—William Charles Wentworth', *Old Times*, July.

Clark, C. Manning (1950), Select *Documents on Australian History 1788–1850*, Angus & Robertson, Sydney.

—— (1973), *A History of Australia*, vol. 3, Melbourne University Press, Melbourne.

—— (1978), *A History of Australia*, vol. 4, Melbourne University Press, Melbourne.

Connolly, C. N. (1982), 'The Origins of The Nominated Upper House in New South Wales', *Historical Studies* 20, April: 53–72.

Cramp, K. R. (1922), *William Charles Wentworth of Vaucluse House*, D. S. Ford, Sydney.

Fifer, D. E. (1987), 'The Australian Patriotic Association 1835–1841', *Journal of the Royal Australian Historical Society* 73(3): 155–72.

J. P. M. (1916), 'Men of the Days Long Past', *The Austral-Briton*, February.

Liston, C. A. (1976), 'William Charles Wentworth—The Formative Years 1810–1824', *Journal of the Royal Australian Historical Society* 62(1): 20–34.

Murphy, Brian (1982), *Dictionary of Australian History*, McGraw-Hill Book Company, Sydney.

Wentworth, William Charles (1835), *An Act to Provide for the Administration of Justice in New South Wales and Van Diemen's Land, and for more effective Government thereof, and for other purposes relating thereto.*

—— (1849), 'Speech On Moving the Second Reading of the University Bill' on 4th October 1849', Government Printer, Sydney.

—— (1860), *How I Became The Governor—of the New Barataria*, Southern Cross Publishing Office, Sydney.

HIGGINS

Higgins' legal judgments may be found in law reports of the period (see the *Commonwealth Law Reports* and *Australian Argus Law Reports*). His judgments in the Court of Conciliation and Arbitration can be found in the *Commonwealth Arbitration Reports*. Most of the other material is referenced here.

Additional Material

Brooks, Brian (1985), 'From Higgins to Hancock: The Boundaries of a New Province for Law and Order', *Journal of Industrial Relations*, December: 472–83.

Higgins, Henry B. (1926), 'Industrial Arbitration', address delivered in the Chapter House of St Paul's Cathedral, 22 March, Melbourne.

—— (1923), 'Fifty Years Hence', address delivered to the Members of Millions Club, 4 December, Sydney.

Kirby, M. D. (1983), 'Industrial Relations, Law Reform and the Constitution', *Journal of Industrial Relations*, March: 103–7.

Macarthy, P. G. (1976), 'Justice Higgins and the Harvester Judgement', in J. Roe (ed.), *Social Policy in Australia: Some Perspectives 1901–1975*, Cassell, Melbourne.

McQueen, Humphrey (1983), 'Higgins and Arbitration', in E. L. Wheelwright and K. Buckley (eds), *Essays in The Political Economy of Australian Capitalism*, vol. 5, Australia & New Zealand Book Company, Sydney.

Mitchell, Richard (1986), 'The High Court And The Preference Power: Wallis and Findlay In The Context Of The 1947 Amendments', *Western Australian Law Review* 16(4): 338–43.

Plowman, David (1986), 'Employers and Compulsory Arbitration: The Higgins Era 1907–1920', *The Industrial Relations Journal*, December: 588–609.

Reiger, Kerreen (1989), 'Clean and Comfortable and Respectable: Working-class Aspirations and the Australian 1920 Royal Commission on the Basic Wage', *History Workshop Journal* 27, Spring: 86–105.

Rickard, John (1993), 'H. B. Higgins: The Reluctant Father of Federation', *Constitutional Centenary* 2(5): 9, 15–16.

MENZIES

A plethora of newspaper articles have been written about Menzies. I could not include all of them here, but have included a selection. APAIS (see 'General Notes' section) is an excellent source for articles on Menzies.

Additional Material

Anthony, Doug (1994), 'Masterful Ming', *Australian*, December 20: 9.

Bunting, John (1988), *R. G. Menzies: A Portrait*, Allen & Unwin, Sydney.

Carroll, John (1985), 'The Battle for Sir Robert Menzies', *Quadrant* 29(1–2): 66–70.

Clark, Manning (1986), 'Flawed Heroes: Billy Hughes, Bob Menzies, Jack Curtin and the first world war', *Australian Society* 5(9): 21–4.

Harris, Max (1981), 'Menzies: The P. M. With no Place in History', *Bulletin* (Sydney), 21 April : 55–6, 58.

Hasluck, Paul (1988), 'Menzies: Our Chief of Men', *Quadrant* 32(10): 20–2.

Hastings, Peter (1988), 'Why Menzies Despised Australia', *Sydney Morning Herald*, October 11: 45.

Hazelhurst, Cameron (1979), 'The Menzies Illusion', *The Age*, 24 February: 17–18.

Kelly, Paul (1978), "Menzies: The Man and the Myth', *National Times*, 22–27 May: 8–9.

Layland, Penny (1994), 'The Menzies Papers', *National Library of Australia News*, November, pp. 3–5.

Manne, Robert (1993), 'Allan Martin's Menzies', *Quadrant* 37(6): 65–8.

Martin, Allan (1990), 'R. G. Menzies and the Murray Committee', in F. B Smith and P. Crichton (eds), Ideas *for Histories of Universities in Australia*, ANU, Canberra.

Martin, Allan (1993), *Robert Menzies: A Life*, assisted by Patsy Hardy, Melbourne University Press, Melbourne.

McQueen, Humphrey (1998), 'A Menzies Revolution', *ABC Radio 24 Hours*, February: 48– 51.

Menzies, Robert (1950), Roy Milne Memorial Lecture, 'The British Commonwealth of Nations in International Affairs', Australian Institute of International Affairs, Canberra.

—— (1970), Inaugural Sir Robert Menzies Lecture, 'The Foundations of Australian Liberalism', speech by Sir Robert Menzies for the Liberal Party of Australia (WA Division), Perth, Tuesday, 12 May.

—— (1944), *Post War Reconstruction in Australia*, Australasian Publishing Co., Sydney.

—— (1967), *Central Power in the Australian Commonwealth: An Examination of the Growth of Commonwealth Power in the Australian Federation*, Cassell, London.

Mills, Stephen (1982), 'Britannia Captivates an Innocent Abroad', *Age*, 24 July, Supplement: 9.

Perkins, Kevin (1968), *Menzies: Last of the Queen's Men*, Rigby, Adelaide.

Robinson, Ray (1966), *The Wit of Sir Robert Menzies,* Leslie Frewin Publication, London.

Whitton, Evan (1981), 'Who Really Founded the Liberal Party? Menzies' Shaky Claims', *Sydney Morning Herald,* 1 August: 37–8.

DOWSE

Much of the publicly available material written by Dowse has been referenced in this book. The National Library holds a significant quantity of her personal papers.

Additional Material

Dowse, Sara (1978), 'Sara Dowse: why I quit', *Australian Women's Weekly,* 1 February 1: 7–9.

—— (1983e), 'Bias Against Women In Job Creation Schemes', *National Times,* 13–19 May: 20.

—— (1984), 'Australia: Women In a Warrior Society', in *Sisterhood is Global: The International Women's Movement Anthology,* pp. 63–8.

—— (1988), 'Getting Started: The Beginning of Canberra Tales', transcript of a talk to staff and students in the School of Communication and Cultural Studies, Curtin University, Perth, *Blast* (Manuka, ACT) 8, Summer: 18–19.

—— (1989d), 'Tilly Devine and the Red Brick Wall', *Australian Society,* April: 6–7.

—— (1991), 'Hard Won Point of View', *Island* (Sandy Bay, Tas.), 47, Winter: 12–15.

—— (1991b), 'Academics fight back—The Association for the Study of Australian Literature is fighting educational policies which disadvantage the humanities', *Australian Society,* August: 42–4.

—— (1994), 'Portents on Piper Street—Discussion of Anne Summers and her book, Damned Whores and God's Police (1982)', *Island* (Sandy Bay, Tas.) 59, Winter: 50–5.

—— (1996), 'Significant Sojourns: Reflection on America and Australia', *Westerly* 41(4): 12–20.

DEAKIN

Deakin has been the subject of a number of newspaper articles and APAIS would prove a useful source for those.

Additional Material

Clark, Manning (1987), *A History of Australia,* vol. 4, Melbourne University Press, Melbourne.

Deakin, Alfred (1995), *And Be One People: Alfred Deakin's Federal Story,* introduction by Stuart Macintyre, Melbourne University Press, Melbourne.

Hirst, J. B. (1987), 'The Private Writings of Alfred Deakin', *Historical Studies* 22(89): 525–46.

LaNauze, John (1960), *Alfred Deakin: Two Lectures,* University of Queensland Press, Brisbane, pp. 37–50.

Macintyre, Stuart (1981), 'Equity in Australian History', in P. N. Troy (ed.), *A Just Society: Essays on Equity in Australia,* Allen & Unwin, Sydney.

Macklin, Robert (1988), *100 Great Australians,* Viking O'Neil, Melbourne.

Macmillan, David (1962), 'Alfred Deakin', in *Great Australians,* Melbourne University Press, Melbourne.

Martin, A. W. (1982), 'Australian Federation and Nationalism: Historical Notes, in R. L. Mathews (ed.), *Policies in Two Federal Countries: Canada and Australia*, Centre For Research on Federal Finance Relations, ANU Press, Canberra.

Oakes, Laurie (1988), 'Many Rifts But Only Two Greats', *Bulletin*, 26 January: 144–6.

Palmer, Vance (1954), *National Portraits*, Melbourne University Press, Melbourne.

Ward, John (1981), 'Colonial Liberalism and its Aftermath: New South Wales, 1867–1917', John Alexander Ferguson Memorial Lecture 1980, *Journal of the Royal Australian Historical Society* 67, September: 81–101.

Wright, Don (1969), 'The Politics of Federal Finance: The First Decade', *Historical Studies* 13, April: 460–76.

—— (1978), 'An Open Wrestle for Mastery: Commonwealth–State Relations', in B. Hodgins, D. Wright, W. H. Heick (eds), *Federation in Canada and Australia: The Early Years*, ANU Press, Canberra.

COOMBS

Apart from Coombs' report on Australian Government Administration, the main works of his that are not referenced in this book relate to his attempts to secure social justice for Aboriginal Australians. APAIS would provide most of these. Paul Smyth and Tim Battin have produced a number of books and articles that deal with the postwar period in which the philosophy that Coombs and others adopted is discussed.

Additional Material

Black, Laurel (1984), 'Social Democracy and Full Employment: The Australian White Paper, 1945', *Labour History* 46, May: 34–7.

Coombs, H. C. (1944), 'Problems of a High Employment Economy', the Joseph Fisher Lecture in Commerce, 29 June, Hassell Press, Adelaide.

—— (1948), 'Are Depressions Necessary?', *Economic Papers* 8, Sydney: 36–53.

—— (1958), 'Conditions of Monetary Policy in Australia', R. C. Mills Lecture, 29 April, Australian Medical Publishing Co., Sydney, pp. 19–40.

—— (1972), 'Matching Ecological and Economic Realities', *Australian Conservation Foundation Occasional Publication* 9, June: 3–18.

—— (1980), 'Technology, Income Distribution and the Quality of Life', CRES Working Paper, Centre for Resource and Environmental Studies, ANU, Canberra.

—— (1991), *Aborigines Made Visible: From 'Humbug' to Politics*, National Library of Australia, Canberra.

Dusevic, Tom (1990), 'The Dreamtime of Nugget Coombs', *Financial Review*, 15 June: 1.

Groenewegen, Peter, and Bruce McFarlane (1990), *A History of Australian Economic Thought*, Routledge, London.

Horne, Donald (1988), 'Nugget: A Planner of Dreams', *Weekend Australian*, 6–7 August: 35–6.

Jones, Carolyn (1993), 'Intelligentsia Has Failed Us', *Australian*, 2 April: 3.

Schedvin, B. (1992), *In Reserve: Central Banking In Australia 1945–1975*, Allen & Unwin, Sydney.

HEWSON

John Hewson was a columnist for *Business Review Weekly* from 1983 to 1986. I have used many of these columns in preparing this book, but could not include references for all of them in this section. Nor have I referenced all of the newspaper articles written about him, as these are too numerous to be readily included here. (Once again, APAIS would be the best means of finding these.)

Additional Material

Hewson, John (1975), *Liquidity Creation and Distribution in the Eurocurrency Markets*, Lexington Books, Massachusetts.

—— (1979), 'The Financing of Budget Deficits', in J. R. Hewson, J. W Neville, J. O. N. Perkins, J. O. Stone, *The Significance of the Budget Deficit*, Centre for Applied Economic Research, Sydney.

—— (1980), 'How Much Independence for the Reserve Bank?' *Economic Papers* 63, February: 70–88.

—— (1990), 'Labor's Cure May Kill the Patient', *Australian Accountant*, February: 42–3.

—— 1990), 'The Challenge of ANZAC for Today's Generation', *Monthly Record* 61(4): 199–200.

—— (1992), 'Hewson Fights Back', *Australian Quarterly* 64(3): 329–38.

—— (1994), 'The Unravelling of Mabo', *Australian Business Monthly*, March: 80–2.

Hewson, John, and J. W. Neville (1985), 'Monetary and Fiscal Policy in Australia', in V. E. Nagy and J. W. Neville (eds), *Inflation and Unemployment: Theory, Experience and Policy-Making*, Allen & Unwin, Sydney.

Hewson, John, and Eisuke Sakakibara (1974), 'The Euro-Dollar Deposit Multiplier: A Portfolio Approach', *International Monetary Fund Staff Papers* 21: 307–28.

—— (1975), 'The Impact of U.S. Controls on Capital Outflows on the U.S. Balance of Payments: An Exploratory Study', *International Monetary Fund Staff Papers* 22: 37–60.

Kitney, Geoff, and Steve Burrell (1990), 'Interview with John Hewson', *Australian Financial Review*, 15 February: 14–15.

INDEX